WITHDRAWN

WITHDRAWN

Famous Biographies for Young People

Books by Dorothy Horton McGee

SKIPPER SANDRA, *A Story of Sailing and Mystery*

SALLY TOWNSEND, PATRIOT

THE BOARDING SCHOOL MYSTERY

FAMOUS SIGNERS OF THE DECLARATION

Famous Signers

OF THE *Declaration*

BY DOROTHY HORTON McGEE

With photographic illustrations

DODD, MEAD & COMPANY

NEW YORK : 1955

To my Mother and the memory of my Father

Acknowledgments

APPRECIATION is extended to Mr. Acosta Nichols of Groton School for advice on the manuscript; to my editor, Miss Dorothy M. Bryan of Dodd, Mead & Company; and to the following for assistance in research: The New Hampshire Historical Society Library; Dr. Stephen T. Riley, Librarian, Mr. Warren G. Wheeler, The Massachusetts Historical Society; Dr. Clifford K. Shipton, Custodian of the Harvard University Archives; Mr. Ernest C. Woodsum, Town Clerk of Braintree; Mr. William C. Edwards, Chairman, Board of Managers of Historical Places, Quincy; Mr. Clarkson A. Collins III, Librarian, The Rhode Island Historical Society; Mr. Thompson R. Harlow, Director, The Connecticut Historical Society; Mr. Arthur S. Maynard, Assistant Librarian, Mrs. Louise H. Zimm, The New York Genealogical and Biographical Society; Dr. R. W. G. Vail, Director, Miss E. Marie Becker, The New York Historical Society; The Staff of the American History Room, The New York Public Library; Miss Lavinia Dobler, Librarian, *Scholastic Magazines;* Mr. Montgomery Schuyler, President, Miss Janet C. Livingston, The Colonial Lords of Manors in America; Mr. John Jay Ide of New York; Mrs. Oliver Allen Campbell of East Norwich, New York; Mr. Alexander J. Wall, Jr., Director, Mrs.

Joseph W. Greene, The New Jersey Historical Society; Dr. Henry L. Savage, Archivist, Princeton University Library; Mr. R. N. Williams II, Director, Mr. Nicholas B. Wainwright, The Historical Society of Pennsylvania; Mr. M. O. Anderson, Superintendent, The Independence National Historical Park Project, National Park Service; Mr. Percy Hamilton Goodsell, Jr., President-General, The Descendants of the Signers of the Declaration of Independence; Gertrude D. Hess, Assistant Librarian, The American Philosophical Society, Philadelphia; Mr. Leon deValinger, Jr., State Archivist, Delaware; Mr. James W. Foster, Director, The Maryland Historical Society; Mr. David C. Mearns, Chief, Manuscripts Division, The Library of Congress; Mr. John Melville Jennings, Director, The Virginia Historical Society; Mrs. Fiske Kimball, Curator, The Thomas Jefferson Memorial Foundation; Mr. W. Frank Burton, State Archivist, North Carolina; Mrs. R. H. Simmons, Secretary, The South Carolina Historical Society; Mrs. Lilla M. Hawes, Director, The Georgia Historical Society; and to the many others who have assisted.

Appreciation is also extended for permission to use material from the following books: *John Witherspoon Comes to America* by L. H. Butterfield, published by the Princeton University Library, 1953; *Robert Morris, Patriot And Financier* by Ellis Paxson Oberholtzer, published by the Macmillan Company, 1903; *Charles Carroll of Carrollton* by Ellen Hart Smith, published by the Harvard University Press, 1945; *The Lees of Virginia* by Burton J. Hendrick, published by Little, Brown and Company, 1935; and *The Declaration of Independence—Its History* by John H. Hazelton, published by Dodd, Mead & Company, 1906.

Contents

Illustrations

The Signatures on the Declaration of Independence

John Hancock

Saml Adams
John Adams
Robt Treat Paine
Elbridge Gerry
Josiah Bartlett
Wm Whipple
Matthew Thornton
Step Hopkins
William Ellery
Roger Sherman
Sam^el Huntington
Wm Williams
Oliver Wolcott

Wm Floyd
Phil. Livingston
Fran^s Lewis
Lewis Morris
Richd Stockton
Jno Witherspoon
Fra^s Hopkinson
John Hart
Abra Clark
Robt Morris
Benjamin Rush
Benj^a Franklin
John Morton

Geo Clymer
Ja^s Smith

Th Jefferson

Geo Taylor
James Wilson
Geo. Ross
Casar Rodney
Geo Read
Tho McKean
Samuel Chase
Wm Paca
Thos Stone
Charles Carroll of Carrollton
George Wythe
Richard Henry Lee

Benj^a Harrison
Thos Nelson jr.
Francis Lightfoot Lee
Carter Braxton
Wm Hooper
Joseph Hewes
John Penn
Edward Rutledge
Thos Heyward Junr
Thomas Lynch Junr
Arthur Middleton
Button Gwinnett
Lyman Hall
Geo Walton.

CHRONOLOGY

1761   Otis' Pleas against Writs of Assistance

1763   Peace of Paris. France cedes to England all of Canada and the region east of the Mississippi
Royal Proclamation. Colonization west of the Alleghenies forbidden

1763-1764
Grenville Program 1. Acts of Trade to be strictly enforced; 2. A Standing Army to be kept in America; 3. New Duties to be levied on coffee, silks, wine, calicoes, etc.

1764   Sugar Act
Stamp Act proposed

1765   Passage of Stamp Act
Patrick Henry's Resolutions passed by Virginia House of Burgesses
Stamp Act Congress held at New York. Nine Colonies represented

1766   Repeal of Stamp Act
Declaratory Act stating right of Parliament to tax Colonies

1767   Townshend Acts 1. New duties levied; 2. Writs of Assistance, Board of Customs Commissioners; 3. Governors' and Judges' salaries to be paid from revenue

1768   British Regiments at Boston

1770   Formation of the Lord North Ministry
Boston Massacre
Townshend Duties repealed, except for tax on tea

1773   Intercolonial Committees of Correspondence established by Virginia
Tea Act
Boston Tea Party

1774 Intolerable Acts 1. Port of Boston closed; 2. Transportation of offenders overseas for trial; 3. Self-government curtailed
Quebec Act
First Continental Congress at Philadelphia. General Association adopted

1775 Virginia adopts Patrick Henry's Resolutions. Liberty or Death speech
April 19—Battles of Lexington and Concord
May 10—Second Continental Congress meets in Philadelphia
Capture of Fort Ticonderoga
June 15—George Washington appointed Commander-in-Chief
June 17—Battle of Bunker Hill
November 12—Capture of Montreal by General Montgomery
December 31—Repulse of Montgomery and Arnold at Quebec
Act declaring Colonists out of the King's Protection

1776 January—*Common Sense* published
March 17—British Evacuation of Boston
March 23—Privateering Resolution approved by Congress
April 6—Ports opened to Foreign Trade
April 12—North Carolina Assembly Instructions to concur in Independence
May 15—New Government Resolution passed by Congress at Philadelphia
Virginia Assembly Instructions to Declare Independence
June 7—Richard Henry Lee of Virginia moves for Independence in Congress
July 2—Independence Resolution passed by Congress
July 4—Declaration of Independence approved by Congress
August 2—Declaration of Independence Signed

CONGRESS VOTING INDEPENDENCE

begun by Robert Edge Pine, finished by Edward Savage

JOHN HANCOCK
by John Singleton Copley

SAMUEL ADAMS
by John Singleton Copley

PHILIP LIVINGSTON
by Benjamin West

ROGER SHERMAN
by Ralph Earl

THOMAS JEFFERSON
by Charles Willson Peale

CHARLES CARROLL OF CARROLLTON
by Sir Joshua Reynolds

BENJAMIN FRANKLIN
by David Martin

JOHN ADAMS
by John Singleton Copley

JOHN WITHERSPOON
by Charles Willson Peale

RICHARD HENRY LEE
by Charles Willson Peale

Declaration of Independence July 4, 1776

Independency Road

THE BOSTON TEA PARTY in December, 1773, was an eruption of the long and bitter quarrel between King George III's British-American subjects and the "Mother Country," Great Britain, over taxation without representation. On the repeal in 1770 of the Townshend duties, the threepenny tax on tea had been retained "to keep up the right," and three years later the British ministry sent ships with surplus East India tea to be sold in the American Colonies. Determined that the tea should not be landed from the three tea ships which arrived in Boston, a band of Patriots, "cloath'd in Blankets with the heads muffled, and copper color'd countenances," in order to look like Mohawk Indians, boarded the hated tea ships at Griffin's wharf on the evening of December 16. Before nine o'clock every one of the three hundred and forty-two chests of tea belonging to the East India Company "was knock'd to pieces and flung over ye sides," into Boston Harbor, as John Andrews described the Tea Party in a letter two days later.

"The die is cast," John Adams wrote to James Warren on December 17. In his diary entry of the same date, he said that the "destruction of the tea is so bold, so daring, so firm, intrepid and inflexible, and it must have so important consequences, and so lasting, that I cannot but consider it as an epocha in history."

Boston's punishment was not long in coming. Early in 1774 the British Parliament passed the "Intolerable Acts," as they were called in America. On June 1, the port of Boston would be closed until the "drowned" tea was paid for, town meetings (except for regular elections) would thereafter be forbidden without permission of the royal governor and other rights of self-government were to be curtailed. A new governor for the Massachusetts Bay Colony, General Gage, arrived in May and an army of about four thousand men was quartered in Boston.

The news of this vengeance upon Boston aroused the sympathy of all the Colonies. Virginia proposed the calling of a General Congress, and on September 5, 1774, forty-four delegates representing twelve of the Thirteen Colonies, all except Georgia, met at Carpenters' Hall in Philadelphia "to deliberate and determine upon wise and proper measures for the recovery of their just rights and liberties."

This First Continental Congress, "such an assembly as never before came together, on a sudden, in any part of the world," was composed of notable delegates, including George Washington, Patrick Henry and Richard Henry Lee in the Virginia delegation, as well as the Patriot "brace of Adamses," Sam and his cousin John from Massachusetts.

Traveling to Philadelphia by coach, the Massachusetts delegates, "four poor pilgrims," were met at Frankfort, about five miles out of the city, by several of the most active Philadelphia Sons of Liberty (resistance groups of Patriots originally formed in the Colonies to oppose the Stamp Act in 1765). They advised the newcomers that "friends of Government" in Boston and New England had represented the Massachusetts men as "desperate adventurers." As John Adams described the interview in a letter to Timothy Pickering in 1822: "We were all suspected of having independence

in view. Now, said they, you must not utter the word independence . . . in Congress or any private conversation."
Warning that the idea of independence was as unpopular in
Pennsylvania and all the Middle and Southern Colonies as
the Stamp Act itself, Dr. Benjamin Rush and the other Sons
of Liberty advised the delegates from the "suffering State" to
be very cautious and not come forward with any bold measures. The Virginians, the Sons of Liberty continued, "are
very proud of their antient Dominion, as they call it; they
think they have a right to take the lead, and the Southern
States, and the Middle States too, are too much disposed to
yield it to them."

The Frankfort advice made a deep impression on the
Massachusetts representatives and, as John Adams stated in
his letter of 1822, gave "a color, complexion, and character,
to the whole policy of the United States, from that day to
this."

Of the Congress which met at Carpenters' Hall from September 5 until its adjournment in October, one member
wrote: "Here are fortunes, abilities, learning, eloquence,
acuteness, equal to any I ever met with in my life." But the
delegates could only act as a committee of advice, having no
legislative powers to bind the Colonies.

On September 17, the Suffolk Resolves—bold resolutions
against British oppression, passed by a convention of towns in
Suffolk County, Massachusetts, and brought to Philadelphia
by Paul Revere, the Patriot express rider—were considered
by Congress. Resolutions of support and sympathy were
adopted by Congress—"enough to melt a heart of stone,"
John Adams wrote to his wife Abigail the next day.

The so-called Galloway plan of union, dangerous because
it conceded to Parliament a share in legislating for America,
was only narrowly defeated by the vote of one colony, then
erased from the record. Instead, the Continental Congress
prepared a declaration of rights, sent a petition to the King

for redress of their grievances, published addresses to the people of England, Canada and the Thirteen Colonies. Finally, they adopted the agreement, known as the "American Association," to suspend all trade with Britain in order to bring pressure upon Parliament. Adjourning on October 26, they were to meet again the following May—if their grievances had not been remedied.

Every question, wrote John Adams to William Tudor on September 29, was discussed with "a moderation, an acuteness, and a minuteness equal to that of Queen Elizabeth's privy council." All this had occasioned "infinite delays." The Massachusetts Patriots had had a difficult time— "We have been obliged," Adams continued, "to keep ourselves out of sight, and to feel pulses, and to sound the depths; to insinuate our sentiments, designs, and desires, by means of other persons, sometimes of one province, and sometimes of another—" But the first united colonial congress had made the cause of Massachusetts the common cause, and nobody had even suggested that they pay for the tea!

In the Virginia Convention of March, 1775, supporting his resolution to put the colony into a state of defense, Patrick Henry made his famous speech for liberty— "Is life so dear or peace so sweet as to be purchased at the price of chains and slavery? Forbid it, Almighty God! I know not what course others may take, but as for me, give me liberty or give me death!" Prophetically he declared, "The next gale that sweeps from the north will bring to our ears the clash of resounding arms."

Less than a month later armed hostilities began at Lexington when the British troops, eight hundred strong, marched from Boston to seize the gunpowder collected by the Massachusetts Patriots at Concord and Acton. Their other objective was to arrest the Patriot leaders, Samuel Adams and John Hancock, who were at the parsonage in Lexington where Hancock had played as a boy.

On the evening of the eighteenth of April, warned by lanterns hung in the North Church tower in Boston that the British troops were on the march, Paul Revere started off from the opposite shore on his famous ride to warn "the country folk to be up and to arm."

As William Wadsworth Longfellow continued the story in *The Midnight Ride of Paul Revere,*

> "The fate of a nation was riding that night;
> And the spark struck out by that steed, in his flight,
> Kindled the land into flame with its heat . . ."

Aroused by Revere, a company of Minute Men on the village green at Lexington answered the enemy fire at dawn on April 19. At Concord,

> "By the rude bridge that arched the flood,
> Their flag to April's breeze unfurled,
> . . . the embattled farmers stood,
> And fired the shot heard round the world"

as it is told by Ralph Waldo Emerson in his *Concord Hymn.*

To the reverberations of this shot the Second Continental Congress met as scheduled on May 10 in Philadelphia—this time in the State House, now known as Independence Hall. On that same day, Patriot forces in the north captured Fort Ticonderoga, on Lake Champlain, which commanded the invasion route to and from Canada.

Among the new faces were those of Benjamin Franklin ("Poor Richard") and John Hancock, who was elected president on Peyton Randolph's return to Virginia. A little later, the "famous Mr. Jefferson" took his seat.

This Congress, still only a committee of *advice,* like the first, began to assume some powers of a national government. Acting on the request of Massachusetts, John Adams made a motion that Congress "adopt the army at Cambridge, and appoint a general." When George Washington realized that

John Adams (always mindful of the Frankfort advice) had him in mind, "from his usual modesty, (he) darted into the library-room." Sam Adams seconded the plan which, after debate, was postponed; but on June 15, George Washington, nominated by Thomas Johnson of Maryland, was elected Commander-in-Chief of the Continental Army, which had been adopted earlier.

Two days later, at Charlestown, Massachusetts, the Battle of Bunker Hill was fought. As the British regulars charged the hill which had been occupied by the Patriots the night before, the American officers gave the command, "Don't shoot until you can see the whites of their eyes!" to conserve the scarce powder supply. The British finally took the hill when the precious powder gave out, but the battle was a moral victory for the Americans because it showed that the colonial militia could stand up successfully to the British regulars.

News of this defeat reached George Washington by courier when the General was about twenty miles outside of Philadelphia, on his way to take command of the American forces at Cambridge.

On July 6, Congress issued a declaration setting forth the causes of taking up arms and stating "before God and the world" their decision to use force "for the preservation of our Liberties." But the paper disavowed "ambitious Designs" of establishing independent states.

Congress supported John Dickinson, leader of the "pacific system," in approving a second petition for redress to the King—that "measure of imbecility," as John Adams termed it. Irritated by Dickinson, who had lectured him for opposing the petition, and by its passage in Congress, Adams wrote two letters avowing his designs for independence and criticizing Dickinson, who "has given a silly cast to our whole doings. We are between hawk and buzzard." Intercepted and published, these letters had a great effect on both sides of the

Atlantic. Colonel Reed, General Washington's secretary, told Adams that Providence seemed to have thrown those letters before the public for the good of the Colonies, for the "whole country had been compelled to turn their thoughts upon it (independence) . . ."

When Congress met in September, after a summer adjournment, Adams found that he and Mr. Dickinson were not even on "bowing terms." For a while following the publication of the letters, Adams was almost universally avoided in the streets of Philadelphia, as if "infected with the leprosy."

The breach was widening between the Colonies and the mother country. In October, Falmouth (now Portland, Maine) was burned by the captain of a British warship, and in November two small American armies were invading Canada, with the sanction of Congress. King George, who had hired German mercenaries for his armies earlier, declared the Colonies out of his protection in December and blockaded the ports. On the last day of the year 1775, the American forces in Canada, under Benedict Arnold and Richard Montgomery, were repulsed at Quebec and Montgomery was killed.

On January 10, 1776, *Common Sense* by Thomas Paine was published in Philadelphia. Widely read throughout the Colonies, this pamphlet had a great influence in turning the minds of the people toward independence.

In Congress, the "moderates," members of Mr. Dickinson's "dilatory system," still held control. On February 13, Mr. Wilson brought in a draft of an address to the constituents of Congress. Richard Smith, a New Jersey delegate, describes this draft in his diary as "very long, badly written and full against Independency."

The "violents" struggled on. During the fall and winter of 1775-1776, independence, a confederation or union of the Colonies and negotiations with foreign powers were John Adams' "constant and daily topics," whenever he was present. Many motions were made and lost, after tedious discussion. Sam Adams, of course, helped, though he rarely spoke in Congress—and George Wythe, too. John Adams wrote: "Mr. Richard Henry Lee, of Virginia, Mr. Sherman, of Connecticut, and Mr. Gadsden, of South Carolina, were always on my side, and Mr. Chase, of Maryland, when he did speak at all, was always powerful, and generally with us."

In his *Autobiography*, under date of February 29, John Adams tells that postponement was the object of the antagonists of his system. A majority of Congress were "either determined against all measures preparatory to independence, or yet too timorous and wavering to venture on any decisive steps." The "violents" could do nothing but keep their eyes fixed on the great objects of free trade, new governments in all the Colonies and independence, grasping every opportunity to advance step by step. The "moderates" seized any excuse "to play cold water on the fire of independence," and clutched at each "airy phantom."

With the aid of cannon taken at Ticonderoga, and careful planning, the American forces under General Washington successfully occupied Dorchester Heights on March 3, threatening Boston. Sir William Howe and the British army evacuated the city on March 17 and sailed north to Halifax, Canada, accompanied by hundreds of Tories who had flocked to Boston for protection. Congress later ordered a gold medal struck for General Washington in honor of this victory.

On March 23 Congress passed the privateering resolution permitting American ships to take enemy shipping. John Adams wrote to General Horatio Gates on the day of this move: ". . . for the future We are likely to wage three Quarters of a War. . . . This is not Independency you know, nothing like it." He continues wryly, "Independency is an Hobgoblin, of so frightfull Mein, that it would throw a delicate Person into Fits to look it in the Face."

"Great things" were done on April 6—Congress approved resolutions opening the ports to foreign trade. But "moderate" delegates clung to the hope of the so-called "peace commissioners," said to be coming from London in the spring or summer. As to whether American liberties could be secured by reconciliation or independence, Robert Morris wrote to Gates on the same day: "We shall quarrel about which of these roads is best to pursue unless the Commissioners appear soon and lead us into the first path . . ."

Less than a week later, on April 12, the Provincial Congress of North Carolina instructed their delegates in the Continental Congress to concur "in declaring *Independency*" —the first colony to use the word itself in its instructions.

On May 6 the "violent" men knew that time was running out for establishing a union and declaring for independence before the British fleet from Halifax, augmented by forces from England, would invade the Colonies and warfare would break out along fifteen hundred miles of coastline. A resolve, written by John Adams, to give Congress full powers to act was instantly defeated in Congress that same day.

Four days later, on May 10, a revised measure, "brought before the Committee of the whole house, in concert between" Richard Henry Lee and John Adams the day before, was adopted by Congress after strong opposition. The resolution recommended the institution of new, independent governments to the Assemblies in all the Colonies where no government "sufficient to the exigencies of their affairs" had been established. The new governments were to be such as should, in the opinion of the representatives of the people, "best conduce to the happiness and safety of their constituents in particular, and America in general."

A committee of three was appointed to prepare a preamble to this resolution. The "violents" managed to place two of their members, John Adams and Richard Henry Lee, on the preamble committee as against only one representative of the "dilatory system," Edward Rutledge of South Carolina.

On May 15 Adams presented his preamble draft, "very short" and not elaborate, by request of his two colleagues and with their "approbation." It urged that all powers of government be exerted under the authority of the people of the Colonies "for the preservation of internal peace, virtue, and good order, as well as for the defence of their lives, liberties, and properties, against the hostile invasions and cruel depredations of their enemies . . ."

After furious debate, this preamble was passed, seven Colonies to five—Maryland abstaining. The preamble and the resolve of the tenth were ordered published.

One of the "moderates," James Duane, who had taken a heated part in the debate, came up to John Adams, accusing him, ". . . You have created a machine for the fabrication of independence."

Looking directly at the speaker, the delegate from Massachusetts smiled and said, "I think it is independence itself, but we must have it with more formality yet."

At Williamsburg, Virginia, on May 15, the General Convention, established on May 6, following the dissolution of the Colonial Assembly, "appealing to the Searcher of hearts for the sincerity of former declarations," adopted the famous resolution instructing the Virginia delegates in the Continental Congress "to declare the United Colonies free and independent States. . . ."

Colonel Nelson left immediately for Congress with this resolution. Thomas Ludwell Lee wrote to Richard Henry Lee on May 18, enclosing "some printed resolves which passed our Convention to the infinite joy of the people here. . . . The British flag was immediately struck on the Capitol, and a Continental hoisted in its room."

On May 27 the resolution was laid before Congress, as was the April 12 resolve of North Carolina. Of the former, General Washington—called from New York by Congress to consult on the impending British invasion of that colony and other enemy war plans—wrote from Philadelphia to his brother, John Augustine Washington, on May 31: "I am so very glad to find that the Virginia Convention have passed so noble a vote, and with so much unanimity . . . many members of Congress, in short, the representation of whole provinces, are still feeding themselves upon the dainty food of reconciliation. . . ."

On the first Friday in June, Richard Henry Lee, the senior of Virginia's delegates and a "violent," stepped out of his brother-in-law's house at Fourth and Locust Streets, Philadelphia, on his way to Congress, meeting at the State House. This distinguished member of the well-known Lee family, described by his close colleague John Adams as "tall, spare, a deep thinker," had represented Virginia in Congress since the second day in 1774. A "gentleman of fine talents, of amiable manners, and great worth," Lee needed that day all his "fluency as easy and graceful as it was melodious" to carry out the instructions sent by the Virginia Convention. Dressed in a light summer coat and breeches, he entered the State House, taking his seat in the white-paneled room. Intently he watched the business of the day begin.

"Friday, June 7, 1776," Charles Thomson, secretary of Congress since September, 1774, recorded in his legible script. John Adams brought in the report of his committee on a letter of May 22 from Esek Hopkins and resolutions regarding it were passed. Adams wrote later in his *Autobiography* that Commodore Hopkins was one of three persons who were at that time "standing subjects of altercation in Congress . . . One design was to divert us from our main object."

The atmosphere grew tense. It was eleven days now since the independence resolution had been laid before Congress. Daily the "moderates" expected the Virginia delegation to act upon it. Lee had talked freely in public of the Continental flag flying over the Virginia capitol. "May God grant it never be lowered," he was quoted as saying, to the fervent agreement of the Adamses.

Time was short. The remnant of the American forces in Canada were in full retreat. General Sir William Howe and his army were expected to land in New York. General Washington had hurried back to defend that city two days before. Another British force under Sir William's brother, Admiral Lord Richard Howe, was headed for the Colonies.

Two further matters of business were brought before Congress and considered. The tension grew almost unbearable.

Mr. Richard Henry Lee then stood up. He was later "heard to say that it was the most aweful moment of his life when he rose to make the motion."

The chair recognized the gentleman from Virginia and the room was startled into silence. Virginia, "the most Antient colony," was risking the lives of her people, her great fortunes, rich plantations and beautiful buildings for the cause of Freedom. Every member knew that Lee, owner of Chantilly, a plantation on the Potomac River, was about to "come out with it."

His pleasant voice constrained, the long-time Liberty man asked leave to present the resolutions "in obedience to instructions from their constituents":

"Resolved That these United Colonies are, and of right ought to be, free and independent States, that they are absolved from all allegiance to the British Crown, and that all political connection between them and the State of Great Britain is, and ought to be, totally dissolved.

"That it is expedient forthwith to take the most effectual measures for forming foreign Alliances.

"That a plan of confederation be prepared and transmitted

to the respective Colonies for their consideration and approbation."

John Adams immediately seconded the motion.

The house being obliged at that time to attend to some
other business, as Jefferson wrote in his notes taken "in my
seat," the proposition was referred to the next day, when the
members were ordered to attend punctually at ten o'clock.

Congress as a committee of the whole debated the resolution furiously on the eighth and again on the tenth of June.
Mr. Dickinson's "dilatory system" against a declaration at
this time was opposed by "the Power of all N. England, Virginia & Georgia," as Edward Rutledge wrote on the evening
of the eighth. No longer hopeful "that we should ever again
be united with Great Britain," the "moderates" nevertheless
urged waiting "to take any capital step" until "the people
of the middle colonies" were ripe for it, so Jefferson recorded
in his notes.

The majority in Congress at that time depended on the
vote of Joseph Hewes of North Carolina, who was against the
independence measure. Samuel Adams rose to his feet and
made a decisive speech, giving the opinion of the people
throughout all the Colonies, gained from his correspondence
with the Patriot leaders, to prove that the "general sense of
all" favored independence. As his cousin John described the
scene, when Sam told of the situation in "North Carolina,
and produced letters and public proceedings which demon-
strated that the majority of the colony were in favor of it,
Mr. Hewes, who had hitherto constantly voted against it . . .
lifting both his hands to Heaven . . . cried out, 'It is done!
and I will abide by it.'"

Joseph Hewes' changed vote swung the majority toward
independence, but the question was quickly eluded by a motion for adjournment. John Adams said that he would give
more for a painting of the "terror and horror upon the faces
of the old majority" at that critical moment than for the

"best piece of Raphael." Another member of the "old ma-jority" deeply affected by Samuel Adams' reasoning was John Morton of Pennsylvania, and he too began to waver in his firm stand against independence.

On June 10, Congress resolved that consideration of the independence resolution "be postponed to this day three weeks." A committee was to be chosen to prepare a Declara-tion of Independence, "so that no time be lost in case the Congress agree thereto."

Explaining the postponement, Jefferson's notes say: "It appearing in the course of these debates that the colonies of N. York, New Jersey, Pennsylvania, Delaware & Maryland were not yet matured for falling from the parent stem, but that they were fast advancing to that state, it was thought most prudent to wait a while for them . . ."

The committee appointed on June 11 to prepare the Declaration consisted of Mr. Jefferson, Mr. John Adams, Mr. Franklin, Mr. Sherman and Mr. Robert R. Livingston of New York.

In his *Autobiography,* John Adams explains the choice of Jefferson, only thirty-three years of age, rather than Lee, the mover of the resolutions, or such veterans as Franklin, Sher-man, Harrison and himself. "Jefferson was chairman because he had most votes and he had most votes because We united in him, to the Exclusion of R. H. Lee in (or)der to keep out Harrison." Jefferson was a very satisfactory compromise chairman—he was a "violent," he had a reputation for wield-ing a "masterly pen," and he was a Virginian. Without the Frankfort advice to place a Virginian at the head of every-thing, Adams reminds us in the 1822 letter to Pickering: "Mr. Jefferson (would never) have been the Author of the declaration of Independence . . ."

At the request of his committee, Jefferson proceeded to make a draft of the paper in the parlor of his lodgings at Market and Seventh Streets. Adams and Franklin, to whom this was submitted, changed a few words, the committee approved it and the draft was laid before Congress on June 28. The composition was read to the members that same day and tabled. Josiah Bartlett of New Hampshire wrote on July 1: "The Declaration before Congress is, I think, a pretty good one. I hope it will not be spoiled by canvassing in Congress."

Since the postponement of June 10 the "violents" had been working desperately to pluck the ripening colonies from "the parent stem."

From Burlington, New Jersey, came welcome news. Jonathan D. Sergeant, a New Jersey delegate to the Continental Congress, wrote to John Adams, on June 15: "We are passing the Rubicon & our Delegates in Congress on the first of July will vote plump. . . . The bearer is a staunch Whig & will answer any questions . . ." Five new delegates from New Jersey were chosen on June 22—Richard Stockton, Abraham Clark, John Hart, Francis Hopkinson and John Witherspoon. Their instructions were to support "the just rights and liberties of America," and if necessary or expedient for this purpose, to join with the other Colonies in declaring independence.

Thomas McKean of Delaware left Congress on June 12 for New Castle, where the Delaware Assembly was in session, to work for independence. Despite the threats of armed Tories in Sussex County, by the seventeenth he had "returned from the Lower Counties (Delaware) with Full Powers," as John Adams wrote to Samuel Chase, a Maryland delegate.

Regarding Maryland, Chase wrote Adams from Annapolis on June 28, telling of the "Unan: Vote of our Convention for *Independence* et et— See the glorious Effects of County Instructions, — our people have fire if not smothered."

This Maryland instruction was "laid before Congress &

read" on the morning of July 1, as shown by the *Journal*. The "generous and unanimous" Maryland vote brought great "pleasure" to the "violents" on this long-awaited day when Congress as a committee of the whole took up consideration of the "resolution respecting independency." Debate raged, with Dickinson speaking against it, and Adams finally answering, after waiting for someone "less obnoxious" to reply. The new delegates from New Jersey appearing at that moment, Adams was persuaded to set forth the arguments again for their benefit in a long, now famous speech. An affirmative vote was then taken in the committee of the whole, as Jefferson tells in his notes: "by the votes of N. Hampshire, Connecticut, Massachusets, Rhode island, N. Jersey, Maryland, Virginia, N. Carolina, & Georgia. S. Carolina and Pennsylvania voted against it. Delaware having but two members present, they were divided . . ." The New York delegates were enjoined from voting by their instructions. At the request of Mr. Edward Rutledge of South Carolina, the final decision was put off until the next day, as he believed that his colony's delegation might join in approving the resolution for the sake of unanimity. Thomas McKean, the "violent" of the two Delaware delegates present, instantly sent an express rider to Delaware at his own expense to summon Caesar Rodney, the third delegate.

The second of July dawned cloudy and threatening and "before ten came on a heavy rain," as Christopher Marshall recorded in his diary. Rodney, riding all night and through the storm, arrived at the State House in Philadelphia in time to turn "the vote of that colony in favour of the resolution." South Carolina concurred and, as Jefferson continues in his notes, "members of a different sentiment attending that morning from Pennsylvania also, their vote was changed so that the whole 12. colonies, who were authorized to vote at all, gave their voices" for the independence resolution!

"Yesterday," John Adams wrote to his wife Abigail on July

3, "the greatest Question was decided, which ever was debated in America, and a greater perhaps, never was or will be decided among Men."

Consideration of the Declaration of Independence was taken up by Congress as a committee of the whole on July 2, and again on July 3 and 4. While the Declaration "underwent abundance of criticism and alteration" in Congress, John Adams fought "fearlessly for every word of it." "Congress," he wrote later, "cut off about a quarter part of it, as I expected they would." Jefferson admitted that the opinions of some were "expressed in acrimonious criticisms on some of its parts, that made him writhe a little." He was sitting by Dr. Benjamin Franklin, who, seeing that he "was not insensible to these mutilations," tried to distract him with an anecdote about a hatter whose proposed sign, "John Thompson, *Hatter, makes* and *sells hats for ready money,*" with a hat portrayed, was reduced by the advice of his friends to "John Thomson" and the pictured hat. Adams, in the 1822 Pickering letter, said he had long wondered why the original draft had never been published, supposing it to be because of "the vehement Philippic against Negro Slavery" it contained.

Jefferson later told a friend that consideration of the Declaration was hastened by an invasion of flies from a near-by livery stable. The members of Congress, who wore knee breeches and silk stockings, were busily employed in "lashing the flies from their legs." Relief was only to be had by approving the Declaration and hurrying from the room, Jefferson recounted gleefully.

More seriously, Jefferson's notes tell that on the evening of the fourth of July, the Declaration was finally "agreed to by the house," beginning with the now famous lines:

"When in the course of human events it becomes necessary for one people to dissolve the political bands which have connected them with another, and to assume among the powers of the earth the separate and equal station to which the laws of nature & of nature's god entitle them . . .

"We hold these truths to be self evident: that all men are created equal; that they are endowed by their creator with certain inalienable rights . . ."

It is said that the old bellman had been stationed in the steeple of the State House ever since Congress had convened in the morning. He had placed a boy at the door below, to give him notice when the Declaration was approved. As the hours passed without any action, the old graybeard shook his head, saying, "They will never do it!" Suddenly a loud shout reached him from below. The boy clapped his hands, crying, "Ring! Ring!" Grasping the rope, the old man rang the bell proclaiming "Liberty throughout all the land . . ."

The Liberty Bell, with its inscription from Leviticus 25:10 —"Proclaim liberty throughout all the land unto all the Inhabitants thereof—" had originally been imported from England for the State House by Isaac Norris, father-in-law of John Dickinson, in 1752. Now its voice is stilled—the last note sounded for the 114th birthday of George Washington— but the haunting phrases of the document it proclaimed so jubilantly on July 4, 1776, still echo around the earth, bringing the dream of liberty to every part of the globe where men are in bondage—a resounding hope to them of freedom under God.

Since the last ringing of the Liberty Bell in 1846, when a previous crack widened dangerously, it has only been tapped with a rubber mallet to mark historical occasions. The Bell is now on display in the Tower Room of Independence Hall in Philadelphia.

New York approved the Declaration on July 9, and Pennsylvania elected a different slate of delegates on July 20 and adopted independence instructions six days later.

The secret domestic journal of Congress shows that on July 19 it was "Resolved That the Declaration passed on the 4th be fairly engrossed on parchment" and signed by every member.

On August 2 the Declaration on parchment was signed by the members present. In his *Life of Benjamin Franklin,* Jared Sparks reports the following conversation when the members were about to sign: "We must be unanimous," said Hancock; "there must be no pulling different ways; we must all hang together."

"Yes," replied Franklin, "we must, indeed, all hang together, or most assuredly we shall all hang separately."

When John Hancock signed in his bold, large script, it is related that he rose from his seat, saying, "There! John Bull can read my name without spectacles, and may now double his reward of £500 for my head. That is my defiance."

John Adams, in a letter written to William Plumer in 1813, stated he believed several "signed with regret," and several others "with many doubts and much lukewarmness."

Except for John Hancock, whose name as president of Congress was on the printed copies of the Declaration, the names of the Signers were not made public until January, 1777, for fear of reprisals against these Patriots.

The Declaration, engrossed on parchment by Timothy Matlack, clearly and symmetrically, is on display in the Exhibition Hall of The National Archives, Washington, D. C. Each one of its fifty-six Signers is mentioned in this book. The longer biographies have been given to those who seemed the more *famous.*

In reading the sketches of the Signers which follow, shall we join Thomas Jefferson in praying that the principles of the document which they signed at the risk of being "exalted on a high gallows" be eternal?

"And for the support of this Declaration, with a firm reliance on the protection of divine Providence we mutually pledge to each other our Lives, our Fortunes, and our sacred Honor." So the Declaration closes and the signatures follow. It is a pledge that each succeeding generation of Americans must make to our Republic under God.

Josiah Bartlett *1729–1795*

Josiah BARTLETT, New Hampshire delegate to the Continental Congress, and his colleague, William Whipple, were the first to vote for "The resolution for independancy," on July 2, 1776. As the Colonies voted in geographical order, starting with the northernmost, the vote of New Hampshire in the affirmative column is recorded at the top of the list on the original manuscript, now in The National Archives, Washington, D. C. The actual mark is a wide dash, evidently made with a quill pen by John Hancock, who, as president, recorded with a similar dash the vote of each colony as it was cast.

Josiah Bartlett had been an active and firmly convinced Patriot long before independence was the prevailing sentiment in New Hampshire. Born on November 21, 1729, in Amesbury, Massachusetts, he received the rudiments of a classical education and started the study of medicine with his relative, Dr. Ordway of Amesbury, when he was only sixteen years old. Working very hard, he soon exhausted the library of his instructor and was given the opportunity to use that of a neighboring clergyman.

In 1750 Dr. Bartlett began to practice medicine at Kingston, New Hampshire. Desperately ill of a fever in 1752, he was cured by treatment of his own after that of the local physicians had failed. This experience taught him the value of freedom from dogmatical rules of practice. Rapidly rising in his profession, he used Peruvian bark with great success during the prevalence of an alarming throat disease in 1754, a course opposed to common usage.

Starting his political life in 1765 as a delegate to the New Hampshire Legislature, Dr. Bartlett served in this capacity until the Revolution. In the Assembly he frequently opposed the royal policy. Hoping to gain his support, Governor Wentworth appointed Bartlett a justice of the peace and, later, in 1770, gave him the command of a militia regiment. Josiah was not won over, however, continuing as a zealous Whig—the term taken from the seventeenth century English political party which upheld the rights of the people against the royal prerogatives. Elected as a delegate from his colony to the First Continental Congress in 1774, Bartlett was forced to decline this office, due to the loss of his house by fire at that time. Because of his activities as a Patriot, Governor Wentworth deprived him of his civil office and militia command in February, 1775.

Later that year, the Governor left the province, ending ninety-six years of royal rule in New Hampshire, and the Committee of Safety, of which Dr. Bartlett was a member, took over government in the colony when the provincial congress was not in session. In August Josiah Bartlett was appointed colonel of a militia regiment.

Chosen by the New Hampshire Provincial Congress for the Second Continental Congress on August 23, 1775, to replace John Sullivan, "now engaged with the Army" as a brigadier general aiding in the siege of Boston, Bartlett produced his credentials in Congress on September 16. Nathaniel Folsom, the other original New Hampshire delegate to the first Congress, was appointed to the chief command of the New Hampshire troops after the Battle of Lexington. Other representatives from New Hampshire were John Langdon, who served in the second Congress until December, 1775, and in 1777 staked his fortune to equip General Stark's brigade for the effort to check Burgoyne's march from Canada; and William Whipple, elected on January 23, 1776, who came to Congress at the end of February, delayed by roads "so extreem bad."

On October 18, 1775, Congress received a request from New Hampshire for advice about governing the colony. "This instruction might have been obtained by Mr. Langdon, or Mr. Whipple," John Adams recounts in his *Autobiography,* but he always supposed it was General Sullivan who suggested the measure to institute a new government, "because he left Congress with a stronger impression upon his mind of the importance of it, than I ever observed in either of the others."

With the permission of Congress, on January 5, 1776, the Assembly of New Hampshire established a government which was, however, only "to Continue During the Present Unhappy and Unnatural Contest with Great Britain. Protesting & Declaring that we Never Sought to throw off our Dependance upon Great Britain . . . And that we Shall Rejoice if Such a reconciliation . . . can be Effected."

Colonel Bartlett, attending Congress at Philadelphia, wrote to John Langdon about the instructions disavowing independence which had been given the Portsmouth representatives in the New Hampshire Assembly: ". . . by the instructions I find the town (Portsmouth) is very much affraid of the idea Conveyed by the frightful word *Independence!* This week a pamphlet on the subject (*Common Sense*) was printed here, and greedily bought up and read by all ranks of people—I shall send you one of them which you will please to lend round to the people; perhaps on Consideration there may not appear any thing so terrible in that thought as they may at first apprehend if Britain should force us to break off

Connections with her." And Bartlett wrote again to Langdon, telling him that *Common Sense* had run to three editions in Philadelphia, had been reprinted in New York and "by the best information it has had a great effect on the minds of many here and to the Southward."

John Langdon, a successful merchant, wrote to Colonel Bartlett from Portsmouth: "Things are pretty much in the same Situation as they were . . . not one word about *independence,* am ready to think he's gone out of Town, and those gentlemen who kept him Company while in Town, seem rather ashamed of them Selves." Langdon had participated in the removal of gunpowder and military stores from Fort William and Mary in Portsmouth Harbor in December, 1774, one of the first overt acts of the American colonists against the property of the Crown.

A poor frontier colony, New Hampshire was torn between the Patriot faction and that which felt the need of Great Britain's protection. Also there was quite a contrary feeling toward the lead of Massachusetts, the rich and powerful neighbor that had absorbed the New Hampshire towns during part of the seventeenth century.

Of the feelings of the delegates in Congress, Edward Tilghman wrote to his father: "There is reason to believe that the disposition of Congress (a majority) are in favor of reconciliation and abhorrent from independency. The division is this: Rhode Island frequently loses a vote, having only two members, and they differing; New Hampshire, Massachusetts, Connecticut, and the Ancient Dominion hang very much together. They are what we call violent, and suspected of independency. . . ."

Colonel Bartlett wrote on June 6 to Nathaniel Folsom: "The affair of declaring these Colonies Independant States . . . must soon be Decided whatever may be the opinion of the Delegates of New hampshire on that matter they think it their duty to act agreable to the minds of their Con-

stituents and . . . Desire the Explicit Directions of the Legislature . . ." On the day of the postponement, June 10,
Bartlett wrote to John Langdon, requesting instructions and
urging that favorable ones "would Carry great weight with
it (independence)."

In his notes concerning the Colonies which were not yet
ready "for falling from the parent stem," Thomas Jefferson
does not list New Hampshire, and rightly, in spite of that
colony's January stand against independence. The New
Hampshire House of Representatives, sitting at Exeter on
June 11, appointed a committee to prepare "a Declaration of
this General Assembly for Independence . . ."

Folsom, who was present in the Council, replied to Colonel Bartlett on the 15th: ". . . I doubt not you will be pleased
to hear that a prety General harmony in the Grand American Cause Prevails here—the vote for independency you will
see is unanim' in both Houses. . . . I wish you the divine
blssing at the Congress—I doubt not if we remain firm &
united we shall under god disappoint the Sanguenary designs
of ouer Enemies—"

The instructions were "to join with the other Colonies in
declaring The Thirteen United Colonies, A FREE & IN-
DEPENDENT STATE . . ."

Over a week later, John Langdon, now being considered
for Congress' agent of prizes in New Hampshire, wrote from
Portsmouth to his colleague Bartlett that he then knew of
none who opposed independence. He continued: "Those
who did some time since, and had like to have overset the
Government, (and would most certainly have done it, had it
not been for a few), have all been appointed to some office,
either in the Civil or Military Department, and those few
who were worthy, entirely left out. Strange conduct this, by
which the Houses have in great measure lost the confidence
of the people. . . ." The Virginia resolutions he liked "well"

—the Virginians "ever have been as firm as Rocks; *near relations to the Yankees.*"

Presenting the situation in the Continental Congress through the eyes of a New Hampshire delegate, Colonel Whipple wrote on June 17: ". . . there is a great change here since my arrival (February 28) as there was in New Hampshire between the time that the powder was taken from the fort and the battle of Bunker Hill . . . Affairs go bravely as you'll see by the papers." A week later he wrote: "The middle colonies are getting in a good way. Next Monday being the first of July, the grand question is to be debated and I believe determined unanimously. May God unite our hearts in all things that tend to the well being of the rising Empire."

New Hampshire's new instructions reached Philadelphia just in time. Writing to Nathaniel Folsom on the evening of July 1, Colonel Bartlett tells that the independence resolve of their colony "came to hand on Saturday, very seasonably, as that Question was agreable to order this Day taken up in a Committe of the whole House & every Colony fully represented; this much I can inform you that it was agreed to in Committe & I make no Doubt but that by next post I shall be able to send you a formal Declaration of Independency setting forth the reasons &c."

The next day, when the colony of New Hampshire was called upon to start the voting, Josiah Bartlett and his colleague, William Whipple, arose to give the first vote for independence!

Following an order of Congress, on July 6 John Hancock sent a copy of the Declaration approved on July 4 to the Assembly of New Hampshire, along with a letter "to request you will have (it) proclaimed in your Colony . . ." Three days later, Colonel Bartlett sent a copy to Weare: "As we were so happy as to agree in sentiments with our constituents, it gave us the greater pleasure to concur with the Delegates of the other Colonies in the enclosed Declaration. . . ."

Meshech Weare, then at Exeter, answered Hancock's letter, assuring him that, although ". . . a very few months since many persons in this Colony were greatly averse to anything that looked like independence of Great Britain, the late measures planned and executing against us have so altered their opinions that such a Declaration was what they most ardently wished for . . . a very few individuals excepted . . ." And he adds as a "P.S." that the Assembly and Committee of Safety were sitting at Exeter where all future communications should be sent. By being directed to Portsmouth, the express rider who brought the Declaration "went thirty miles out of his way."

Josiah Bartlett is thought to have been the second to sign the Declaration on August 2, following John Hancock. Bartlett's signature, just under the pledge of "our Lives" in the text, is at the head of the extreme right-hand column of names on the priceless parchment—a signature which might have hanged him!

William Whipple, the other New Hampshire delegate present, signed directly below Bartlett. Descended from the Whipples of Ipswich, Massachusetts, this Signer was born in Kittery, Maine, then part of Massachusetts. Benjamin Rush, in his "characters" of the Signers, describes Whipple as "an old sea captain, but liberal in his principles and manners; and a genuine friend to liberty and independance." Whipple was commissioned a brigadier general in 1777 and commanded a brigade of New Hampshire troops at the battles of Saratoga and Stillwater. After the surrender of Burgoyne on October 17, he signed the articles of capitulation with Colonel James Wilkinson on behalf of General Gates and he was one of the officers in charge of conducting the British troops to their encampment on Winter Hill, near Boston. In 1778 he participated in General Sullivan's expedition to Rhode Island.

A member of the New Hampshire Assembly, 1780-1784, Whipple was appointed justice of the State Superior Court in June, 1782. Justice of the peace and quorum in 1784, he was acting in this capacity at the time of his death, the following year.

At the bottom of the extreme right-hand column is the name of Matthew Thornton, the third New Hampshire delegate to sign. A member of the New Hampshire Council when independence was approved, he was elected by that state to the Continental Congress in September, to replace John Langdon, but did not present his credentials in Philadelphia until November 4. A native of Ireland, Thornton came to the Colonies with his father when he was about three or four years old. Following a classical education, he studied medicine and started practice in Londonderry, New Hampshire, soon becoming wealthy. As a surgeon, he accompanied the New Hampshire troops in the expedition against Louisburg in 1745. He was an active Patriot and was chosen president of the provincial convention or Congress which assembled in April, 1775, after Lexington. Speaker of the Assembly in 1776, he was made a judge of the Superior Court of New Hampshire that year, serving until 1782, besides his two terms in the Continental Congress. In 1779 he moved to Exeter, and then settled on a farm at Merrimack, retiring from medical practice. A state senator and a member of the Council, he also wrote political articles for the newspapers. Of this Signer, who died in 1803, Benjamin Rush, a Pennsylvania Signer, wrote: "Matthew Thornton. A practitioner of physic, of Irish extraction. He abounded in anecdotes, and was for the most part happy in the application of them. He was ignorant of the world, but was believed to be a sincere patriot and an honest man."

Josiah Bartlett, according to Rush, was a "practitioner of physic, of excellent character, and warmly attached to the liberties of his country." Appointed general naval agent in June, 1776, Bartlett left Congress for a while, as his health was failing, and did not resume his seat until 1778. He was with General Stark at the Battle of Bennington, as New Hampshire's medical agent, when the Green Mountain Boys and Continental troops defeated Burgoyne's raiding party on August 16, 1777. Bennington, in the former New Hampshire Land Grant territory, was then headquarters for the newly-formed Vermont Council of Safety.

Justice of the State Superior Court in 1782, Bartlett became chief justice six years later. An active member of the state convention that adopted the federal Constitution in 1788, he declined an election to the United States Senate the following year, due to his advanced age. President of the state in 1790, he became the first governor of New Hampshire under the new state constitution in 1793.

Josiah Bartlett married his cousin, Mary, daughter of Deacon Joseph Bartlett of Newton. Her father was for many years an Indian captive, taken in the attack on Haverhill in 1708. Besides five daughters, Governor and Mrs. Bartlett had three sons, all of whom became physicians and also carried on their father's spirit of devotion to the affairs of their country. Josiah, Jr., was elected a United States Representative. Four other children died in infancy. Bartlett had grandsons, too, who became physicians. A cousin of Josiah's, Enoch Bartlett of Dorchester, Massachusetts, gave his name to the Bartlett pear which is so popular in this country.

Chiefly instrumental in founding the New Hampshire Medical Society, Governor Bartlett served as its first president. Dartmouth College conferred on him a degree of Doctor of Medicine.

A statue of New Hampshire's Signer Bartlett was erected on July 4, 1888, at Amesbury, Massachusetts, his birthplace, and dedicated to his countrymen.

John Greenleaf Whittier composed a poem in honor of Josiah Bartlett, entitled *One of the Signers,* which was read on this occasion. One verse is:

> "Amidst those picked and chosen men,
>   Than his, who here first drew his breath,
> No firmer fingers held the pen
>   That wrote for liberty or death."

Samuel Adams *1722–1803*

SAMUEL ADAMS OF BOSTON is credited with having done more than any man in organizing the forces of revolution in the years immediately preceding the War of Independence. As James Otis' strength and vigor declined, Adams came more to the fore in molding and directing public opinion in his community. "For seven years before the commencement of the war (i.e. from 1768)," he said to Benjamin Rush, "independence has been the first wish of my heart."

Sam was born in Boston on September 27, 1722. His father, Deacon Samuel, was a Boston Adams, two generations away from the Braintree freehold and three from the original settler, Henry Adams of England, who had emigrated to Braintree in 1638. Deacon Adams, a prosperous brewer and merchant, served in the Massachusetts Bay Assembly, was a justice of the peace, deacon of the Old South Church, and town selectman. Once he had been elected to the governing council but was vetoed by the royal governor. He lived in a handsome house on Purchase Street, overlooking the water.

After eight years at the Boston Latin School, where he became proficient in Latin and Greek, young Samuel was sent by his father to Harvard at the age of fourteen. There he received a thorough classical education from the college which required that its students lead "sober, righteous and godly Lives." In 1740, the year of the religious revival called the Great Awakening, Samuel graduated, ranking fifth in his class. The rank or standing of each boy was decided upon during his freshman year and was based solely on his father's political and social position. Sam continued at Harvard, receiving his Master of Arts degree in 1743, on which occasion he spoke on the bold subject of his thesis, the affirmative of "whether it be lawful to resist the Supreme Magistrate, if the Commonwealth cannot be otherwise preserved."

Deacon Adams was financially ruined by the Land Bank in 1741, as were most of the mechanics and artisans, men of the ropewalk and shipyard. Among these were the so-called "radical" element whose club, the Boston Caucus (possibly derived from caulkers), was a political power. The senior Adams was their friend and organizer. His son followed in his political footsteps.

He also helped his father with the newspaper, *The Independent Advertiser,* started by Rogers and Fowle in 1748 "to defend and state the Rights and Liberties of Mankind," and so gained experience in political writing. Deacon Adams died later that year and the paper went out of existence in December, 1749.

Sam did not have his father's success in business. Placed after college as an apprentice with Thomas Cushing, a leading Boston merchant whose son was later a member of the Continental Congress, he lasted only a short while. Then, with capital given him by his father, he failed miserably on his own as a merchant, always preferring politics.

In 1756 he was elected tax collector for Boston. His accounts were always in arrears and he was later sued for his easy methods in collecting!

When James Otis, after his electrifying opposition to the Writs of Assistance, was elected to the House of Representatives in 1761, Samuel Adams became his right-hand man.

Sam's artful pen was a great asset and, though not a member
of the Legislature, his influence was growing. In town meetings he carried great weight and he belonged to many political clubs, always including the Boston Caucus. This was
described by his "cousin Adams" in February, 1763, as meeting in the garret of Tom Dawes' house—"selectmen, assessors,
collectors, wardens, fire-wards and representatives, are regu-
larly chosen before they are chosen in the town. . . . They
send committees to wait on the merchant's club, and to
propose and join in the choice of men and measures." He
mentions Adams and Cooper and others as members who
"smoke tobacco till you cannot see from one end of the garret
to the other."

In the spring of 1764 Sam drafted the annual instructions
to the town's representatives in the Assembly, just as his father had many years before. Besides Otis, the representatives
were Royall Tyler, Oxenbridge Thacher and Thomas Cushing. Opposing Lord Grenville's program and the Sugar Act
—taxing for revenue for the first time, instead of regulation
of trade—Sam asked: "For if our Trade may be taxed why not
our Lands? Why not the Produce of our Lands & everything
we possess or make use of? This we apprehend annihilates our
Charter Right to govern & tax ourselves. . . . It strikes at our
Brittish Privileges . . ." If taxed without legal representation,
he continued, "are we not reduced from the Character of free
Subjects to the miserable State of tributary Slaves?" He further requested that the weight of the other Colonies be added
to Massachusetts, as they were all embarked in "this most
important Bottom," so that the "united Applications of all
who are aggrieved" might bring "Redress."

Samuel Adams was living then on old property of his father's at the South End of Boston, down by the docks, where
he was in the midst of his friends. His first wife, Elizabeth
Checkley, had died in 1757, leaving two children, Samuel and
Hannah. Three others died in infancy. In December, 1764,

Sam married Elizabeth Wells, whose loyalty and skill in household management kept the family in some comfort, despite their meager income. In the household then were the two children, a freed slave girl and a big Newfoundland dog named Queue.

Though shabby to the point of extreme poverty, Sam Adams knew everybody in his beloved Boston and was an invaluable ambassador, from the highest circles to the lowest—excepting the circle of the Governor and his "court" party! Writing a great deal himself, Sam also looked over Otis' writings, "to pour a little oil in them." He was incorruptible, having little regard for money or power. Always an extremely pious man, he was a regular churchgoer, attending Dr. Samuel Cooper's Brattle Street Church. Dr. Cooper was one of the Patriot Congregational ministers later known to the Tories as the "black regiment."

On August 14, 1765, resentment in Boston against the coming enforcement of the Stamp Act in November burst out in a mob riot and the hanging in effigy of the stamp collector from the Liberty Tree, a large oak in Hanover Square. A spectator who said he saw "Adams under the tree of liberty" asked him who and what the effigies were. Sam replied that "he did not know—he could not tell—he wanted to inquire." But it was generally thought that he had been involved. Adams became one of the leading Sons of Liberty —Patriot groups whose name was derived from Barré's pro-American speech in Parliament during the Stamp Act debate. Wilkes-Barre, in Pennsylvania, was named by the Patriots in his honor and that of John Wilkes.

In September, Sam Adams was again chosen to draft instructions for the delegates in the Assembly and he urged them, in opposing the Stamp Act, to have "the inherent, unalienable Rights of the People" asserted and recorded so that posterity might never charge them "with the Guilt of tamely giving them away." And the "best Oeconomy" was urged "in expending the publick money."

To fill the vacancy caused by the death of Oxenbridge Thacher, an acclaimed Patriot, the Boston town meeting elected Sam Adams to the Assembly, where he soon became influential and known as Otis' chief lieutenant—though heavily in arrears in tax money! Popular on committees, he usually had "a set of resolves, ready cut & dryed" for consideration when appointed.

The hated Stamp Act, requiring stamp duties on internal business, having given the Colonies a common cause for action, James Otis followed Adams' suggestion of the previous year and proposed an intercolonial congress to the Massachusetts Assembly. Representatives from nine British Colonies met in New York in October, 1765, as a result of this motion, and sent petitions to King and Parliament.

While Otis was in New York at the Stamp Act Congress, Adams wrote a series of resolves for the Massachusetts Assembly: "That there are certain essential rights . . . which are founded in the law of God and nature" and that the foregoing resolves be kept so "that a just sense of liberty and the firm sentiments of loyalty be transmitted to posterity."

James Otis had written of natural law under God two years before in his *The Rights of the British Colonies Asserted and Proved* and Adams emphasized these God-given rights upon which the American Republic was later founded.

Boston's two rival "mobs" were brought together and consolidated by the beginning of November. From that time on they acted as a "trained Mob," of which Sam Adams was said to be the keeper.

In December, John Adams, in commenting on a meeting of the Monday night club, "warm to have the courts open," without using the hated stamps, described Sam in his diary. "Adams, I believe, has the most thorough understanding of liberty and her resources in the temper and character of the people, though not in the law and constitution; as well as the most habitual, radical love of it, as well as the most correct, genteel and artful pen. He is a man of refined policy, steadfast integrity, exquisite humanity, genteel erudition, obliging, engaging manners, real as well as professed piety, and a universal good character, unless it should be admitted that he is too attentive to the public, and not enough so to himself and his family."

On receiving the news of the Stamp Act repeal in May, 1766, the Sons of Liberty celebrated. Plans included "such illuminations, bonfires, pyramids, obelisks . . . fireworks as were never before seen in America." Sam Adams felt in his "humble Opinion the Fate of the Colonys turnd" upon the "Union" formed to oppose the Act, as he wrote to Christopher Gadsden of South Carolina in December. But his fears were aroused by the Declaratory Act, accompanying the repeal, stating that the British Parliament had "full power and authority to make laws . . . to bind the colonies and people of *America*, subjects of the crown of *Great Britain*, in all cases whatsoever."

Becoming clerk of the Assembly on May 28, 1766, Sam Adams continued to serve in that body until 1774. He composed, as well as recorded, state papers and wrote many political articles, signed with different names, such as Puritan and Candidus, most of which appeared in the *Boston Gazette*, that "most factious paper in America." The opposition complained that all his work seemed "in general designed for the Press & for that Purpose only." As clerk and head of a recess committee, he exerted great influence for the Patriot cause and built the spark lighted by James Otis into a "perpetual flame."

From as early as 1758, Samuel Adams made it a constant rule to watch the rise of every brilliant genius, "to court his friendship" and "to fix his affections and reflections on the side of his native country." These included, to name a few,

Dr. Joseph Warren who fell at Bunker Hill, John Hancock, later president of Congress, and Josiah Quincy, the Boston Cicero who, though mortally ill, traveled to England in 1774 to present the Patriot side. As Peter Oliver later complained, Hancock became as close to Adams as the "Rattles are affixed to the Tail of the Rattle Snake."

In opposition to the Townshend Acts of 1767, the Massachusetts Assembly approved the famous "circular letter" of February 11, 1768, and copies were sent to the other Colonies, asking their "Sentiments." This letter, proposed by Otis and Adams, denied Parliament's power to raise revenue through external taxes or duties and opposed the plan to use this revenue to pay the salaries of the royal governors and colonial judges, making these officials independent of the colonial assemblies. The letter stated that the Townshend measures were "Infringements of their natural & constitutional Rights" because Parliament "by those Acts grant their Property without their consent." Sam Adams denied the Tories' charge that the resolution was "procured by surprise in a thin house."

John Adams wrote to William Tudor in March, 1819, that the circular letter and other papers approved by the Assembly in early 1768 "demonstrate the rough cast of James Otis and the polish and burnish of Samuel Adams." Otis had told him that he gave the material to Sam "to quieu whew them."

To the Patriots, Sam "smoothed with an oily brush"; while to the royal governor, "every dip of his pen stung like a horned snake."

The circular letter brought enthusiastic responses from other Colonies. These were published in the *Gazette*. From Parliament in June came a demand that the House rescind the resolution which had given rise to this "flagitious attempt to disturb the public peace." The House refused—ninety-two to seventeen—and was dissolved by the Governor. To commemorate "the Glorious Ninety-two," Paul Revere made a silver bowl and the Philadelphia Legislature sent a song to the *Gazette,* praising the Ninety-two and referring to the Seventeen as "slaves ingrained." This song must have been a welcome selection for the singing societies organized by Sam Adams among the Boston mechanics which, the Tories charged, trained more revolutionaries than songbirds.

The riot of June 10 on the seizure of Hancock's sloop *Liberty* led off a summer of increasing tension, due to the expected arrival of British troops. Adams advocated resistance to military rule. In September, at Otis' suggestion, the Boston Town Meeting called a convention of all the Massachusetts towns, and on Sam Adams' motion approved a Fast Day to pray for divine aid. The convention assembled in Faneuil Hall, before the troops arrived, and only voted to send the King another copy of the February House Petition. But this extra-legal institution, of which Samuel Adams was clerk, drew the colony together and was the forerunner of the Massachusetts Provincial Congress.

Landing unopposed, the British regiments garrisoned Boston while Sam Adams and other Patriots worked on in opposition to this "military tyranny." There was a danger that he, with Otis and Hancock, would be hung in England for treason and they came "within an hair's breadth of it."

The highly charged atmosphere exploded on March 5, 1770, into the Boston Massacre, of which Paul Revere made the well-known engraving. A mass meeting, held the next day, sent Sam Adams and a committee to the acting governor to demand the removal of the British troops. In the Council Chamber of the State House, hung with "glorious portraits" of two kings and "little miserable likenesses" of Puritan governors ."in obscure corners," Sam Adams, "a plain, simple, decent citizen, of middling stature, dress, and manners," made his plea before Lieutenant Governor Hutchinson and the Council, resplendent in white wigs and English scarlet cloth cloaks, as John Adams described the scene in an 1817 letter to William Tudor. Hutchinson, Sam's long-time foe, and the British commander agreed to remove one regiment, whereupon Samuel Adams arose "with an air of dignity and majesty . . . stretched forth his arm, though even then quivering with palsy," and said in a decisive and harmonious voice that "nothing short of the total evacuation of the town by all the regular troops" would satisfy the people or preserve the peace. After some hesitation, it was agreed to evacuate all troops and these forces were later described by Lord North as "Sam Adams' two regiments."

Sam Adams also opposed the Townshend Acts by promoting the nonimportation agreement, adopted by Boston merchants in March, 1768, by which importation of British goods was suspended until the Acts should be repealed. And he worked hard to reach the people through the *Gazette,* published by Edes and Gill. In his diary entry for September 3, 1769, John Adams tells of spending the evening with Samuel Adams, Otis, Gill and another Patriot, "preparing for the next day's newspaper—a curious employment, cooking up paragraphs, articles, occurrences, &c., working the political machine!"

When, except for the tax on tea, the Townshend Acts were repealed in March, 1770, Sam Adams had a difficult time rousing people to the dangers still present. *"Fair promises,"* he warned, writing as Candidus on September 30, 1771, were only to lull them "into that *quietude* and *sleep* by which *slavery* is always preceeded. . . . While treachery and imposition is the fort of any man, let us remember, *there is always most danger when his professions are warmest."* The Whig party split and declined to such a low point that members finally demanded that Adams and Hancock reconcile their aims. To prove complete agreement, Hancock commissioned Copley to paint their portraits, and the two pictures, shown in this book, were hung side by side in Hancock's drawing-room.

Following the news, in 1772, that the colonial judges of the Massachusetts Superior Court were to be paid by the Crown from the customs revenue, making them independent of the Assembly, Sam Adams established the Boston Committee of Correspondence on November 2. Stating their rights under "the laws of God and nature," and their grievances, the Boston Committee invited the sentiments of the other towns of the province. The response was very heartening. Scrolls of resolves from the surrounding towns arrived in Boston, sent by almost a hundred local committees. In March, the Virginia Legislature passed a motion, instituted by Jefferson, to make the committees of correspondence intercolonial.

In the early summer of 1773, Adams received a packet of letters written by Hutchinson and obtained somehow by Benjamin Franklin in London. On June 16, Sam read the letters aloud before the Legislature, and the House passed resolves holding the Governor and Oliver responsible for the "Misery" brought to Massachusetts.

When the hated tea ships appeared in Boston Harbor later that year, feeling ran high. Hutchinson refused clearance papers, insisting that the duty be paid. On December 16 Patriots crowded into the Old South Meeting House to hear his answer to a last appeal for a clearance. As the candles were being lighted, a refusal came, and Sam Adams solemnly declared: "This meeting can do nothing more to save the country." This was the signal which started the Boston Tea Party described in the Prologue. John Adams claimed he did not know any of the names of the participants but wrote that they were "no ordinary Mohawks."

News of Boston's punishment, the Port Bill, came in May. A town meeting was held on May 13 and Adams and the Committee immediately spread word of their plight. Paul Revere rode south with the important letters to the other Colonies. On June 2 further acts of Parliament were proclaimed—the Murder Bill, ordering disturbers of the King's peace to be transported out of the province for trial, and an act taking away the colony's self-government.

On June 5 the Committee of Correspondence sent out Sam Adams' Solemn League and Covenant, asking that the Colonies take an oath against importation of British goods and against exportation to Great Britain as well, until the Port Act was repealed. This measure was not then approved.

About this time the new royal governor, General Gage, attempted to buy or threaten Sam Adams away from the Patriot cause, warning through an emissary that he was empowered to send Adams to England to stand trial for treason. Adams replied that he trusted he had long since made his *"peace with the King of Kings"* and that no personal consideration could induce him to abandon the "righteous cause of my country." Governor Hutchinson had known it was useless to try bribery—"Such is the obstinacy and inflexible disposition of the man," he explained to a friend.

On June 17, in the Massachusetts House, then meeting in exile in Salem, Samuel Adams made a motion that a "General Congress of deputies meet at Philadelphia." Five delegates—Thomas Cushing, James Bowdoin, Samuel Adams, John Adams and Robert Treat Paine—were named. The Tory members present were locked in but one escaped to warn the Governor. From outside the locked door, the Governor's messenger ordered the meeting dissolved. "Stand your ground," said Sam to the watchman while business was concluded. It is said the key was in his pocket. This was the last Provincial Assembly to convene in Massachusetts under royal authority.

On August 10, Sam Adams and his fellow delegates assembled at the house of Thomas Cushing, with the exception of James Bowdoin who was unable to go. A group had gathered to see them off and the scene was gay as a splendid coach drew up to the door. But fear ran underneath—Governor

Gage might seize the four delegates. Sam Adams' head was forfeit.

As the coach set off, in full view of the British regiments, Sam was handsomely dressed. New wig, new red cloak, new cocked hat, shoes with silver buckles, silk hose, and gold-headed cane stamped with the emblem of the Sons of Liberty —all presented anonymously by certain of the Patriots. The importance of a well-dressed delegation at Philadelphia was recognized. Representing the other Colonies there were delegates of large fortunes and estates.

When the Philadelphia Sons of Liberty and others met the Massachusetts delegation at Frankfort, they revealed that Samuel Adams had been represented as "a very artful, designing man, but desperately poor, and wholly dependent on his popularity with the lowest vulgar for his living." As to the importance of the Frankfort advice to let Virginia take the lead, Pickering, in *Political Essays* 1812, stated that Adams assured him it was the deciding factor in the choice of Jefferson to write the Declaration—"with a significance of countenance, in making the remark, which distinguished that wily politician."

At the Congress, Adams supported the motion to have the sessions opened with prayer. When the Suffolk Resolves were passed by Congress, Adams felt America would aid Boston "to the utmost." He helped defeat Galloway's Plan of Union, which he feared because of the control over the Colonies it gave to the "Mother-State." Of Adams, Galloway said, he "eats little, drinks little, sleeps little, thinks much, and is most decisive and indefatigable in his objects." In the Association passed by this Congress was some of the spirit of Sam's Solemn League and Covenant, although it did not go as far as he wished.

In April, 1775, Adams feared the imminent arrest of the top Patriots, and with John Hancock he was in hiding at Lexington when Gage started hostilities. Heading south for the opening of the second Congress on May 10, Sam was persuaded by his cousin John to learn to ride. After a painful beginning, he became proficient and this ability served him in good stead later when Congress was forced to flee from Philadelphia to escape capture.

In that Congress, Sam, a "violent" man, pushed for independence when he could. Although very active in debates and "out-of-doors," he did not speak often in Congress. But on that occasion of extreme importance—during the debate on Lee's June 7 motion—the speech he made in regard to support for independence in the different Colonies, as told in the Prologue, swung the majority of Congress to independence. Due to Adams' eloquence, Morton of Pennsylvania changed his vote to independence on July 1. Surely this was one of the occasions when Adams' "feelings raised him . . . upon his toes at the close of his sentences," as Rush said happened frequently.

Of his character, Rush, who knew him well, wrote: "He was near sixty years of age when he took his seat in Congress, but possessed all the vigor of mind of a young man of five and twenty. He was a republican in principle and manners. . . . He dreaded the undue influence of an individual in a Republic, and once said to me 'Let us beware of continental and State great men.' He loved simplicity and oeconomy in the administration of government, and despised the appeals which are made to the eyes and ears of the common people in order to govern them. He considered national happiness and the public patronage of religion as inseparably connected; and so great was his regard for public worship, as the means of promoting religion" that, when there was no service in the chapel of Congress he attended divine service in the German church in York while the governing body met there, although not understanding a word of German. "His morals were irreproachable, and even ambition and avarice, the usual vices of politicians, seemed to have no place in his breast. . . . both friends and enemies agree in viewing him as one of the most active instruments of the American Revolution."

Adams continued in Congress until 1781 and served on the committee to prepare a plan of confederation. In 1779 he was a member of the convention which framed the 1780 Massachusetts constitution. He also was a member of the state convention that ratified the Constitution of the United States. Lieutenant governor of Massachusetts in 1789, he served as Governor from 1794 to 1797. He died in 1803.

"Mr. Adams was born and tempered a wedge of steel to split the knot of *lignum vitae,* which tied North America to Great Britain. Blunderheaded as were the British ministry, they had sagacity enough to discriminate from all others, for inexorable vengeance, the two men most to be dreaded by them, Samuel Adams and John Hancock . . ." John Adams wrote to William Tudor about these Patriots. James Otis' name would have been included, too, had he not been incapacitated by a blow on his head which aggravated his instability. These three "were the first movers, the most constant, steady, persevering springs, agents, and most disinterested sufferers and firmest pillars of the whole Revolution. I shall not attempt even to draw the outlines of the biography of Mr. Samuel Adams. Who can attempt it?"

In June, 1775, when it became known that Adams and Hancock were excluded from Governor Gage's general pardon of the twelfth, Adams' renown in the Colonies increased. He was styled by Thomas Jefferson, "the Man of the Revolution."

No Patriot had greater faith in America's future in the discouraging early days of the struggle for liberty. Samuel Adams had "long been of Opinion that America herself under God must finally work out her own Salvation."

Adams, who early navigated by the "polestar of independency," has left our Republic a lodestar to follow:

"May the administration of the federal government, and those of the several states of the union, be guided by the unerring finger of Heaven!"

John Hancock *1737–1793*

JOHN HANCOCK is known to everyone who has ever studied the Declaration of Independence as the writer of the big bold confident signature immediately under the text. "Put your John Hancock here" is a phrase which now stands in our language for signing on dotted lines. When Hancock signed as President of the Continental Congress, "at the risk of our lives, our fortunes and our sacred honor," he was putting on an uncharted line his life, already proclaimed forfeit; a fortune which was one of the largest in America; and his honor—long risked for his native land.

This Patriot was a direct cause of the Battle of Lexington —part of General Gage's plan of action having been to arrest him and Samuel Adams. John's grandfather, the Reverend John Hancock, was pastor of the Congregational Church in Lexington, Massachusetts, for many years and it was in his former parsonage that John was being entertained that eventful night of April 18, 1775. The Patriot's father, also a John, was minister of the Congregational Church at Braintree, Massachusetts, from 1726 until his death in 1744. The Signer's mother, Mary Hawke Hancock, was left almost penniless at her husband's death, with three small children, Ebenezer, Mary and John to raise. Her brother-in-law, Thomas

[50]

Hancock, and his wife, Lydia Henchman Hancock, took the seven-year-old John to live with them in their mansion on Beacon Hill, in Boston. A merchant of great wealth, Thomas Hancock made the boy his heir.

Handsomely dressed, John attended the Latin School, and during vacations was taken in the Hancock chaise down to his grandfather's parsonage at Lexington for the country air. When restless there, he was driven over to the parsonage at Bedford where his uncle and aunt, the Reverend Nicholas and Lucy Hancock Bowes, lived with their children. These young cousins made John's visits very merry and he was given the best the parsonage afforded. He was even allowed to dip his quill pen in his uncle's "inkstand dish" when displaying his penmanship.

Sometimes his cousin, Lucy Bowes, would be visiting her grandparents at Lexington when John was there and the two children would romp over the Lexington hills, peer into the old church belfry or make mud pies at its base. Young John also was kept in touch with his mother, brother and sister.

John Hancock went to Harvard, graduating in the class of 1754, and then entered his uncle's firm as a clerk. He worked hard and in 1760 was sent abroad to represent the business house in London. He is said to have been presented to the newly-crowned George III, who gave him a gold snuff-box. If true, this gift must have been much regretted a few years later.

After his return to America, John was taken into partnership by his uncle, on January 1, 1763, "having had long Experience of his Uprightness, & great Abilities for Business. . . ." The firm were importers, merchants and ship-owners. They exported products of the whale fisheries, supplied the British garrisons at Annapolis and Chignecto, Nova Scotia, on the Bay of Fundy, and did some financing, since there were then no banks in the province.

John Hancock dressed elegantly, as suited his position. A

dandy of the day, he wore a shirtfront trimmed with fine lace with a large brooch pinned in it, gold-laced coat of red or blue broadcloth, breeches of green or red velvet or satin ones of white, lilac or blue, and fine shoes with buckles of silver or gold.

Stricken by apoplexy at the old State House while serving as a member of the Governor's Council, Thomas Hancock died on August 1, 1764. He left a large fortune to his nephew, to carry on the business, and John Hancock made plans to expand it. Interesting records of his transactions and his readiness to help others are found in his letter book, marked on the flyleaf with the famous autograph.

In March, 1765, John Hancock was named a selectman of Boston, as his uncle had been before him. In addition to this new responsibility, he was trying that spring to reach an agreement with William Rotch of Nantucket about the whale oil trade.

In late August, Hancock wrote to his London agents, telling them of the riots caused by the general dissatisfaction over the Stamp Act and warning them that "it is a Cruel hardship upon us & unless we are Redressed we must be Ruin'd. . . ." He urged the agents to promote the colonists' interests with the London merchants or else "the fatal Effects of these Grievances you will very Sensibly feel; our Trade must decay . . ." His ship *Liberty* carried this letter to England on her first voyage.

In September, Hancock, as a selectman, must have approved the new instructions drawn up for the Boston representatives, protesting the Stamp Act. These included the charge that this act weakened "the best Security of our Lives Libertys and Estates . . ." A move to economize by giving up the garrisons on the eastern frontier that Hancock's firm supplied apparently did not pass, as he was still provisioning Annapolis and Chignecto the next year.

Writing to his London agents just before the dreaded enforcement of the Stamp Act, John Hancock declared he would not "send one Ship more to Sea nor to have any kind of Connection in Business under a Stamp" and that a copy of this letter would remain in his Letter Book to show posterity and his children that he did not consent to this "Cruel Act" and submit to "Slavery."

In December, Hancock's ship, the *Boston Packet,* sailed without a stamp. Although the Stamp Act was in effect, the customs officers cleared the ship, certifying that no stamps were available. The law courts, however, were still closed to business and Hancock served with Adams in preparing a petition to the Governor, asking that the courts proceed without using stamps.

Determined to abide by the "United Resolves" of the principal merchants and traders of Boston and the province, Hancock wrote his agents that he would "not import one single manufacture of Great Britain" until the "grievous" Act was repealed. Business was largely suspended during the winter. The Patriots exerted a strong influence—"Hancock and his crew" they were labeled.

On May 16, a copy of the Repeal arrived in Boston, brought by a Hancock ship, and was joyfully celebrated.

When the question of a new representative for Boston came up before the May, 1766, elections, John Rowe, a successful Patriot merchant, was suggested, but Samuel Adams, looking up to the Hancock mansion, is reported to have said, "Is there not another John who would do better?" Hancock was elected.

Of his fortune at that time, John Adams reported that "not less than a thousand families were, every day in the year, dependent on Mr. Hancock for their daily bread. Consider his real estate in Boston, in the country, in Connecticut, and the rest of New England. Had Mr. Hancock fallen asleep to this day (1817), he would now awake one of the richest men. . . ." But Adams continued that "no man's property was ever more entirely devoted to the public."

John Hancock, who had nothing to gain and everything to lose, again concurred in nonimportation during the spring of 1768, to protest the Revenue Acts of 1767. When his ship *Liberty* docked later, she had on board some Madeira wine, but this had been ordered seven months previously. The import duties were evaded, as was the custom, and the cargo of Madeira was unloaded while the revenue officer was forcibly held. As punishment for evading the duties, Hancock's sloop was seized on June 10 by a boarding party from the *Romney,* a British warship, newly arrived from Halifax. A mob gathered in protest and destroyed a small boat belonging to a customs man.

A town meeting was called and a committee was appointed to wait on the Governor and request the removal of the *Romney.* John Hancock served on this committee and also on the one which called the convention of Boston towns in September. As the Assembly had been dissolved by the Governor, it seemed imperative to meet before the expected British regiments arrived.

In the Boston *Gazette,* Hancock's letter of November 12 refuted a charge made in that paper that he had sought by letter to supply the British regiments which had arrived in Boston the end of September.

The case of the sloop *Liberty* was brought up in Admiralty Court, and Hancock secured John Adams as counsel. These legal proceedings against him only served to increase his popularity and he was re-elected as selectman and representative in the spring of 1769.

After the Boston Massacre in 1770, John Hancock served with Samuel Adams on the committee appointed to secure the removal of the British troops.

In 1772, he contributed handsomely to the new Brattle Street Church, ordering glass from England and reserving the right to build a mahogany pulpit. Some years earlier he had provided a collection of books for the Harvard Library, in his uncle's name and his own.

Hancock, who may have had an interest in two of the ships sent to Boston with East India tea in the fall of 1773, dispatched his trusted agent, William Palfry, to New York and Philadelphia at the beginning of December to communicate the Boston feeling about tea. On December 21, he wrote to his London agents, telling them that all of the tea had been thrown into the salt water and that "No one circumstance could possibly have taken place more effectively to unite the Colonies than this manouvre" of sending the taxed tea to be sold in America, which was universally resented and detested.

In March of 1774, John Hancock delivered the Massacre Oration, speaking out boldly against British oppression. In May he was re-elected to the General Court or Assembly, and the town took action in regard to the Boston Port Bill for "annihilating the trade of this town."

The Governor revoked Colonel Hancock's appointment as Commander of the Cadets in August. Gage's order for the General Court to convene on October 5, later countermanded, resulted in an assembly of about ninety. These resolved themselves into a provincial congress of which John Hancock was made chairman. He was elected president of the second Provincial Congress, opening at Cambridge the first of February, 1775. He made a motion on the fourth day that Colonel Roberson deliver four field pieces and two mortars to the Committee of Safety. Two of these—known as the Hancock and the Adams—are to be seen today at the Bunker Hill Monument, in the summit chamber.

In March, Colonel Hancock's mansion was twice molested by British soldiers but he was not swerved from attending the second session of the Provincial Congress, which assembled in Concord on March 22, and presiding as president until the adjournment on April 15. Because of the threatening situation in Boston, it appears that John Hancock and Samuel Adams went immediately to the parsonage of the former's cousins, Reverend and Mrs. Jonas Clark, at Lexington—previously the home of John's grandfather, where he had so often visited as a boy. Madam Hancock and her young friend, Dorothy Quincy, were there, too.

As Longfellow tells about the events of that fateful night of April 18, and of the ride of Paul Revere to arouse the Patriots:

> "It was one by the village clock,
> When he galloped into Lexington . . ."

Hancock and Adams were driven over to seek refuge at the Woburn Precinct parsonage. But a false alarm prevented their staying there and the two Patriots were guided through the woods by Cuff, the parsonage Negro slave, to the home of Amos Wyman, in Billerica.

To avoid arrest by General Gage, Hancock, a newly-elected delegate, and Adams proceeded immediately on their journey to Philadelphia for the opening of the Second Continental Congress on May 10, without venturing near Boston.

From Worcester, on April 24, Hancock wrote to the Committee of Safety, very much worried about what was happening and what measures were being taken. He asked for all particulars of the Battle of Lexington, the conduct of the troops from the nineteenth, "the certainty of their firing first," so that he could spread the information on the trip and especially at Philadelphia.

In Congress, John Hancock was popular with both "violents" and "moderates" and he was elected president of that body on May 24, when Peyton Randolph of Virginia retired. Hancock and Adams having been hunted by General Gage in the raid on Lexington, Benjamin Harrison of Virginia is said to have remarked, as he conducted Hancock to the president's chair, that "We will show Britain how much we value her proscriptions."

While he was nominating George Washington as Commander in Chief, John Adams saw that Mr. Hancock was listening to him with visible pleasure until he revealed his choice as Washington. Then "Mortification and resentment were expressed as forcibly as his face could exhibit them," since the president himself had wanted the post. But the next day, in writing to Elbridge Gerry, Hancock referred to Washington as a fine man, and three years later he named his son John George Washington Hancock.

After the scare of Lexington, John's aunt, Madam Hancock, and Dorothy Quincy went to visit Mr. and Mrs. Thaddeus Burr in Fairfield, Connecticut. Dorothy, or "Dolly" as the now president of the Continental Congress called her, married John Hancock on August 28, 1775. The wedding was celebrated at Fairfield and the young couple went to live in Philadelphia. It is said that Aaron Burr, a cousin of the Thaddeus Burrs, came to visit at Fairfield earlier that summer. Madam Hancock thwarted his efforts to distract the young lady from her fiancé. Dorothy Hancock was a second cousin once removed of Abigail Adams. She grew up in Braintree and her sister Esther had married Jonathan Sewall, John Adams' best friend before the Revolution divided them.

The following winter President Hancock sent some resolutions to General Washington with a covering letter. He recounted that the last one, relative to an attack on Boston, was passed after a serious debate and added, "May God crown your attempt with success . . . though I may be the greatest sufferer."

After the evacuation of Boston by the British in March, 1776, Hancock heard that his house was not much damaged, his furniture was in "tolerable order," and his family pictures were untouched.

The "moderates" had worked to influence Hancock. John Adams tells in his *Autobiography,* under date of March 15, that Mr. Harrison of Virginia "had courted Mr. Hancock, and Mr. Hancock had courted Mr. Duane, Mr. Dickinson, and their party, and leaned so partially in their favor, that Mr. Samuel Adams had become very bitter against Mr. Hancock . . ." And it was a blow to the "violents" when Hancock nominated Harrison of the "cold party," to the important chairmanship of the committee of the whole in March, instead of Samuel Ward, a long-time Liberty man.

On June 11, Hancock wrote to Washington that Congress, in a committee of the whole, had been deliberating two days on "three capital matters, the most important in their nature of any that have yet been before us . . ."

As soon as the Declaration of Independence was passed on July 4, copies, on which appeared only the names of the president and the secretary of Congress, were printed and sent by Hancock to the different Colonies and to General Washington. On the sixth, Hancock wrote to the latter, asking that he have the enclosed declaration proclaimed to the army, and saying that now they would "trust the event to that Being, who controls both causes and events. . . ."

When John Hancock put his bold signature on the parchment bearing the Declaration on August 2, presumably the first to sign, he is quoted as remarking, "I write so that George the Third may read without his spectacles."

In the face of the advancing British army, Congress fled from Philadelphia to Baltimore on December 12. It was an especially anxious time for the president of Congress, as a baby daughter had recently been born. She was named Lydia for his aunt, and she lived only a few months.

The Congress returned to Philadelphia in February, 1777, and John Hancock served as president until October of that year. He continued to be a member of Congress until 1780.

As a major general of militia, he commanded the Massachusetts troops in the Rhode Island expedition of 1778. He was a member of the convention which framed the Massachusetts constitution and was elected the first governor of the state, serving from 1780 to 1785, and again, after two years, until his death in 1793. As Governor he presided over the Massachusetts Convention which ratified the Constitution of the United States in 1788.

Rush wrote that Hancock was "fond of the ceremonies of public life," his conversation was "desultory, and his manners much influenced by frequent attacks of the gout . . . he was a disinterested patriot, and made large sacrifices of an ample estate to the liberties and independance of his country."

"Of Mr. Hancock's life, character, generous nature, great and disinterested sacrifices, and important services . . . I should be glad to write a volume," John Adams declared.

Those who feel that the *John Hancock* on the Declaration is written too large might remember that the document was then considered by many to be a death warrant. Also, if any should read, among other documents of these heroic times, a love letter to his "Dearest Dolly," they will find that the signature after "forever yours" equals in size that with which he risked everything he had for the cause of liberty under God.

John Adams *1735–1826*

OF JOHN ADAMS and his cousin Samuel in the Continental Congress, Thomas Jefferson wrote: ". . . in the discussions on the floor of Congress he (Samuel Adams) reposed himself on our main pillar in debate Mr. John Adams. these two gentlemen were verily a host in our councils. comparisons with their associates, Northern or Southern, would answer no profitable purpose, but they would suffer by comparison with none."

John Adams, Signer of the Declaration and later second President of the United States he had helped so devotedly to build, was the fifth generation of the Adams family to live in Braintree, Massachusetts, farming the land, practicing frugality and thrift. Henry Adams, the first of the line in the New World, emigrated from England in 1638. John's grandmother, Hannah Bass Adams, was a granddaughter of John Alden and his wife Priscilla, who had said, "Speak for yourself, John!" when he had called to promote Miles Standish's courtship of this spirited young lady. John Adams wrote of his father as "a deacon of the church, and a selectman of the town, almost all the business of the town being managed by him in that department for twenty years together; a man of strict piety, and great integrity . . ." John's mother Susanna, "a pious Woman," was a daughter of Peter Boylston. Her uncle, Zabdiel Boylston, who lived in a mansion in Brookline, had, with Cotton Mather, introduced the smallpox inoculation to Massachusetts in the terrible epidemic of 1721. John, born on October 30, 1735, in the Adamses' one and a half-story house, was the oldest of three sons.

Growing up in Braintree, he went to Dame School and to Mr. Cleverly's Latin School. His free time was spent "in making and sailing Boats, in swimming, skaiting, flying kites and shooting, in marbles, Nine-pins, Bat and Ball, Football &c. &c. &c. Quoits, Wrestling and sometimes Boxing and what was no better running about to Quiltings and Huskings and Frolicks and Dances . . ." Following the custom of his own father, Deacon Adams saved for years to send John to Harvard as his share of patrimony, intending him for the Congregational ministry. After preparing with Joseph Marsh, John entered the college in 1751, in a freshman class of twenty-four. Sam Quincy, a Braintree neighbor, was a sophomore; also John Hancock, originally from Braintree. As indicated before, class listings in those days were based on family standings, and the next spring John was graded fourteenth, possibly due to the stature of the Boylstons. His second cousin Samuel had been fifth of twenty-two some years before, but Sam's father had been a member of the Massachusetts Legislature and had held several offices in Boston.

John worked hard at Harvard and read avidly. In his *Autobiography* he tells that "The last two years of my residence at college produced a club of students . . . who invited me to become one of them. Their plan was to spend their evenings together in reading any new publications, or any poetry or dramatic compositions that might fall in their way. I was as often requested to read as any other, especially tragedies, and it was whispered to me and circulated among others that I had some faculty for public speaking, and that I should make a better lawyer than divine . . . My inclination was soon fixed on the law."

Soon after graduating in July, 1755, John, not yet twenty, went to Worcester as Latin master for the grammar school there. Worcester was "immersed in politics" and talk of war. General Braddock and his forces, along with young George Washington, had been routed at Fort Duquesne in July by the French and their Indian allies. Reflecting on this and other events, John wrote to his cousin, Nathan Webb, ". . . if we can remove the turbulent Gallicks (French), our people . . . will in another century become more numerous than England itself. Should this be the case . . . the united force of all Europe will not be able to subdue us. The only way to keep us from setting up for ourselves is to disunite us. Divide et impera. Keep us in distinct colonies. . . ."

In November the new schoolmaster started a diary into which he poured his philosophical thinking, as well as his activities. He thought a great deal on religion and transcribed religious tracts into a copybook. The diary entry for March 14, 1756, mentions "Mr. Franklin, of Philadelphia, a prodigious genius, cultivated with prodigious industry." Of his school, adjustment to which he had found very hard, John writes the following day: "In this little state . . . I have several renowned generals but three feet high, and several deep projecting politicians in petticoats. I have others catching and dissecting flies, accumulating remarkable pebbles, cockle shells &c . . . Some rattle and thunder out A, B, C, with as much fire and impetuosity as Alexander fought, and very often sit down and cry as heartily upon being outspelt, as Caesar did, when at Alexander's sepulchre he recollected that the Macedonian hero had conquered the world before his age. . . ."

John conjectures a great deal about his future and on April 29 the diary says: "Our proper business in this life is not to accumulate large fortunes, not to gain high honors

... but constantly to improve ourselves in habits of piety and virtue." Another conclusion is: "From a sense of the government of God, and a regard to the laws established by his providence, should all our actions for ourselves or for other men primarily originate; and this master passion in a good man's soul, like the larger fishes of prey, will swallow up and destroy all the rest."

He is often discouraged with his progress and writes in July: "I am resolved to rise with the sun, and to study the Scriptures on Thursday, Friday, Saturday, and Sunday mornings. Noons and nights I intend to read English authors. ... May I blush whenever I suffer one hour to pass unimproved."

Deciding on a legal career, John Adams engaged to study law with a Worcester attorney, Mr. Putnam, for two years and teach school at the same time. When this period was up, he went to Boston to seek admission to the bar, unhappily without a recommendation from his patron, who had neglected to give him any. But Mr. Jeremy Gridley offered to sponsor him and advised him in regard to law to "pursue the gain of it enough to keep out of the briers, but give your main attention to the study of it," and also "not to marry early." John and Sam Quincy "were sworn" as attorneys on November 6, 1758.

John's first writ was rejected, to his embarrassment. He especially didn't want to be laughed at by Bob Paine, a law student who had once lived at Weymouth and would one day be a Signer, too. Of his efforts to get started, John wrote that he had to "dig treasures with my own fingers; nobody will lend me or sell me a pickaxe." But he worked increasingly hard, always continuing his studies, and soon began to get ahead.

The war with France ended in September, 1760, with the fall of Montreal, and all Canada with it, to the British. George III ascended the British throne in October and shortly afterward instructions were sent to America to enforce strictly the Acts of Trade and Navigation. A Salem customs official applied to the Massachusetts Superior Court for writs of assistance or search warrants to aid in locating contraband. Sixty-three merchants, foreseeing ruin, petitioned against the writs and a hearing was set for February, 1761.

Feeling about the writs was violent, and John Adams and Samuel Quincy were delighted to be permitted to attend the hearing, although they were not yet barristers. James Otis and Oxenbridge Thacher defended the petition before the five judges arrayed in "rich robes of scarlet English broadcloth," cambric bands and immense judicial wigs. John Adams took notes of the proceedings, which are the only existing on-the-spot record of this far-reaching event.

The handsome Council Chamber in the Town-house or Old State House was tense with excitement. At the lawyers' table, John Adams, "lost in admiration," moved his quill pen across the paper as James Otis spoke—" a flame of fire—"

"This writ is against the fundamental principles of law ... A man who is quiet, is as secure in his house, as a prince in his castle" except by special, not general, search warrants for felonies upon process and oath.

"An act against the Constitution is void; an act against natural equity is void. . . ."

John Adams' minutes were no better an account of Otis' speech "than the gleam of a glow-worm to the meridian blaze of the sun," he later wrote. "Then and there the child Independence was born."

The writs were granted the following November, but Otis was elected to the Massachusetts Assembly in May as a hero for proclaiming the rights of British subjects.

John's first public service was as surveyor of highways in Braintree. He was elected to the office in March, 1761. His father died in May of that year, greatly mourned by his family and all of Braintree.

After a long engagement, John Adams married Abigail Smith, daughter of Parson and Mrs. Smith of Weymouth, on October 25, 1764. Mrs. Smith was a daughter of Colonel John Quincy of Wollaston, one of the most important men of Suffolk County. He had represented Braintree in the Massachusetts Assembly for forty years, and had been a member of the Governor's Council and speaker of the House longer than anyone in the colony.

Citizens of Boston, indignant over the Stamp Act and its threatened enforcement on November 1, rioted on August 14, 1765. They ransacked Lieutenant Governor Hutchinson's house some evenings later. John Adams, upset by Britain's action, prepared a new set of instructions regarding the Stamp Act for the Braintree representative in the Assembly. These instructions were adapted by forty towns of the province for their own use. One of the paragraphs "worthy to be wrote in letters of gold" follows:

"We further recommend the most clear and explicit assertion and vindication of our rights and liberties to be entered on the public records, that the world may know, in the present and all future generations, that we have a clear knowledge and a just sense of them, and, with submission to Divine Providence, that we never can be slaves."

Another piece from John's pen was arousing interest, the essay "On Canon and Feudal Law," published in the Boston *Gazette* by installment. This had originally been written by John for Mr. Gridley's Sodality, a small club. "I say RIGHTS," it reads, "for such they (the people) have, undoubtedly, antecedent to all earthly government,—*Rights*, that cannot be repealed or restrained by human laws—*Rights*, derived from the great Legislator of the universe."

In December, 1765, along with Jeremiah Gridley and James Otis, John Adams—for the town of Boston—petitioned the Governor in Council to open the courts of law, closed since the hated Stamp Act had gone into effect on November 1.

The Board refused the petition, declaring it was a matter for the judges, but Samuel Adams encouraged his cousin, saying he hoped "that Braintree, finding the eyes of Boston were upon me, would fix theirs on me too, next May (at elections)."

Of Christmas of that year, John's diary reads: "At home thinking, reading, searching, concerning taxation without consent; concerning the great pause and rest in business."

"They (the British leaders) know not the character of Americans," he writes later, and on January 1, 1766, "This year brings ruin or salvation to the British colonies . . . Britain and America are staring at each other; and they probably will stare more and more for some time."

News of the repeal of the Stamp Act on March 18, 1766, received in the Colonies in May, was joyously celebrated. In Braintree, John Adams was apprehensive over the wording of the Declaratory Act passed shortly before, giving Parliament full powers over the Colonies. "What is the end and design of that bill?" John, now a selectman, wondered.

Urged by his friends there, in April, 1768, John Adams and Abigail, "his partner," moved to Brattle Square, in Boston, with their children, Abigail, not yet three, and John Quincy, born in July, 1767. John's law practice increased and clients were forthcoming from his friends among the Sons of Liberty. When John Hancock's sloop *Liberty* was seized on June 10 by the British warship *Romney* for non-payment of import duties, he engaged John Adams as his counsel.

A town meeting was called on the fourteenth and John Adams was asked to draft new instructions for the four Boston representatives. They called for resolutions condemning as an enemy every person "who shall solicit or promote the importation of troops at this time." While remaining sub-

ordinate to Parliament "in all cases of necessity . . . it is our
unalterable resolution, at all times to assert and vindicate
our dear and invaluable rights and liberties, at the utmost
hazard of our lives and fortunes. . . ."

Not long after this, John's old friend, Jonathan Sewall,
with whom he had carried on a newspaper controversy opposing Sewall's defense of Governor Bernard, offered him, on
behalf of Bernard, the office of Advocate-General in the Admiralty Court. John declined this lucrative post with the
Crown party.

Adams was away on law business when the convention was
held in September and the British troops landed. A regiment drilled in front of his house during the fall and winter.
In his *Autobiography* he tells that the "spirit-stirring drum
and ear-piercing fife" aroused him early every morning and
the indignation they excited was soothed but "not allayed
by the sweet songs, violins and flutes, of the serenading Sons
of Liberty under my windows in the evening. . . ."

The following May, 1769, John, now living on Cold Lane
by the Mill Pond, was once more the draftsman of instructions for the Boston representatives. "The debates of our
assembly must be free," he wrote. Protesting against the
juryless admiralty courts, he quoted from the Magna Carta:
"No freeman shall be taken or imprisoned . . . but by lawful
judgment of his peers. . . ."

In June, John argued an impressment case—four American
sailors accused of murder while resisting kidnaping into the
British Navy. With the eyes of all New England upon him,
a verdict of justifiable homicide in necessary self-defense was
rendered by the special vice-admiralty court.

The always increasing tension between the Boston townspeople and the British regulars snapped on the fifth of
March, 1770. John Adams, at a club meeting, heard a ringing of bells about nine in the evening. Rushing out to help

if it should be a fire, he heard that British soldiers had fired on the inhabitants, killing some and wounding others.

The next morning he was approached to take the defense of Captain Preston of the British Army, said to have given the order to fire. As the man could obtain no other counsel, John took the case for a binder of one guinea, risking his popularity with the American cause to uphold law in Massachusetts Bay. Josiah Quincy, Jr., an ardent Patriot, agreed to serve as junior counsel.

In June, John Adams was elected a Boston representative and, summoned to Faneuil Hall, was sworn in. "At this time," he states in his *Autobiography,* "I had more business at the bar than any man in the Province." He was throwing away "bright prospects" for endless labor and anxiety "if not to infamy and to death." Mrs. Adams burst into tears but was very willing "to share in all that was to come, and to place her trust in Providence."

In October, John Adams and Josiah Quincy argued the case of Captain Preston against Sam Quincy, elder brother of Josiah, and Robert Treat Paine. The prosecutors were well known to John Adams. Preston was acquitted and John Adams was successful in the two companion trials of the eight British soldiers who had fired on the crowd and of the Tory sympathizers also; but the stigma of his having defended these British soldiers made him suspect to some of the Liberty party.

Exhausted from the endless work and worry of these trials, John retired from public life and moved back to Braintree. On April 20, 1771, a week after his return, he wrote in his diary: ". . . shall divide my time between Boston and Braintree, between law and husbandry;—farewell politics."

In the late fall of 1772, the Adams family returned to Boston for the winter, and John's diary entry for the first day of 1773 states that his resolutions to devote himself to private life are a comfort—"Peace, be still, my once anxious heart."

Then suddenly Massachusetts received word that her five judges of the Superior Court henceforth would be paid by the crown, not the people. John Adams, stung by this blow and publicly challenged to dispute it, published eight articles in the *Gazette* on the independence of English judges. Sam Adams' newly-organized committees of correspondence brought John further back into politics.

Fearing the influence of these committees, Governor Hutchinson charged in the Massachusetts Legislature that allegiance to Britain was at stake. John Adams was asked to revise the House answer, removing the "roses and flowers" and adding "legal and constitutional" principles. As to the Governor's charge that no line could "be drawn between the supreme authority of Parliament and the total independence of the Colonies," Adams' revised reply stated that the representatives could not undertake to draw a line without the consent of the other Colonies "in Congress." The paper was passed with difficulty, due to this last assertion, but less than two months later, as has been told, the Virginia House of Burgesses voted to make the committees of correspondence inter-colonial.

John Adams' election to the Council in May was vetoed by the Governor. "Not a check but a boost," the lawyer said.

By December, as Abigail Adams wrote on the fifth, "The Tea that bainfull weed is arrived." John Adams was away the night of the Boston Tea Party. "What measures will the Ministry take in consequence of this?" he asked in his diary.

Only one judge refused to renounce the King's grant. Fearing that the man might be removed from the bench by violence, John proposed impeachment. Assuming the power of Parliament, the Massachusetts House formally accused the Tory sympathizer on February 14. At the next session of the Superior Court, the jurors refused to take the oath and serve under him, and the Court never met again under royal jurisdiction.

News of punishment for the Tea Party came on May 10. As described in the Prologue, the Port of Boston was ordered closed on June 1—to be starved into submission.

Although John was again elected to the Council, he was vetoed by the new governor, General Thomas Gage. On the second of June the other "Intolerable Acts" were proclaimed. John Adams was acting as moderator of a town meeting in Boston on the seventeenth when, at Salem, where the Assembly was gathered in exile, Sam Adams proposed that a General Congress of deputies meet at Philadelphia. Five delegates from Massachusetts were chosen. Among them—John Adams.

Three days later he wrote in his diary: "There is a new and grand scene open before me; a Congress. This will be an assembly of the wisest men upon the continent, who are Americans in principle. . . . I feel myself unequal to this business."

To a friend who tried to dissuade him from going to the Congress, Adams said he "had passed the Rubicon; swim or sink, live or die, survive or perish with my country, was my unalterable determination."

He traveled southward to Philadelphia by coach with his fellow delegates, Sam Adams, Robert Treat Paine and Thomas Cushing. (Bowdoin remained home.) On the way John tried to learn what he could and size up the people he met. They were going into strange country, they must be cautious. A letter from Joseph Hawley, Patriot leader of western Massachusetts, reminded the delegates of this. There were men in the Southern Colonies, he wrote, "of as much sense and literature as any we can . . . boast of."

Robert Treat Paine, descended from a Connecticut Governor, was educated to be a clergyman and afterward became a lawyer. He served in the Massachusetts Provincial Congress as well as in the Continental Congress. Attorney-general of the State for many years, he was appointed a judge of the State Supreme Court in 1790. His fellow Signer Rush complained that he had a certain "obliquity of understanding" which prevented his seeing "public objects" in the same light as other people. Though called the "Objection Maker" in Congress, he was notwithstanding a "firm, decided, and persevering patriot" and eminently useful to that governing body, particularly on committees.

The reception and advice received by the Massachusetts delegates at Frankfort has been described in the Prologue. In the First Continental Congress, the Massachusetts men moved cautiously. John and Sam Adams represented their colony on the grand committee to prepare a Declaration of Rights. John Adams insisted that the law of nature—God's law by which man is born to liberty—be retained "as a Resource to which we might be driven by Parliament much sooner than we expected."

As adopted, including "the immutable laws of nature," the Declaration read: "Resolved N. C. D. 1. That they are entitled to life, liberty and property, and they have never ceded to any sovereign power whatever a right to dispose of either, without their consent."

In subcommittee, John Adams also helped to decide what authority should be ceded to Parliament. Liking his phrases, "the necessity of the case" and "excluding all ideas of taxation, external and internal," John Rutledge of South Carolina suggested that Adams produce something that would unite them. Though the committee was not fully satisfied, they agreed to what he drew up, and "upon this," as Adams' *Autobiography* recounts, "depended the union of the Colonies."

Convinced by the passing of the Suffolk Resolves that "America will support Massachusetts or perish with her," John Adams was frightened when the treacherous Galloway Plan of Union was tabled by a vote of only six colonies against five.

On October 28, the Congress over, John Adams started for

home, where he served for Braintree in the Provincial Congress. He wrote, as Novanglus, a series of papers opposing articles written by Massachusettensis, a Tory adherent, "to expose the wretched policy of the whigs." The last of Mr. Adams' papers was not published because of the outbreak of hostilities on April 19 at Lexington and Concord, "which changed the instruments of warfare from the pen to the sword."

John Adams, his three previous colleagues, and John Hancock arrived in Philadelphia on May 10, 1775, for the assembling of the Second Continental Congress, to take up the cause of Massachusetts, still convinced "that the die was cast, the Rubicon passed."

Adams' role in the nomination of George Washington as Commander-in-Chief and the setting up of the Continental Army is told in the Prologue. He was also vitally concerned in the request of Massachusetts, read before Congress on June 2, for advice on the formation of a civil government. On this occasion Adams spoke of the urgency of setting up new governments in the Colonies, which were "not huddled up in a hurry, by a few chiefs." Congress advised Massachusetts to elect an assembly to run the colony "until a Governor of His Majesty's appointment will consent to govern the Colony according to its charter."

One of Adams' two letters (mentioned in the Prologue) which were intercepted by the British and caused such a furor among both colonists and Britons was written to his wife— "We have a constitution to form for a great empire . . . a standing army of twenty-seven thousand men to raise, pay, victual and officer . . ." The other letter, to James Warren, described Dickinson as "A certain great Fortune and piddling Genius," and continued, "We ought to have had in our Hands a month ago the whole Legislative . . . to have raised a naval Power, and opened all our Ports wide; to have arrested every Friend to Government . . . as Hostages for the poor victims in Boston, and then opened the Door . . . for Peace and Reconciliation."

Home during the August adjournment of Congress, Adams found that his brother Elihu had died of an epidemic in camp. Fearful for his family, John had to return to Philadelphia to his duties in Congress as the disease spread.

Favoring a Navy, John Adams worked and debated that October to have Congress create one. In the end, a naval committee was appointed, including Adams and Stephen Hopkins of Rhode Island.

In his *Autobiography* for September, John Adams writes: "Almost every day I had something to say about advising the States to institute governments" and that three measures, "independence, confederation, and negotiations with foreign powers, particularly France, ought to go hand in hand, and be adopted all together. . . ." More about the "violents' " long, weary struggle that winter is told in the Prologue.

Though John Adams liked the arguments in favor of independence in Thomas Paine's *Common Sense,* he sensed the impious streak in the author and disagreed with his plan for government. Dreading the effect of the latter on the people, he wrote down his own, published as *Thoughts on Government, in a letter from a gentleman to his friend* (George Wythe). Adams' plan influenced the future New York, Virginia, North Carolina, New Jersey and other state constitutions.

"All his publications . . ." wrote Benjamin Rush, "discover a strong predilection for republican forms of government. To be safe, powerful and durable he always urged that they should be composed of three legislative branches, but that each of them should be the offspring directly or indirectly of the suffrages of the people."

As the independence party rose, John Adams' moves led directly to the Declaration and his actions are described in the Prologue. There the realization of his dream of independence is presented. As to his second hope—the Articles of Confederation—these were adopted by Congress on November 15, 1777, after long consideration by the committee appointed in June, 1776. Of his third objective—the Treaty of Alliance with France—this was signed in February, 1778, bringing desperately needed hope to the Americans after the frightful winter at Valley Forge.

From his experience in government on the state and national level, John Adams went on to a career abroad. Serving in the American Congress until November, 1777, he went to France as Commissioner to the French Court, but the treaty had already been concluded. He returned home and served as a member of the Convention which framed the Massachusetts Constitution of 1780, drafting that instrument on a sub-committee.

Chosen on September 27, 1779, as minister plenipotentiary for negotiating treaties of peace and commerce with Great Britain, he signed the preliminary treaty in November, 1782. He had secured recognition of the United States from Holland earlier that year, as well as a treaty of amity and commerce—the first foreign alliance since the French Treaty.

This "profound and enlightened patriot" who had felt himself "unequal" to the business of the First Continental Congress went on to serve as Minister to the Court of St. James, Vice-President during George Washington's two terms—and President of the United States, 1797-1801.

Defeated by Thomas Jefferson for re-election, Adams left the White House after four stormy years as president, to return to the peace and quiet of his home in Quincy.

The Signer's eldest son, John Quincy Adams, over whose education he had watched with such care, writing home from the Continental Congress ". . . teach them to Scorn Injustice, Ingratitude, Cowardice and Falsehood. Let them revere nothing but Religion, Morality & Liberty," became the sixth President of the United States.

John Adams died on the fourth of July, 1826, a few hours after Thomas Jefferson. It was the fiftieth anniversary of the Declaration of Independence. Worrying about the country's future he had written earlier in his *Autobiography*: "However the good sense and integrity of the majority of the great body of the people came into my thoughts, for my relief, and the last resource was after all in a good Providence."

Elbridge Gerry *1744–1814*

ELBRIDGE GERRY was elected to represent Massachusetts in the Continental Congress on January 18, 1776, in the place of Thomas Cushing. He set out for Philadelphia with John Adams, who wrote in his *Autobiography* that "Mr. Samuel Adams, Mr. Gerry and myself now composed a majority of the Massachusetts delegation, and we were no longer vexed or enfeebled by divisions among ourselves, or by indecision or indolence."

The "violents" desperately needed a majority in the delegation at that time, so they could work toward independence. The Massachusetts instructions, passed at the election, could have been construed as either for or against a separation. Their representatives were empowered to join "with the Delegates from the other American Colonies, to concert, direct, and order such further measures as shall to them appear best calculated for the recovery and establishment of American right and liberties."

The son of a wealthy merchant, Elbridge Gerry was born in Marblehead, Massachusetts, on July 17, 1744. His father, Thomas Gerry, had emigrated to the Colonies from Newton, England, in 1630. His mother, Elizabeth Greenleaf of Marblehead, was the daughter of Enoch Greenleaf.

When his preparatory studies were finished, Gerry entered Harvard, graduating in 1762. He took his Master's degree three years later and the subject chosen provided a chance for him to give his patriotic views on the Stamp Act and other oppressive revenue measures. Entering business, he amassed a considerable fortune.

Election to the General Court in 1772 started his public career. He took his seat on May 27 and was chosen on the Committee of Correspondence the next year. He helped to carry through the resolutions on the removal of Governor Hutchinson and was a member of the first Provincial Congress of his colony. Very active in this body, he served on the important committees of safety and supplies.

These two committees, tradition says, were sitting at Arlington on the day preceding the Battle of Lexington, and Mr. Gerry, with Colonels Lee and Orne, decided to remain until the next day. In the middle of the night they were alarmed by the arrival of the British troops, on their way to Concord. As the main body of the enemy came to the house where the Patriots were lodging, a file of soldiers was detached and ordered to surround the place. With great difficulty, Gerry and the colonels escaped and concealed themselves in a cornfield until the search was over. They then came out of hiding and spread the alarm among the citizens.

Gerry, a great friend of General Joseph Warren, spent the night before the General's departure for Bunker Hill in the same bed with him. Warren is said to have had a presentiment of his fate on the "awful heights" which he confided to his friend.

Gerry, who had taken his seat in Congress at Philadelphia on February 9, received the following word from Major Joseph Hawley, important member of the Massachusetts Assembly: "I have read the pamphlet entitled, 'Common Sense, addressed to the Inhabitants of America,' and every sentiment has sunk into my well-prepared heart . . ." If independence is resolved upon, he continued later, "what will hinder but that we may instantly commence a trade not only with Holland, France, and Spain, but with all the world? . . . Independence, in short, is the only way to union and harmony, to vigour and despatch in business; our eye will be single, and our whole body full of light; anything short of it will, as appears to me, be our destruction, infallible destruction, and that speedily."

It was presumably these communications which drew forth Gerry's letter of March 26 to James Warren, the president of the Massachusetts House, which met at Watertown: "You are desirous of knowing what capital measures are proposed in congress. I refer you to . . . what is done concerning privateering . . . This will not in itself satisfy you, and *I hope nothing will, short of a determination of America to hold her rank in the creation, and give law to herself* . . . I sincerely wish you would originate instructions, expressed with decency and firmness—your own style—and give your sentiments as a court in favour of independency. I am certain it would turn many doubtful minds, and produce a reversal of the contrary instructions adopted by some assemblies. Some timid minds are terrified at the word independence . . . the fruit must have time to ripen in some of the other colonies . . ."

Gerry's business ability proved invaluable in his work for Congress. During the spring he served on several important committees. These included the standing committee on the treasury, the one that provided the means for furnishing supplies to the army; another devoted to the issue of bills of credit; still another on the best methods of legislating the business of Congress, and several more. The committee on supplies, consisting of Lewis and Sherman in addition to Gerry, attended General Washington at New York and as a result of their mission some measures of reform in regard to the furnishing of clothing, to the administration of the Quartermaster General's department and to the plan of hospital establishments, plus other military matters, were approved by Congress.

Gerry continued to work hard for independence, urged on by Hawley, who wrote on May 1: "The Tories dread a declaration of Independence, and a course of conduct on that plan, more than death. They console themselves with a belief that the Southern Colonies will not accede to it. My hand and heart are full of it. There will be no abiding union without it."

On the twentieth, following the new government resolution of May 15, Gerry sent word to Warren: "It appears to me that the eyes of every unbeliever are now open; that all are sensible of the perfidy of Great Britain, and are convinced there is no medium between unqualified submission and actual independency . . . Amidst all our difficulties, you would be highly diverted to see the situation of our 'moderate gentlemen'. . . . They are coming over to us . . ."

But the struggle was far from finished. Of the postponement of the June 7 resolution, Gerry told Warren that its purpose was "to give the Assemblies of the Middle Colonies an opportunity to take off their restrictions and let their Delegates unite in the measure." On the twenty-fifth he wrote again to the Massachusetts Assembly president: "I think we are in a fair way to a speedy Declaration of Independency . . . it appears to me that there is not a doubt of any Colony on the continent, except New York and Maryland. These will not impede us a moment. I do not affirm that either of these is of the neuter gender; but . . . am persuaded the people are in favour of a total and final separation, and will support the measure, even if the Conventions and Delegates . . . vote against it. Since my first arrival in this city, the New-England Delegates have been in a continual war with the advocates of Proprietary interests in Congress and this Colony (Pennsylvania) . . . but I think the contest is pretty nearly at an end. . . ."

On July 2, before Congress met for the second day of debate on Lee's postponed motion, Gerry wrote to Warren: ". . . yesterday was agitated in Congress the great question of Independency; and as the facts are as well known at the Coffee-House of that city as in Congress, I may go on to tell you that, in a Committee of the whole House, it was carried by nine Colonies." And on July 5, Gerry, enclosing a copy of the Declaration "for yourself, and another for Major Hawley," faithfully reported to Warren: "I have the pleasure to inform you that a determined resolution of the Delegates from some of the Colonies to push the question of Independency has had a most happy effect, and, after a day's debate, all the Colonies, excepting New York . . . united in a declaration long sought for, solicited, and necessary . . ." Hawley acknowledged the copy from Northampton: "No one thing made the Declaration of Independence indispensably necessary more than cutting off traitors."

It is alleged that "Mr. Gerry . . . as slender and spare as Mr. Harrison was vigorous and portly, stood beside him at the table, while signing the Declaration. He (Harrison) turned round to him with a smile, as he raised his hand from the paper, and said, 'When the hanging scene comes to be exhibited, I shall have all the advantage over you. It will be over with me in a minute, but you will be kicking in the air for an hour after I am gone.' " But this must be put down as pure fable because Gerry left Congress on July 16 and could not have signed until his return, to Philadelphia, probably early in September.

Gerry continued in Congress until 1781, contributing invaluable aid in its military and financial affairs. Amidst all the critical work is the record in the *Journal* of November, 1777: "That a committee of three be appointed, to collect and digest the late useful discoveries for making molasses and spirits from the juice of cornstalks, and report a plan for communicating the said discoveries to the inhabitants of the several states." Mr. Gerry was chairman but there is no mention of any findings of this committee!

Again a member of Congress in 1783, Gerry was a delegate to the Constitutional Convention in 1787. He served in the Congress of 1789 as a Republican representative and was re-elected. In 1797, he was sent by President John Adams, with John Marshall and Charles Cotesworth Pinckney, on a mission to France, which became known as the XYZ affair. Disgusted with their treatment by the government of the Directory, Marshall and Pinckney sailed for home, while Gerry remained a while longer in the vain hope of some success.

In 1808 a town meeting was called in Boston in protest over the attack of the British ship *Leopard* on the American frigate *Chesapeake,* and at the last moment Mr. Gerry was asked to preside. Though he had not yet recovered from a serious illness, he agreed to "yield to the call that is made on me, as I hold it to be the duty of every citizen, though he may have but one day to live, to devote that day to the good of his country."

Gerry was governor of Massachusetts from 1810 to 1812. During his administration a bill was passed re-districting the state on alleged partisan lines. One of these new districts was thought to resemble a salamander, thus giving rise to the term "Gerrymander."

In 1812 Gerry was elected vice-president of the United States on the Democratic-Republican ticket with James Madison as president. He died in office on November 23, 1814, thus fulfilling his pledge to serve his country "though he may have but one day to live."

Elbridge Gerry married Ann Thompson in 1786. Of their three sons and six daughters, Emily Louise Gerry, who lived until December, 1894, was the last surviving child of a Signer.

During Gerry's first year in the Continental Congress,

John Adams described him as "an old bachelor, and what is worse, a politician, and is worse still, a kind of soldier . . ." Rush says of Gerry that "he knew and embraced truth when he saw it. He had no local or state prejudices" and was "a genuine friend to republican forms of government."

Stephen Hopkins *1707–1785*
William Ellery *1727–1820*

Stephen hopkins, representing Rhode Island, was a veteran of the first continental assembly—the Albany Congress of 1754—at which Benjamin Franklin was the only other future Signer. Except for Franklin, Hopkins was the senior member of the Continental Congress in experience as well as years.

He was born in Providence (the part later called Scituate) on March 7, 1707. His ancestor, William Hopkins, had married the aunt of Benedict Arnold, the first governor of Rhode Island. Stephen's mother was the granddaughter of one of the first Baptist ministers of Providence. He had little opportunity for schooling but his vigorous mind and determination helped him to acquire an education—self-taught. Engaged in farming until 1742, he then moved to Providence and went into the mercantile business. He also did land surveying.

Public life started for Hopkins in 1732, when he was chosen to represent Scituate in the General Assembly, being re-elected, with one interval, until 1738. Again a representative in 1741, he became speaker of the House. Ten years later he was chosen Chief Justice of the colony.

The Albany Congress followed and in 1755 Hopkins was elected Governor of Rhode Island. Alternating terms, first with William Greene and then with Samuel Ward, his bitter political rival, he served until 1768. He raised a volunteer corps during the French and Indian War when Montcalm invaded northern New York.

On June 15, 1774, Hopkins—then Chief Justice and representative in the Provincial Assembly—was elected, with Samuel Ward, as a delegate to the First Continental Congress.

In October of 1775, one of the Rhode Island delegates presented the resolutions of their General Assembly on the establishment of a fleet. After opposition, the idea was taken up in a different form. Governor Ward wrote home that he had great hopes for the project of a fleet because "Dr. Franklin, Colonel Lee, the two Adamses, and many others would support it." On October 30, Stephen Hopkins, with John Adams, Mr. Hewes and Mr. Lee, were added on a committee for "fitting out armed vessels." To John Adams, this naval committee—the origin of the United States Navy—provided the pleasantest part of his labors in Congress. "Mr. Lee, Mr. Gadsden, were sensible men, but Governor Hopkins of Rhode Island, above seventy years of age, kept us all alive." When the business of the evening was over, he shared with the others his "wit, humor, anecdotes, science, and learning. He had read Greek, Roman, and British history, and was familiar with English poetry, particularly Pope, Thomson, and Milton." Esek Hopkins, his brother, was appointed first captain or commodore of the fleet.

Samuel Ward—Hopkins' fellow governor, fellow chief justice and fellow delegate to the Congress, although eighteen years younger—had early taken up the American cause. He was active in the founding of Rhode Island College, now

Brown University. Governor at the time of the Stamp Act, he was the only colonial governor who refused to take the required oath to enforce it. His brother Henry was secretary of the province, officially Rhode Island and Providence Plantations, from 1760 to 1797 and took part in the Stamp Act Congress in New York. A suit brought against Samuel Ward by Hopkins for slander was later defaulted.

Of the adoption of the New Hampshire resolution on government, passed on news of the King's refusal to receive Dickinson's petition, Ward wrote too optimistically: "Thank God, the happy day, which I have long wished for, is at length arrived; the southern colonies no longer entertain jealousies of the northern; they no longer look back to Great Britain . . . One of the gentlemen, who has been most sanguine for pacific measures, and very jealous of the New England colonies, addressing me in the style of *Brother Rebel,* told me he was now ready to join us heartily. . . . Our resolutions will henceforth be spirited, clear, and decisive," Ward predicted. "May the Supreme Governor of the universe direct and prosper them!"

In Congress, on January 6, 1776, Ward received a letter from General Greene, in camp before Boston, recommending a declaration of independence and urging a "call upon the world, and the great God who governs it, to witness the necessity, propriety, and rectitude thereof."

But Rhode Island's instructions straddled the issue and their delegates were not always united on measures of independency, as the Tilghman letter recounted: "Rhode Island frequently loses a vote, having only two members, and they differing." In February, 1776, a letter written by Ward urged that Paine's *Common Sense* should be reprinted and distributed at public expense, if necessary; so it appears that it was Hopkins who leaned temporarily toward reconciliation.

In March, President Hancock started nominating Harrison as chairman of the committee of the whole instead of Ward, whom he previously had promoted. Adams wrote that Ward "was become extremely obnoxious to Mr. Hancock's party, by his zealous attachment to Mr. Samuel Adams and Mr. Richard Henry Lee." Unfortunately, Governor Ward caught smallpox and died on March 25, and the "violent" men "lost an honorable, a conscientious, a benevolent, and inflexible patriot."

Stephen Hopkins, now sole delegate, wrote to Governor Cooke, making "queries concerning dependance or independence." The Rhode Island General Assembly, on May 4, passed instructions which were still indecisive but voted at the same time for an act discharging the inhabitants of the colony from allegiance to the King. This act gave Hopkins "little room to doubt what is the opinion of the Colony." In the place of Ward, William Ellery, an "excellent member," was chosen for Congress, and he reached there on May 14.

Rhode Island joined with the other New England Colonies in supporting the Lee resolution, passing it on July 2, and the Declaration on July 4.

When the signing "on parchment" took place on August 2, Stephen Hopkins' signature was shaky, but he was known to have palsy which rendered him almost unable to write. A letter penned by Ellery to the Governor of Rhode Island on June 8 hoped that the correspondence between the delegates and the colony, interrupted by Ward's death and "the great inconvenience which attends Mr. Hopkins in writing," might be resumed.

Stephen Hopkins was chosen on the committee which drafted the Articles of Confederation for the United States and he served in Congress until 1779—very active and almost constantly a member of some important committee. Rush says he had "an original understanding, extensive reading, and great integrity. He perfectly understood the principles of liberty and government, and was warmly attached to the independance of his country. . . . He disliked hearing long letters read him from the generals of our armies, and used to say 'he never knew a General Quillman good for anything.' "

Hopkins' first wife was Sarah Scott. On her death he married a widow, Anne Smith, who was a member of the Society of Friends, and Mr. Hopkins was a regular attendant at Meeting during his life. Two of his children died in tragic accidents.

By his own efforts, Hopkins became a distinguished mathematician and he was helpful in the observation of the planet Venus in June, 1769. He moved for a public library in Providence in 1750, and later for free schools there. He was a member of the American Philosophical Society, founded by his fellow Signer, Benjamin Franklin. He died in 1785, a self-taught colonist who had helped in the building of the United States.

William Ellery, the new delegate who signed just below Hopkins, was born in Newport, Rhode Island, in 1727. His father, of the same name, was a Harvard graduate. He became a successful merchant in Newport and served as judge, senator and lieutenant governor of the colony. Prepared mostly by his father, Ellery entered Harvard, graduating in 1747, at the age of twenty. He engaged in business and public life and in 1770 began the practice of law. He was married twice and had seventeen children. One of his descendants was Richard Henry Dana, the author of *Two Years Before the Mast*.

Ellery often described his signing of the Declaration of Independence a little over two months after he entered Congress in this way in later years: "I was determined to see how they all looked as they signed what might be their death warrant. I placed myself beside the secretary, Charles Thomson, and eyed each closely as he affixed his name to the document. Undaunted resolution was displayed in every countenance"—

including, of course, his colleague Hopkins of the shaky penmanship.

Ellery's signing at the risk of his fortune proved only too realistic, as Newport was captured by the British in December, 1776, and during their occupation, which lasted three years, his house was burned and nearly all of his property was destroyed. In 1778, Mr. Ellery left Congress briefly to assist in a plan to drive the British out of Newport, but the project failed. He was able, however, to obtain some relief from Congress for the distress brought to the Rhode Islanders by the British occupation. He served also on committees to resolve certain difficulties among the American Commissioners to Europe, to arrange some matters connected with the admiralty courts and many others.

In 1784, while acting as a judge of the Rhode Island Supreme Court, he was on the committee to which the definitive Treaty of Peace with Great Britain was referred. In 1785, working with Rufus King of New York, he made strong efforts to have slavery abolished in the United States.

After the new government under the Constitution was in operation, William Ellery was appointed collector for the port of Newport, near the place where Rhode Island had early displayed her Patriot sympathies by the successful evasion and destruction of a British revenue schooner, the *Gaspee,* in 1772. Now, events having run full cycle, one of the colonists who had done so much for the Patriot cause—and lost his own property in the effort—was serving liberated Newport according to the laws and government it had taken the War of Independence to establish.

Rhode Island, founded by Roger Williams who sought religious freedom, helped found a Union seeking freedom of worship.

Roger Sherman *1721–1793*

Roger sherman of connecticut was one of the five men chosen to serve on the committee of Congress to prepare the Declaration of Independence on the postponement of Lee's June 7 motion. Thomas Jefferson, the committee chairman and author of the immortal document, wrote of Sherman: "I served with him in the old congress, in the years 1775 and 1776: he was a very able and logical debater in that body, steady in the principles of the revolution, always at the post of duty, much employed in the business of committees, and, particularly, was of the committee of Doctor Franklin, Mr. J. Adams, Mr. Livingston, and myself, for preparing the Declaration of Independence. Being much my senior in years, our intercourse was chiefly in the line of our duties. I had a very great respect for him. . . ."

Roger Sherman's qualifications and right to merit this distinction were without question. The significant part of this American success story is that he rose to such prominence from the humblest beginnings entirely by his own efforts.

Captain John Sherman, the Signer's great-grandfather, emigrated to the Colonies from England about 1635, settling in Watertown, Massachusetts. Roger's parents, William, a cordwainer and farmer in modest circumstances, and his wife,

Mehetabel Wellington Sherman, were living in Newton when Roger was born on April 19, 1721. He was named for his maternal great-grandfather, Roger Wellington.

The Shermans moved to Stoughton in 1723. After his father's death in 1741, Roger took over the responsibilities of educating his younger brothers, two of whom became clergymen.

Not forgetting to mention that Roger Sherman was born in Massachusetts, John Adams said of this "most cordial" friend: "Destitute of all literary and scientific education, but such as he acquired by his own exertions, he was one of the most sensible men in the world. The clearest head and the steadiest heart."

Early apprenticed to a shoemaker, Roger worked faithfully at that trade until he moved the family to New Milford, Connecticut, in 1743, where he became a merchant. He traveled there on foot, carrying his tools.

Sherman continued his studies every chance he had and it is said "that he was accustomed to sit at his work with a book before him, devoting to study every moment that his eyes could be spared from the occupation in which he was engaged." He became proficient in mathematics, logic, geography, philosophy, theology, and especially law and politics.

Skill in mathematics led to his being appointed county surveyor in 1745. A few years later he was supplying astronomical calculations for an almanac published in New York City. In 1754 he was admitted to the bar as a result of his legal studies, and he began the practice of law.

The following year he was elected to the Connecticut Colonial Assembly at the age of thirty-four, commencing a public career which was to continue all his life.

Roger Sherman first married Elizabeth Hartwell, daughter of Deacon Joseph Hartwell of Stoughton, and they had seven children. Following her death, Roger moved to New Haven in 1761. Soon afterwards he was made a justice of the peace, and in 1765 a judge of the Court of Common Pleas. He served, too, as treasurer of Yale University for many years, receiving the honorary degree of Master of Arts.

In 1766 he was elected an assistant or member of the Council, the upper house of the Legislature, where he served for nineteen years. In Connecticut, under their Charter granted by Charles II in 1662, the freemen elected their own governor and lieutenant governor and did not have to contend with a royal governor.

The Stamp Act caused a violent reaction in Connecticut and Sherman "co-operated with his fellow-(council)members in the general opposition to parliamentary supremacy." He was made a judge of the Superior Court in May, 1766, officiating until 1789.

In August, 1774, Roger Sherman and Joseph Trumbull, son of Governor Jonathan Trumbull, the "Brother Jonathan" whose Christian name became synonymous with a Patriot, were elected delegates to the First Continental Congress. Eliphalet Dyer and Silas Deane had been named before, and Titus Hosmer was added as an alternate in November. So was Jonathan Sturges.

When the Massachusetts delegates, on their way to Congress at Philadelphia, stopped at Isaac Bear's tavern in New Haven, Roger Sherman came to see them. John Adams' diary for August 17 records of this staunch Patriot: "He is between fifty and sixty, a solid, sensible man. He said he read Mr. Otis' Rights &c. in 1764, and thought that he had conceded away the rights of America. He thought the reverse of the declaratory act was true, namely, that the Parliament of Great Britain had authority to make laws for America in no case whatever. He would have been very willing that Massachusetts should have rescinded that part of their Circular Letter where they allow Parliament to be the supreme Legislative over the Colonies in any case."

With Dyer and Deane, Sherman attended the opening day

of Congress, September 5. Immediately active in debates and in committee, he was described as speaking "often and long, but very heavily and clumsily."

When the Second Congress opened in May, 1775, Sherman was a delegate. Joseph Trumbull was not re-elected, but he was appointed commissary general of the army in July, 1775. It was his brother, John Trumbull, who later painted "The Declaration of Independence," which is reproduced as an illustration in this book. In October new delegates were named for Connecticut. They were Oliver Wolcott and Samuel Huntington, with William Williams as alternate.

Describing Sherman as a debater, John Adams wrote in his diary that "generally he stands upright, with his hands before him, the fingers of his left hand clenched into a fist, and the wrist of it grasped with his right. But he has a clear head and sound judgment; but when he moves his hand in anything like action,—it is stiffness and awkwardness itself, rigid as starched linen or buckram; awkward as a junior bachelor or a sophomore."

Placed on a committee to examine army accounts, including a contract for shoes, Sherman charged that the price was exorbitant, which he proved by specifying the cost of the materials and workmanship. Never embarrassed by his humble origin, he explained to the committee that he was by trade a shoemaker.

John Adams wrote that during the long, hard struggle for liberty, from the autumn of 1775 through the spring of 1776, —Mr. Sherman of Connecticut "was always on my side."

On June 11, Sherman was appointed to the committee to prepare the Articles of Confederation which were finally ratified by the States on March 1, 1781, as well as to that for drafting the Declaration of Independence. Of his work on the Declaration draft, Jefferson said that the committee approved his (Jefferson's) draft; Adams that he did not remember that Sherman criticized anything.

On June 14 instructions to the Connecticut delegates were "to propose to that respectable body to declare the United American Colonies free and independent States . . ." The May 15 Virginia Resolution to that effect had appeared in Connecticut newspapers a week before.

In approving the independence motion on July 2 and the Declaration on the fourth, Roger Sherman was risking his life and honor and the hard-earned fortune he had amassed by constant work and thrift and plain living. Although very comfortably off, especially in comparison with his fellow Connecticut citizens, he did not waver. It was estimated by Dyer in 1775 that there were "not ten men, in the Colony I come from" that were "worth" twelve thousand pounds.

As Rush described Sherman: "He was so regular in business, and so democratic in his principles that he was called by one of his friends 'a republican machine.' Patrick Henry asked him in 1774 why the people of Connecticut were more zealous in the cause of liberty than the people of other States: he answered 'because we have more to lose than any of them.' 'What is that' said Mr. Henry. 'Our beloved charter' replied Mr. Sherman. He was not less distinguished for his piety than his patriotism. He once objected to a motion for Congress sitting on a Sunday upon an occasion which he thought did not require it, and gave as a reason for his objection, a regard of the commands of his Maker."

Roger Sherman, though very active in Congress, also served on the Connecticut Committee of Safety. In 1783 he was associated with Judge Richard Law in revising the statutes of the state, and in 1784 he was elected mayor of New Haven, continuing in this office during his lifetime.

With Dr. Samuel Johnson and Oliver Ellsworth, Sherman was chosen as a delegate to the Constitutional Convention of 1787, in Philadelphia. He took a very considerable part in the debates—General Charles Cotesworth Pinckney, among others, is our authority for this. The three Connecticut delegates joined in restraining the tendency of the majority to overrule the rights of states and individuals in the establishment of a strong government. A contemporary wrote of Sherman: ". . . if he suspects you are trying to take him in, you may as well catch an Eel by the tail."

Sherman was of great service in securing the approval of the Constitution in his state, as the author of a series of papers issued under the signature of "A Citizen," and as a member of the Connecticut convention which ratified the document.

While a representative in Congress in 1790, he supported an anti-slavery petition. The following year he became a senator, serving until his death in 1793.

By his second marriage to Rebekah Prescott of Danvers, Massachusetts, he had eight children. Among his descendants were Senators William M. Evarts, George F. Hoar, Governor Roger S. Baldwin, Judge John Trumbull and Chief Justice Simeon E. Baldwin.

As a young man Roger Sherman had joined the Congregational Church in Stoughton, and, with all his other interests, he never neglected his study of theology. "The volume which he consulted especially was the Bible: it was his custom to purchase a Bible at the commencement of every session of congress, to peruse it daily, and to present it to one of his children on his return." Among his friends were Dr. Jonathan Edwards, Dr. Trumbull and President Witherspoon of Princeton.

Mr. Macon of Georgia said that "Roger Sherman had more common sense than any man he knew," and Thomas Jefferson remarked that Sherman "never said a foolish thing in his life."

Perhaps more enduring than any words cut in marble are those of Jonathan Edwards: "In short, whether we consider him in public or private life, whether we consider him as a politician, or a christian;—he was a great and good man. The words of David concerning Abner, may, with great truth, be applied on this occasion; *know ye not, that there is a great man fallen this day in Israel.*"

Also voting on independence for Connecticut was Samuel Huntington of Norwich, a fourth-generation American, known as "a sensible, candid and worthy man." His grandfather, Deacon Joseph, was a founder of Windham, where Samuel was born in 1731, one of ten children. Like Sherman, he had become a lawyer with very little formal education and had served as a member of the Assembly and on the Council. Elected to the Second Continental Congress, he served until 1783, and was president of that body from September, 1779, to July, 1781, succeeding John Jay. He was Chief Justice of the Connecticut Supreme Court in 1784 and lieutenant governor the following year. He became Governor of the state in 1786, serving until his death ten years later. His wife, Martha, daughter of the Reverend Ebenezer Devotion, had died in 1794.

Roger Sherman's strong influence for independence was felt beyond Connecticut in far-off Georgia. One of the Georgia delegates to Congress was his friend, Lyman Hall, a Connecticut man by birth and an early Patriot. A North Carolina delegate once complained of the close connection between the two colonies, saying "Georgia always votes with Connecticut."

Oliver Wolcott *1726–1797*

THAT OLIVER WOLCOTT rose to high eminence in the colony of Connecticut—even that he helped this colony to become one of the free and independent United States of America—was not surprising. The first Wolcott of this line, Henry, an Englishman of considerable property who emigrated to the New World in 1630, was a founder, with John Mason, of Windsor, Connecticut, and served in the first general assembly of the colony. His eldest son Henry was a patentee of Connecticut under the 1662 Charter. Oliver's grandfather was the youngest son, Simon, a farmer; his father was Roger, apprenticed to a mechanic at twelve. By industry and frugality, Roger Wolcott acquired a competent estate. As a major general heading the Connecticut troops in 1745, he was second in command under Sir William Pepperell at the capture of Louisburg. He also achieved high civil honors, becoming governor in 1751. Although without formal education, he published a volume of poetry after retiring from public life and engaged in religious meditation.

For two centuries after the first settlement of Connecticut, some of the Wolcott family were members of the Assembly, judges of the Superior Court, or magistrates. That Oliver Wolcott, Roger's youngest son, reached the family standard,

[96]

though not unexpected, was due to his own efforts to make the most of his opportunities and his continuing hard work and sacrifice.

Oliver, whose mother was Sarah Drake Wolcott, was born on November 20, 1726, at Windsor. Among his fourteen brothers and sisters were Ursula, who married Governor Matthew Griswold; and Erastus, brigadier general and judge of the State Supreme Court. Oliver graduated from Yale in 1747, receiving a commission as captain in the army from Governor Clinton of New York the same year. Raising a company of volunteers, he served on the northern frontier until his regiment was disbanded at the Peace of Aix-la-Chapelle.

For a while Oliver studied medicine with his brother, Dr. Alexander Wolcott, but he turned to public life on being appointed the first sheriff of Litchfield County in 1751, the year his father became Governor of Connecticut. Elected assistant or councillor in 1771, he was annually retained in office until 1786. He also served as judge of the County Court of Common Pleas and as judge of probate for the Litchfield district. In July, 1775, he was appointed by the Continental Congress a commissioner of Indian affairs for the northern department, to try to induce the Indian nations to remain neutral during the war. At the same time, controversies over the boundaries between Connecticut and Pennsylvania, and Vermont and New York menaced American harmony. Wolcott was helpful in compromising these issues.

Elected a delegate to the Continental Congress, he took his seat on January 16, 1776. Connecticut instructions then were to resolve upon measures "for the defence, security and preservation of the rights and liberties" of the United Colonies.

Writing to Samuel Lyman on February 3, Wolcott said, "common Sence Operates pritty well, but all Men have not common Sence . . ." This was the day before the letter of a "moderate" indicated that Connecticut, New Hampshire,

Massachusetts and Virginia "hang very much together" and are "what we call violent."

With Sherman, Samuel Chase, John Adams, George Wythe and Edward Rutledge, Wolcott spoke against a move to publish an oration in which it was declared that the sentiment of Congress was to continue "in a Dependency on G Britain." The motion was withdrawn.

A month later Wolcott wrote to Andrew Adams: "the World We shall not Covet but so much of America as may be needfull for us, I hope We shall injoy without any earthly controul . . . some People will still please themselves with the delusive Phanntom of Commissioners coming over, with the Proffers of Peace—but I believe it is Very certain they have nothing in their Hands but Pardons for Rebells . . ." Wolcott's spelling was erratic but never his patriotic intentions! "The british Court mean only to have America under their feet . . . The important Crisis which must stamp the Character of America must be Near—and I do not perceive that it's approach produces but Very few sad faces—"

The "few sad faces" were very vigorous in opposing John Adams' government motion, which was finally passed, however, on May 15. Wolcott wrote about it the next day: "The news is Inclosd—a Revolution in Government, you will perceive is about to take effect—"

The day the Lee motion was postponed until July he felt that "Every Thing is tending to the lasting Independency of these Colonies . . . By the blessing of God I enjoy health . . ." But illness caused him to leave Congress the end of June. On July 1 he was in New York and he reached his Connecticut home on the fourth.

During the celebration in New York of the Declaration of Independence, the equestrian statue of George III, "solid lead gilded with gold," on Bowling Green was pulled down. One of Wolcott's letters tells that "the Statue was broken in pieces and the metal transported to Litchfield (as) a place of safety." In the rear of Wolcott's house there "the ladies of this village converted the lead into cartridges for the army." Wolcott's family helped. 10,790 was the score for Mary Ann, his eleven-year-old daughter who later married Senator Chauncey Goodrich; and Frederick, not yet nine, made 936 bullets!

There seems to have been no official proclamation of the Declaration in Connecticut. In the minutes of the Council of Safety for July 11, William Williams, alternate delegate to Congress, recorded: "Congress Declaration of Independency received in a letter from Colonel (Joseph) Trumbull to me."

A little later, Williams was chosen to replace Wolcott in Congress and he set out for Philadelphia, reaching there in time to sign the Declaration, probably on August 2.

William Williams was born at Lebanon, Connecticut, in 1731, the son of the Reverend Solomon and Mary Porter Williams. Graduating from Harvard in 1751, he lived at home, studying theology with his father, for about a year. In 1755, during the French war, he accompanied his relative, Colonel Ephraim Williams, founder of Williams College, for whom Williamstown is named, on the expedition to Lake George, during which the colonel was killed. William Williams became town clerk of Lebanon in 1752, continuing in this office for forty-four years. He was a representative and later a councilor in the Assembly for more than forty years, the speaker for many years. In 1771 he married Mary Trumbull, daughter of the distinguished governor, Jonathan Trumbull, and they had three children. Williams was a deacon of the Congregational Church and a judge. A merchant with a lucrative business, he did not hesitate to devote himself and his property to the interests of his country. At the beginning of the war he visited almost every family in Lebanon to procure clothing, lead (often weights removed from precious clocks), and especially blankets for the soldiers.

When Continental currency could not buy necessary services, on one occasion Mr. Williams put up over two thousand dollars in specie of his own—and lost the whole amount.

In the dark days of December, 1776, Williams is said to have remarked that he expected to be hung, should the British win, because he had published hostile essays in the papers and signed the Declaration. To a compatriot who felt he was secure from the gallows, as he had done neither of these, Williams replied, "Then, sir, you ought to be hanged for not doing your duty." Of Williams, Rush wrote: "A well meaning weak man, and often misled by state prejudices." This time the irrepressible commentator appears to have been too caustic.

Throughout the war Williams' house was open to the American soldiers who passed through Lebanon, and he gave up his dwelling to the officers of a French detachment stationed there for the winter of 1780-1781.

In 1788 he was a member of the Connecticut convention which ratified the Constitution and strongly advocated its adoption. After our present form of government was established, he often observed that no person could possibly conceive the troubles that were encountered in obtaining our independence but those who achieved it. Saddened by the loss of his oldest son, he died on August 2, 1811.

Replying to a request from General Washington for more aid in defending New York in 1776, Governor Trumbull and the Council of Safety ordered fourteen regiments under Brigadier-General Oliver Wolcott "to march without loss of time." From Litchfield, Wolcott, recovered from his illness, wrote: "I shall most cheerfully render my country every service in my power." A few of these regiments took part in the action at Kip's Bay on September 15.

Wolcott returned to Congress in Philadelphia in October and he must have signed the parchment Declaration then or later. He went with Congress when it fled to Baltimore in December. During the summer of 1777 he was active in military matters. After aiding General Putnam on the Hudson River with reinforcements, he joined the northern army and was assigned to the command of a militia brigade which took part in the defeat of General John Burgoyne. It is said that among their supplies were cartridges of "melted majesty," converted at the Wolcott Litchfield home.

In February, 1778, Oliver Wolcott attended Congress, then sitting at York, Pennsylvania. He was again elected in 1780, continuing until 1784. As a commissioner of Indian affairs, he helped to negotiate a treaty of peace with the Six Nations. Elected lieutenant governor of Connecticut in 1786, he served in this post until he was made governor ten years later. He died in office the following year.

Oliver Wolcott's wife, Laura Collins Wolcott, whom he married in 1755, helped to make his public service possible. She educated the children and managed their small farm with frugality and courage during her husband's long absences in the war. Due to her skill, his property was preserved. Of their five children, Oliver achieved the most prominence. He was appointed Secretary of the Treasury by President Washington in 1795, succeeding Alexander Hamilton. Elected Governor of Connecticut in 1817, he served for ten years.

Of Oliver Wolcott, the Signer, Rush said: "A worthy man of great modesty, and sincerely attached to the interests of his country." Oliver was a strong link in the Wolcott family line of representative Americans.

Philip Livingston *1716–1778*
Lewis Morris *1726–1798*

"To the manor born," Philip Livingston, descended from Scottish earls, was a distinguished Patriot of a famous family. Described in 1774 as one of the "two great families in this Province (New York), upon whose motions all their politics turn," the Livingstons had "virtue, and abilities as well as fortune"—*and a Manor* to lose for supporting the Patriot cause.

Robert Livingston, the first lord of Livingston Manor, was the son of a Scottish Presbyterian minister who had been banished from Scotland for nonconformity and had taken his family to live in Rotterdam. After his father's death, Robert emigrated to America in 1673 and settled in Albany, New York. This colony, originally founded as New Netherland by the Dutch in 1622, captured by the British in 1664 and returned to them after a brief Dutch recapture in 1773, was a propitious place for a young Scot who spoke Dutch fluently. He married Alida Schuyler, of a leading Dutch family, who was the widow of a Van Rensselaer. Land holdings which Robert Livingston acquired by purchase and grant were constituted in 1686 as the manor and lordship of Livingston, with the privilege of holding a manor court, or court-baron, in which a lord exercised his own jurisdiction, as well as other manorial rights. Running about fourteen miles along the east bank of the Hudson River, north of the Dutchess County line, the tract extended to the Massachusetts border. At one time it comprised about 160,000 acres.

Philip, the Signer, was born on January 15, 1716, in Albany. He was the fifth son of Philip, the second lord, and his wife, Catherine Van Brugh of Albany. Among his brothers and sisters were Robert, the third lord; Sarah, who married William Alexander, Lord Stirling, one of Washington's generals; Peter Van Brugh, "extremely staunch in the (Patriot) cause, and very sensible"; and William, delegate to the Continental Congress and Governor of New Jersey. A member of the Assembly for many terms, the second lord and his wife entertained in style at his three residences in New York, Albany and the Manor during their later years.

Graduating from Yale in 1737, young Philip was referred to in 1746 as one of the fifteen persons in the colony of New York who had a college education. After graduation, he became an importer in New York City, and Sir Charles Hardy said in 1755 that "among the considerable merchants in this city no one is more esteemed for energy, promptness, honesty, and public spirit, than Philip Livingston." Elected one of the seven aldermen of New York City in 1754, he served for nine years. Chosen as a member of the Assembly from the city and county of New York for 1759, he was re-elected until its dissolution in 1769, and while a legislator identified himself with the rising opposition to the arbitrary measures of the mother country. In September, 1764, Philip drew up an address to Lieutenant Governor Colden, protesting the tax program: ". . . Such must be the deplorable state of that wretched people, who, (being taxed by a power subordinate to none, and in a great degree unacquainted with their circumstances,) can call nothing their own . . . still hoping that a stop may be put to those measures, which . . . will oblige us to think that nothing but extreme poverty can preserve us from the most insupportable bondage."

The following year, Philip Livingston was one of his colony's delegates to the Stamp Act Congress, held in New York City. Francis Lewis, a Signer, and Judge Robert R. Livingston, Philip's cousin, also represented the colony of New York.

In October, 1768, Livingston was elected speaker in the Assembly of the province. Resolutions asserting the rights of the Colonies were passed in December and a correspondence was begun with the other provinces. As a result, the royal governor dissolved this Assembly on January 2, 1769. Appointed to the next Assembly as the member from Livingston Manor, Philip was unseated by the Tories as a non-resident, since he lived in New York City.

In 1774 he was elected a delegate to the First Continental Congress by the New York City committee of fifty-one, along with Isaac Low, John Alsop, James Duane, and John Jay. The New England delegates passing through New York on their way to Philadelphia were anxious to meet and assess the stand of the New York delegates and gauge the temper of the province. John Adams was told that one party feared civil war, that another was "intimidated lest the levelling spirit of the New England colonies should propagate itself into New York." Of the delegates, Adams wrote in his diary: "Mr. Alsop is a soft, sweet man. Mr. Duane has a sly, surveying eye . . . very sensible, I think, and very artful." Mr. Jay "a young gentleman of the law, of about twenty-six . . . a hard student and a good speaker." Philip Livingston, who remained a member of Congress until his death in 1778, was described by the diarist as "a downright, straightforward man," also "a great, rough, rapid mortal. There is no holding any conversation with him. He blusters away . . ." On

August 24, Cushing and Paine went to Long Island to dine with Philip Livingston at his country house on Brooklyn Heights, while the two Adamses "sent our excuse, that we were not very well; it was raw and wet."

Concerning New York politics another Massachusetts man, Josiah Quincy, Jr., had heard earlier from George Clymer that patriotism "then seemed to have taken but shallow root in some places, particularly at New York, where political principles truly are as unfixed as the wind. One year sees the New Yorkers champions for liberty, and the next hugging their chains."

At Congress, Livingston was appointed to the committee to prepare the address to the people of Great Britain. Two more New York delegates were added to the delegation, John Haring and Henry Wisner. In November, 1774, Livingston was elected to the New York City committee of sixty, successor to the powerful committee of fifty-one. The sixty issued a call in March for an election of deputies to a provincial convention to be held in New York City on April 20, to choose delegates for the Second Continental Congress. Those selected, on April 22, were Philip Livingston, serving as president, Robert R. Livingston, Alsop, Simon Boerum, George Clinton, Duane, Willam Floyd, Jay, Francis Lewis, Philip Schuyler, Wisner and Lewis Morris of Morrisania. The next afternoon news of the Battles of Lexington and Concord reached New York City, and first the committee of one hundred, successor to the sixty, and then the newly organized Provincial Congress took over the government in the colony.

Philip Livingston was elected to the third New York Provincial Congress which convened on May 14, 1776, the day before the Continental Congress passed the resolution for new governments in each colony. Concerning this resolution and its preamble, R. R. Livingston wrote from Philadelphia to John Jay in New York: "It has occasioned a great alarm here . . . some points of the last importance are to be agitated (as we imagine), very early . . . You have by this time sounded our people, I hope they are satisfied of the necessity of assuming a new form of Government . . ."

Duane also wrote to Jay: "There seems therefore no reason that our Colony shou'd be too precipitate in changing the present mode of Government. . . . Above all, let us see the conduct of the middle colonies before we come to a decision: It cannot injure us to wait a few weeks . . ."

In New York, on May 29, the "Committee of Mechanics in union" publicly declared that should the Provincial Congress instruct the delegates in the Continental Congress to "cause these United Colonies to become independent of Great Britain, it would give us the highest satisfaction; and we hereby sincerely promise to endeavour to support the same with our lives and fortunes." The Provincial Congress answered that it could not instruct the delegates on the "momentous question" until it was brought before the Continental Congress.

Philip Livingston attended the Provincial Congress on June 8, and two days later a letter dated June 8 was received from Floyd, Wisner, R. R. Livingston and Lewis. Evidently written before the debate of that day on Lee's independence motion, it read: "Your Delegates here expect the question of Independence will very shortly be agitated in Congress. Some of us consider ourselves as bound by our instructions not to vote on that question. The matter will admit of no delay. . . ." This was taken up at once, "with closed doors." Both Livingston and Jay were present at the discussion.

On the evening of the eleventh, resolutions were passed stating that the Provincial Congress had no power to take any action on independence and recommending that the freeholders, besides authorizing their deputies at the next election to vote on the subject of government, inform them "relative to the great question of Independency . . ." The delegates in Philadelphia were advised and replied to the Provincial Congress that they had taken "no steps inconsistent with their intention as expressed in their letter, by which" the delegates would be careful to regulate their "future conduct."

Following the postponement of Lee's motion, Robert R. Livingston was chosen on the committee to prepare the Declaration of Independence, the only representative of the "dilatory system" among the five members.

New York had had a turbulent spring and in June was disturbed by the disclosure of an armed conspiracy and a plot against General Washington's life, said to stem straight from the royal governor himself, William Tryon, now safe on board a British warship in the bay.

As July 1 approached, the arrival of a British invasion fleet threw the city into a panic and the Provincial Congress adjourned to White Plains. Although his property and business were further jeopardized, Philip Livingston set off for Philadelphia, arriving by July 3.

Edward Rutledge wrote to John Jay in New York on June 29, asking him to come immediately to Congress: "Clinton has Abilities but is silent in general . . . Floyd, Wisner, Lewis and Alsop tho' good men, never quit their chairs. . . ." Jay replied that "plots, conspiracies, and chimeras dire" detained him.

Jefferson's notes of July 1 tell that the Independence resolution was carried in the committee of the whole. ". . . the delegates from New York declared they were for it themselves & were assured their constituents were for it, but that their instructions having been drawn near a twelvemonth before, when reconciliation was still the general object, they were enjoined by them to do nothing which should impede that object. they therefore thought themselves not justifiable in voting on either side, and asked leave to withdraw from the question, which was given them."

The New York delegation, joined by Philip Livingston,

also refrained from the vote which approved the Declaration on July 4, in accordance with their instructions.

At White Plains, on July 9, the newly-elected Provincial Congress received the Declaration, referring it to a committee of Jay, Abraham Yates, John Sloss Hobart and two others. That same evening a resolution was reported and adopted unanimously, approving independence and stating that the members of the New York Congress would "at the risk of our lives and fortunes, join with the other colonies in supporting it."

General Washington, who had come in April to fortify New York City, gave an order on July 9 regarding the celebration of Independence: "The several brigades are to be drawn up this evening on their respective Parades, at six Oclock, when the Declaration of Congress . . . is to be read with an audible voice. The General hopes this important Event will serve as a free incentive to every officer, and soldier, to act with Fidelity and Courage, as knowing that now the peace and safety of his Country depends (under God) solely on the success of our arms . . ." The brigades were formed in hollow squares and in the middle of one the Commander in Chief, on horseback, listened while an aide read the matchless proclamation in a clear voice, under the guns of the enemy ships and in view of the British troops occupying Staten Island. It was during this evening that the King's statue was brought down. Later the royal governor wrote from his safe vantage point on board the warship *Duchess of Gordon,* ". . . every vestige of Royalty, as far as has been in the power of the Rebels, done away . . ."

"Molten Majesty" was a great help in the desperate scarcity of lead. Collections of lead weights from windows were made in New York, and Philip Livingston was among those contributing.

At the Signing in Philadelphia on August 2, Livingston, Lewis and Floyd were present to inscribe their names. The

British forces at New York had built up great strength, so they were literally risking everything they had, as was Morris, too, a post-signer.

Less than one month later, Philip Livingston's elegant country house on Brooklyn Heights was the scene of a conference between George Washington and his generals, at which it was decided that Long Island must be evacuated by the American troops, who had suffered serious defeat in the Battle of Long Island on August 27. A painting by John Ward Dunsmore shows this scene, the prelude to the miraculous withdrawal of the Patriot forces across the river to New York City, aided by a favorable wind change and a screening fog.

Livingston's beautifully built house, with its marble fireplaces, one of which is to be seen in the painting, was used by the British as a naval hospital. Long neglected, it was later destroyed by fire.

On the failure of Howe's peace conference in September, the British troops occupied New York City, and Philip Livingston's house on Duke Street, as well as his extensive business interests, fell into the hands of the invaders.

In May, 1777, Livingston was chosen a state senator under the New York State Constitution adopted in April. In September he attended the first meeting of the new legislature at Kingston, where he was elected again to the national Congress.

Philip Livingston married Christina Ten Broeck, daughter of Colonel Dirck and Margaret Cuyler Ten Broeck, and they had five sons and four daughters. After the loss of New York City in the autumn of 1776, he and his family lived in exile. They were even endangered in their retreat at Kingston when the British burned that city in 1777.

Not long before his death, Philip Livingston sold a portion of his remaining property to sustain the public credit. Aware of his failing health, he took his seat in Congress in

May, 1778. Congress had then retreated to York, Pennsylvania, after the capture of Philadelphia by the enemy. Livingston died on June 12, at York, with only his son Henry at his bedside, so he did not live to return to New York City after the evacuation of the British in 1783, and try to rebuild his way of life and properties there. His country estate of about forty acres on Brooklyn Heights (the mansion stood on Hicks Street, a little south of Joralemon Street) is now divided into city blocks. The low-lying view of Manhattan it commanded is now studded with skyscrapers. Some of these tall buildings stand near the site of Livingston's New York house.

But Philip Livingston's forward-looking part in the city's life is still carried on. He was a charter member of the New York Society Library, established in 1754 by a weekly club, and first president of the St. Andrew's Society. He was an organizer of the Chamber of Commerce, incorporated in 1770, and one of the first governors of the New York Hospital, chartered the following year. A "firm believer in the sublime truths of religion," Philip Livingston, a graduate of Yale, aided in 1746 in founding the professorship of divinity at that college which although no longer active, still furthers the religious aims of its donor!

Lewis Morris, another New York Signer, was the third lord of the "mannour of Morrisania," a tract bounded on the south and west by the East and Harlem Rivers in what is now Bronx County. He had inherited the manor and its rights from the second lord, his father, Lewis Morris. The first lord of the same name added a prayer in his will "that the good God may always protect, direct and influence" his children "to act as becomes them." Lewis Morris I was Chief Justice of New York 1702-1728, and the first Governor of New Jersey, as separate from New York, from 1738 until his death in 1746.

The Signer was born at Morrisania in 1726. At sixteen he went to Yale, studying languages, mathematics and religion under Dr. Clapp. He graduated in 1746. After that he managed his estate, and in 1749 he married Mary Walton. They had six sons and four daughters; three sons took part in the Revolution as officers with the American army.

Morris was made brigadier general of the Westchester County militia on June 7, 1776, and served with his brigade. He also attended the New York Provincial Congress that summer. Back in Congress in Philadelphia, he wrote to Jay on September 8 that he was very anxious about the situation in New York. A week later New York City fell to the British, and Morrisania was soon overrun by enemy soldiers.

In regard to resuming his command, Morris wrote from Philadelphia to the Committee of Safety: "Since my arrival at Philadelphia, the State of N York has had no more than a representation in Congress, and as the Gentlemen of the Committee for Indian Affairs were mostly out of Town, the whole of that necessary business has devolved upon me— My family have been obliged to desert their home, and meeting with them in this place, altogether unprovided, I have been under the necessity of delaying the time of my Stay untill I could fix them in some Situation where they could be accommodated . . . I shall prepare to set out with all possible expedition for West Chester . . ." During this stay at Congress, Morris signed the Declaration—and so gave away his political rights under English law to his tiny principality.

The farms, woodlands, mansion and stock of Morrisania were in the path of the victorious British army and were all occupied, damaged and despoiled. One thousand acres of woodland on navigable waters was too tempting a prize for the enemy to resist.

Cut off from his estate until the evacuation in 1783, Morris was obliged to make many personal sacrifices. On his return to Morrisania he found himself impoverished not only by the ruin there but by the loss of other holdings as well. In 1777 he relinquished his seat in Congress to his half-brother, Gouverneur Morris, but he continued to serve in the state senate and in the militia.

Rush's tribute to this Signer reads: "Lewis Morris. A chearful amiable man and a most disinterested Patriot. He had three sons at one time in the army. He suffered the loss of many thousand pounds by the depredations of the British army upon his property near New York without repining. Every attachment of his heart yielded to his love of his country."

William Floyd *1734–1821*
Francis Lewis *1713–1802*

IN ADDITION TO its partial claim on Philip Livingston because of his country mansion on Brooklyn Heights, Long Island can boast of two Signers: William Floyd, whose house still stands at Mastic, in Suffolk County; and Francis Lewis, whose residence at Whitestone was located almost exactly where the southern span of the Bronx-Whitestone Bridge now rests.

William Floyd belonged to the fourth generation of his family in the Colonies. Richard Floyd I, the first of the line, emigrated from Wales in 1654, settling at Setauket, in the town of Brookhaven. He was very successful in agriculture, became a judge of Suffolk County and served as a colonel of militia. His son, Richard II, married Margaret Nicoll, daughter of Matthias Nicoll, Colonial Secretary, Mayor of New York City and judge. Their second son, Nicoll, of Mastic, Long Island, and his wife, Tabitha Smith, were the parents of the Signer, born on December 17, 1734. Among their seven other children were Ruth, who married General Nathaniel Woodhull, president of the Provincial Congress, who died from the effects of his capture in the Battle of Long Island; and Richard IV, who was a Loyalist and emigrated to the province of New Brunswick, Canada, at the conclusion of the Revolutionary War.

William Floyd had an elementary education and at nineteen was called upon to assume management of the home farm, on the death of his father. His life was spent surrounded by an extensive group of relatives, including the leading families of the county. He enjoyed hunting game and entertaining hospitably in the large white house at Mastic.

The eastern end of Long Island was settled mostly by colonists from New England who were Dissenters; for example, Southold was established in 1640 and Southampton later that year. An active spirit of resistance to British oppression developed there, in which William Floyd joined. In 1774 he was elected a delegate to the First Continental Congress and took his seat in Carpenters' Hall on the opening day.

A member of the provincial convention of April, 1775, he was chosen a delegate to the Second Continental Congress and served on numerous committees, including that to procure supplies for the army. He continued as a delegate to Congress until 1783 with one intermission.

Previous to his election, Mr. Floyd had been appointed to a command in the Suffolk County militia. Upon his return home, he found Eastern Long Island menaced by an invasion from a naval force, gathered in Gardiner's Bay to obtain supplies for the British army. He assembled his command and marched toward the point of attack. The enemy then abandoned their plans.

On September 7, 1775, the several Committees of Suffolk elected William Floyd colonel of the First or West Regiment of the Suffolk County militia. Colonel Floyd's report on this regiment, given in April, 1776, indicates a total of 1030 men.

"The Minute Men, and those Enlisted and to be Enlisted
into the Continental Service" to be taken from the total enrollment, it reads. "The Regiment is about two-thirds furnished with bayonets and the others are getting them as fast
as they Can Get them made; they are furnished with half
pound of powder and two pound of Ball per man . . . they
are pretty Industrious in fixing their accoutrements . . ." and
in a short time should be "tolerably well prepared," Floyd
concludes.

Service in Congress called him, and he left for Philadelphia on April 23—not to return to Long Island for about
seven years, because of enemy occupation.

In Congress, he and Francis Lewis joined with the other
New York delegates in signing the letters of June 8 and 17
regarding their instructions on the question of independence.
On June 29 he shared with Wisner, Lewis and Alsop in Rutledge's description of the New York delegates, who "tho'
good men, never quit their chairs." On July 2 Floyd signed,
along with Lewis and his other fellow delegates, a letter to
the New York Provincial Congress in the handwriting of
George Clinton which stated that independence "this Day
will be finally determined in the House— We know the line
of our Conduct on this Occasion; we have your Instructions,
and will faithfully pursue them— New Doubts and Difficulties however will arise should Independency be declared; and
that it will not, we have not the least Reason to expect nor
do we believe that (if any) more than one Colony (and the
Delegates of that divided) will vote against the Question;
every Colony (ours only excepted) having withdrawn their
former Instructions, and either positively instructed their
Delegates to vote for Independency; or to concur in such
Vote if they shall judge it expedient— What part are we to
act after this Event takes Place . . . "

A note, also dated July 2, written and signed by Wisner,
reports: "Since writing the inclosed the question of inde-

pendance has Been put in Congress and Carried in the afirma-
tive without one Desenting vote (New York, of course, not
voting) I therefore Beg your answer as quick as posable to
the inclosed."

The approval of the Declaration by New York's Provincial
Congress was officially reported to the Continental Congress,
and on August 2 Floyd and Lewis signed with Livingston—
only too truly jeopardizing their families and actually signing
away their Long Island property.

As the enemy swept eastward down the island, General
Floyd's wife and family were forced to flee to Connecticut,
across Long Island Sound, as were many other Long Island
Patriots. His mansion house and farm were seized by the
British and he was cut off from any income from his property
until the evacuation, almost seven years later.

With the aid of friends, Mrs. Floyd and her children
reached Middletown, Connecticut, as refugees from Long
Island. In June, 1779, General Floyd's overseer was granted
permission by the Governor of Connecticut to go to Long
Island after certain property belonging to Floyd. The following year Floyd petitioned the General Assembly of
Connecticut that, as he was "in the publick Service at Philadelphia" when the enemy took Long Island and so was
unable to save his personal property and as Governor Tryon
had allowed his estate to be taken over by two Tories who
had appropriated stock, household furniture, farming uten-
sils, beds, "beding," and other clothing he "prays he may
obtain a permit to Send on to Long Island Some Carefull
persons" to bring off such of his effects as they may find. This
request was granted. British permission for the undercover
raid on Floyd's own property was not asked!

From 1777 until 1783, Floyd was appointed state senator
for the southern district, then within the British lines. At
last, on April 1, he wrote General Clinton of his coming return to his Long Island estate, and in 1784 he was elected

state senator from the same district. He was a representative in the First Congress under the Constitution and served as a presidential elector in 1792, 1800 and 1804.

At the close of the war, William Floyd bought a large tract of land at Westernville, in Oneida County, and, with his family, went there to live in 1803. His first wife, Hannah Jones, having died in 1781, he married Johanna Strong of Setauket. Among his children were Colonel Nicoll Floyd, a member of the New York Assembly; Mary, the wife of Colonel Benjamin Tallmadge, who, as chief of General Washington's secret service in New York, was instrumental in the disclosure of André and the Arnold plot to surrender West Point; and Ann, who married George Clinton, son of New York's first governor.

William Floyd, in Rush's estimate, was "A mild and decided Republican. He seldom spoke in Congress, but always voted with the zealous friends to liberty and independance."

Francis Lewis was an adopted Long Islander, having been born in March, 1713, at Llandaff, South Wales, the son of an Episcopal clergyman and his wife, who was the daughter of the Reverend Doctor Pettingal, also an Episcopalian minister. An only child, orphaned at the age of four or five, Francis was put under the care of a maiden aunt. Strongly patriotic, she had him taught Cymraeg, the Welsh language, and he also learned Gaelic in Scotland. Later he received a classical education at Westminister School in London, and then entered the counting-room of a London merchant. Coming of age at twenty-one, Lewis converted his patrimony into merchandise and embarked for New York, arriving there in the spring of 1735.

He went into business with a Mr. Annesley and, after working for a short period in Philadelphia, established his residence in New York. He married Elizabeth Annesley, sister of his partner, in 1745, and they had seven children, of whom only three lived to maturity.

Francis Lewis' business interests caused him to travel extensively in Europe. He was twice in Russia, visited the Orkney and Shetland Islands and was twice shipwrecked on the coast of Ireland.

During the French and Indian War, Lewis, as agent for supplying the British troops with clothing, was present at Fort Oswego in 1756 when it was attacked by Montcalm. Surrendering, the garrison were made prisoners of war and Lewis fell to the share of the warrior chief of the Indian forces. Legend, now disproved, said that a similarity between the Iroquois and Cymraeg languages gained the interest of the chief and Lewis was sent to Montreal, to be returned to his family without ransom. But, instead, he was shipped in a cartel to France to be exchanged. At the close of the war the British government granted Lewis five thousand acres of land in consideration of his services to the military.

Long active in the American cause against the oppressive acts passed by the British government, Lewis served as a member of the Stamp Act Congress at New York in 1765, as did Philip Livingston. On the attempt to put the Stamp Act into operation, Lewis, an early Son of Liberty, retired from business, to remain at his country seat at Whitestone, Long Island, where he continued to reside until 1771. Anxious to set up his son, also Francis Lewis, in business, he took him on a purchasing trip to England and returned toward the end of 1771 with a large quantity of dry goods, establishing the firm of Francis Lewis and Son. At the start of the Revolution in 1774, he again retired from active business to stay on Long Island.

Like Livingston, Lewis was a member of the committees of fifty-one, sixty, and one hundred. On April 22, 1775, he was elected by the provincial convention a delegate to the Second Continental Congress, and his business abilities made him a valuable member of the committees on which he served. On November 9, he signed the secret pact by which every member of Congress pledged himself "under the ties of virtue honor & love of his country not to divulge directly or indirectly any matter or thing agitated or debated in Congress before the same shall have been determined, without leave of the Congress . . ."

A member of the third New York Provincial Congress, Lewis wrote from the city on May 2, 1776: "As our election for Delegates is to be on the 14th instant, I shall defer my return to Philadelphia till that is over." Re-elected, he set out for Philadelphia on June 1.

Less than a month after the Signing of the Declaration, the enemy invaded and took Long Island. General Morris' anxious letter to Jay about New York explained: "I should have gone off this day but Mr. Lewis has taken flight toward that Place in quest of his family, that were on Long Island, and there remain only three of us."

In retaliation for his signing for American independence, Lewis' Long Island property was destroyed, including his books and papers. Mrs. Lewis was taken prisoner and kept in close confinement. This unhappy situation was brought to the attention of Congress in November, and she was finally exchanged, through the influence of General Washington, for the wife of the British paymaster-general and one other woman. Unfortunately, her health was ruined and she died about two years later.

Francis Lewis was re-elected to Congress in 1777, and in 1779 he was appointed commissioner of the board of admiralty and also became a vestryman of Trinity Church. Colonel Morgan Lewis, his son, served in the Continental army and became a lawyer after the war. He was Chief Justice of the State Supreme Court in 1792, and was elected governor in 1804. His wife, Gertrude, was the daughter of Judge Robert R. Livingston, and the sister of Robert R. Livingston of Clermont who, while ambassador to France, was later instrumental in the Louisiana Purchase. With Robert Fulton he promoted the first successful steamboat, the *Clermont*.

Of Francis Lewis, Rush wrote: "A moderate Whig, but a very honest man, and very useful in executive business."

Richard Stockton *1730–1781*

Besides endangering his family, his honor and his fortune, Richard Stockton signed away his health and his life when he affixed his name to the Declaration of Independence. Captured by the British in November, his health was broken by ill treatment while a prisoner. He did not live to see the surrender of Lord Cornwallis at Yorktown on October 19, 1781, nor the signing in November, a year later, of the Preliminary Articles of Peace.

The first Richard Stockton emigrated from England prior to 1660 and after residing a while at Flushing, Long Island, settled in Burlington County, New Jersey, on a large tract of land. His son Richard accompanied the family to New Jersey but settled in Piscataway. About 1700 he purchased six thousand acres, which included the present site of Princeton. His house, "Morven," is owned by the State of New Jersey and may become the official residence of the governors of New Jersey. John, son of the second Richard, was one of the first presiding judges of the Court of Common Pleas for Somerset County, under the royal government. Largely instrumental in bringing the College of New Jersey (Princeton University) to Princeton in 1756, he was one of its most generous patrons. John and his wife, Abigail Phillips Stockton, were the parents of the Signer, Richard, born at Morven on October 1, 1730.

Richard, the Signer, studied classical science with the Reverend Doctor Samuel Finley at his West Nottingham Academy, now at Colora, Maryland, for about two years and then went to the College of New Jersey, then located at Newark. He graduated at the first annual commencement in 1748, at which time Aaron Burr, Sr., was president of the college. Then he studied law with David Ogden of Newark, was admitted to the bar in August, 1754, and became a counsellor in 1758. He rose rapidly in his profession. In 1766 the Reverend Doctor John Rodgers, a fellow College of New Jersey trustee, wrote of Stockton: ". . . a Gentn. of Genius & Learning, & you may assuredly depend upon his Intelligence as a Person of the strictest Probity. He is an eminant Lawyer & at the Head of his Profession in the Province of New Jersey . . ." Although he lived at Morven, Stockton also took cases in Pennsylvania, becoming acquainted with Dickinson, Shippen and Chew.

After he had earned a considerable fortune, Stockton traveled abroad in 1766 and 1767, visiting England, Scotland and Ireland and meeting the important men of the day. Presented to the King at the Court of St. James, he gave his majesty a written address from the trustees of the College of New Jersey regarding the repeal of the hated Stamp Act.

In November, 1766, Richard Stockton was requested by the College of New Jersey trustees to visit Dr. Witherspoon, newly-elected president of that institution at his home in Paisley, Scotland, and prevail upon him to accept the post. In the trustees' letter to Witherspoon, Stockton is described as "a Gentleman of Fortune & Figure in his Profession of the Law, of distinguished Abilities, & Influence here, and a warm Friend to the interests of Religion & Learning. He is tho'ro'ly acquainted with the state of our affairs religious & political . . ."

Stockton visited Witherspoon the end of February, 1767, and persuaded him that he should become president of the College of New Jersey, but Mrs. Witherspoon flatly rejected the idea. Stockton returned to Edinburgh, obtained the support of some friends of the Witherspoons for his mission, and was presented with the freedom of the city. Benjamin Rush, a young American student, then took over the project to persuade the Witherspoons to accept the call to Princeton, and finally succeeded.

Back in America, Stockton was given a seat in the executive council in 1768. He resided at Morven, managing his extensive and fertile landed estate. In 1774, he became a judge of the New Jersey Supreme Court.

In 1752 Richard Stockton had married Annis Boudinot, sister of Elias Boudinot, who was chosen president of Congress in 1782. Their children were Julia, twins Mary and Susan, Richard, Lucius Horatio and Abigail, the youngest born in September, 1773.

As the breach widened between the Colonies and England, Richard Stockton took the Patriot side. The New Jersey Assembly, on July 21, 1774, declared that their people and the whole country "detest all thoughts of an independence." The colony was represented in the First Continental Congress in September by James Kinsey, William Livingston, John de Hart, Steven Crane and Richard Smith. At an election on February 14, 1776, Jonathan D. Sergeant and John Cooper were substituted for Kinsey and Crane. Instructions were given to the delegates on March 2 to study the measures of the British ministry "which are uncertain, extraordinary, and new almost every week" and "to join in the general voice of the United Colonies."

Jonathan Sergeant, one of Stockton's law students, left Congress for Princeton the beginning of April because, as he wrote to John Adams, he felt that he "may be more useful here or there . . . My head achs & my Heart achs. I tremble for the Timidity of our Counsels." Five days later he wrote again to Adams—that he feared the colony would be *misrepresented* by the current delegation, one of whom had declared himself a candidate for the Provincial Convention in order that "he may control the mad Fellows who now compose that Body." And Sergeant charged that "every Creature that can lisp against Independence, which in other Words, in my Opinion, is every Creature who would wish to give up the quarrel" would be pushed into the convention.

As told in the Prologue, Sergeant and the other Patriots were successful in swinging New Jersey to their side and the five new delegates elected—including Richard Stockton—were all independent "Souls." Sergeant wrote briefly—on "the only white Piece of Paper in Bristol"—that the people of New Jersey "were quite in the dark as to the Sentiments of their Delegates until lately. . . . Our new ones I trust will not deceive us." Samuel Adams commented later on this "new sett" to Richard Henry Lee: "All of them appear to be zealously attached to the American Cause . . ."

Richard Stockton and his colleagues made a dramatic entrance on their appearance in Congress on July 1, when Lee's independence motion was reconsidered. John Adams described the scene in a letter: "In the previous multiplied debates which we had upon the subject of Independence, the Delegates from New Jersey had voted against us, their Constituents were informed of it and recalled them and sent us a new sett on purpose to vote for Independence. Among those were Chief Justice Stockton and Dr. Witherspoon. . . . the Jersey Delegates appearing for the first time, desired the question might be discussed." The writer continued that on so public a question "so long disputed in Pamphlets News Papers and every fireside" the "new sett" could not be uninformed and must have made up their minds. They had not been inattentive to what was passing abroad but they did not feel like giving their opinions until they heard "the

sentiments of Members there. Judge Stockton was most particularly importunate, till the members began to say let the
Gentlemen be gratifi'd and the Eyes of the assembly were
turned upon me and several other of them said come Mr.
Adams you have had the subject at heart longer than any of
us, and you must recapitulate the arguments. . . ."

John Adams then made a famed speech. Richard Stockton's opinion of it was given by his son years later in a letter
to Adams which read: "I have just alluded to my Father and
shall take leave to mention an anecdote . . . I well remember
that on his first return home from Congress in the summer
of 1776 after the 4th of July he was immediately surrounded
by his anxious political Friends who were eager for minute
information in respect of the great event which had just
taken place—Being then a Boy of some observation and of
very retentive memory I remember these words addressed to
his Friends—'The Man to whom the Country is most indebted
for the great measure of Independence is Mr. John Adams of
Boston—I call him the Atlas of American independence—
He it was who sustained the debate. . .' "

All five New Jersey delegates voted "plump" on July 2, as
prophesied by Sergeant. News of the passing of the Declaration on the fourth was sent the following day by John Hancock to the New Jersey Convention and it was proclaimed at
Trenton on July 8, together with the new state constitution
adopted the week before.

Richard Stockton may not have actually signed before
August 9, when he was chosen on a committee in Congress.
On July 19 he had written to Thomas Jefferson from Trenton that he "waited upon the New Jersey Convention—and
proposed to them the agreeing to furnish 2000 men for the
increase of the flying Camp . . ."

Signing also was Richard Stockton's new son-in-law and
old friend, Dr. Benjamin Rush of Pennsylvania, who had

married the Stocktons' eldest daughter Julia in January, 1776.

In September, Stockton was a candidate for governor of the state, receiving on the first ballot the same number of votes as William Livingston. By a re-vote, Livingston was elected, and Stockton was chosen chief justice but declined. On the twenty-sixth, with George Clymer of Pennsylvania, he was appointed by Congress to a committee to inspect the northern army. Proceeding to Albany, Saratoga and other places concerned, they carried out their mission and reported back to Congress.

It was then necessary for Stockton to remove his wife and family to a place of safety, as Morven, in Princeton, was on the direct route of the British army sweeping down into New Jersey. He took them to Monmouth County, after helping the retreating Americans as long as possible. On November 30, he and his friend, John Covenhoven, at whose house he had sought refuge, were captured at night by a party of Loyalists. Deprived of his possessions, he was removed to New York by way of Amboy. At Amboy he was exposed to extreme cold and thrown into the common jail and this, plus subsequent poor treatment in New York, ruined his health. The Congress, distressed at the news of his treatment, directed General Washington, if the report proved true, to "send a flag to general Howe remonstrating against this departure from that humane procedure" and "to know of general Howe whether he chooses this shall be the future rule for treating all such, on both sides, as the fortune of war may place in the hands of either party."

His constitution having been materially impaired, Stockton was only able to give occasional counsel and advice to his country after his release. His large fortune was greatly diminished by the depreciation of Continental currency and by the destruction visited on his property by the enemy army. Morven had been used as military headquarters in late 1776.

His library, one of the best in the country, was destroyed. Benjamin Rush, his son-in-law, wrote to Lee after the Battle of Princeton: "The whole of Mr. Stockton's furniture, apparel, and even valuable writings have been burnt." Years later, Stockton's widow was still trying to locate those priceless papers which would have revealed so much of this Patriot's services to our country.

His lands laid waste, Stockton was forced to ask temporary aid from friends. His health declined steadily and he died on February 28, 1781.

To his children, his last words were: ". . . to subscribe to the entire belief of the great and leading doctrines of the Christian religion . . . divine faith accompanied with an habitual virtuous life, and the universality of the divine providence." He begged them to remember that " 'the fear of God is the beginning of wisdom.' "

Of his father-in-law, Rush wrote: "An enlightened politician and a correct and graceful speaker. He was timid where bold measures were required, but was at all times sincerely devoted to the liberties of his country."

Mrs. Stockton was known for her literary talents. Her Pastoral on the subject of Lord Cornwallis' capture, addressed to General Washington after the surrender at Yorktown, was acknowledged by him in a letter. Her composition "Welcome, Mighty Chief, Once More!" was sung by young ladies of Trenton while strewing flowers in front of General Washington as he passed through that city on his way to New York, just before his first inauguration as President.

Many of Richard and Annis Boudinot Stocktons' descendants were prominent in the service of the Republic which he did not live to see established. Their son Richard was a lawyer and United States Senator. A grandson, Robert Field Stockton, a naval officer, helped secure California for the United States and the city of Stockton in that state is named for him. A great-grandson, John Potter Stockton, served as minister to Rome and United States Senator.

In the letter of thanks to Mrs. Stockton General Washington said: "Your favor of the 17th conveying to me your Pastoral on the subject of Lord Cornwallis' capture has given me great satisfaction. . . . I have only to lament that the Hero of your Pastoral is not more deserving of your Pen; but the circumstance shall be placed among the happiest events of my life."

John Witherspoon *1723-1794*

THE REVEREND Doctor John Witherspoon, sixth president of Princeton University, then called the College of New Jersey, earned honors in religion, education and statesmanship. The present president of Princeton, Dr. Harold W. Dodds, wrote of him: "Truly, in the life of this man is to be found at once a profound lesson and a master key to the history of his day"—and to any day, present or future, we might add. The reputation of this eminent Scottish theologian was so revered in this country that he was called to be president of the College of New Jersey, the New Light Presbyterian seminary, by a Board to whom he personally was unknown.

A lineal descendant of the Reverend John Knox through his mother, John Witherspoon was born on February 5, 1723, in the parish of Yester, Scotland, of which his father James was minister. After attending school in Haddington, John went to the University of Edinburgh at the age of thirteen and was educated for the ministry there from 1736 to 1743. In 1745 he became minister at Beith, and twelve years later transferred to Paisley, where the well-known shawls were woven. A spectator at the Battle of Falkirk in 1746, he was captured by the rebels and briefly imprisoned in a castle.

Two years later he married Elizabeth Montgomerie, and of their ten children only five survived infancy.

Shortly after entering the ministry, Witherspoon was involved in the controversy between the Moderate or liberal wing of the Scottish Kirk and the Popular or orthodox party, eventually becoming the leader of the Popular minority. His first publication, a satirical piece, *Ecclesiastical Characteristics* (1753), attracted the notice of the Reverend Samuel Davies who, with Gilbert Tennent, was in Scotland the following year to raise funds for the College of New Jersey. In his diary, Davies (later president of the college) says of Witherspoon's pamphlet: "I think the humour is nothing inferior to Dean Swift." The mission of the two men was successful and served to create a bond between the Popular wing and the New Light Presbyterians in America.

Witherspoon's many writings gained him wide recognition and in 1764 the University of Aberdeen gave him the degree of Doctor of Divinity. Two years later he was elected president of the College of New Jersey and the letter inviting him to accept that office mentions the "great Ends your Compliance will answer to Religion & Learning in general thro'out all the Colonies—" and tells of the "populous & healthy Country," explaining that the loss of Burr, who had brought the college to Princeton in 1756, and of his successors, Jonathan Edwards, the Reverend Davies and Doctor Samuel Finley "in the compass of a few years" was due to causes not attributable to the Princeton climate!

As told in the preceding chapter, Richard Stockton followed up this letter in person in February, 1767, and persuaded Witherspoon to accept but his wife rejected the idea to the point of illness. Another negotiator, Benjamin Rush, studying medicine in Edinburgh, refused to give up. He wrote of Witherspoon, "His appearance in the pulpit is solemn and graceful. His sermons are loaded with good sense and adorned at the same time with all the elegance and beauty that language can give them." To Witherspoon, Rush wrote on March 25: "All America waits . . . with trembling impatience for your answer . . ."

It was Rush who finally overcame Mrs. Witherspoon's objections, and for a second time her husband was elected to the presidency. In August, 1768, the Witherspoons reached Princeton. The students illuminated Nassau Hall with candles in every window, and a warm welcome was given the new president, who had brought over three hundred books for the college library.

Witherspoon immediately began to reorganize the college. Among his first steps were the reviving of the grammar school, the inaugurating of post-graduate work, putting the financial accounts in order and raising funds. Following the first commencement over which he presided he wrote to Rush, who was still abroad: ". . . there was a vast Concourse of People Ministers from all quarters Ladies & Gentlemen from N. York & Philadelphia. After an inaugural Oration by me in Latin . . ." Attendance was greatly increased that fall, and within a year after that Witherspoon had traveled into New England and south to Virginia in behalf of the college. He made progress, too, toward uniting the Presbyterian schism.

Among the innovations that he introduced in the college curriculum, then dedicated to educating Presbyterian ministers, were the Scottish system of lectures, extending the study of mathematics, improving the science course, introducing French and history as studies and expanding his lectures in moral philosophy to include government, politics and international law.

Witherspoon served as minister in the Princeton church. In addition to his renown as a preacher and his religious leadership, he began to have a political influence, too, among the great numbers of Scotch-Irish who had emigrated to this country. He early turned to the Patriot side and as the difficulties with Britain increased, his political influence with these Presbyterians was of extreme importance. As Moses Coit Tyler says in his *Literary History of the American Revolution:* "He seems to have come at the right moment, to the right place, in the right way."

By 1770 the Princeton students were openly demonstrative for the cause of the Colonies. The seniors, who included Dr. Witherspoon's son, James, appeared dressed in cloth of American manufacture at the commencement exercises in the fall. James Witherspoon's oration defended the thesis that the people were bound to resist the King if he ignored the laws of the State or treated his subjects cruelly. Seven years later, at the Battle of Germantown, James was to give his life for this principle.

For the activities at Princeton and for his friendship with Patriot leaders, John Witherspoon was severely criticized. One of the college trustees wrote: "Our clergy unhappily have gone distracted, and Dr. Witherspoon is at the bottom of it."

"He is as high a son of liberty as any man in America," John Adams wrote of Witherspoon in his diary during his stay in Princeton on the way to the Continental Congress in late August, 1774. He told of going to a service in the college chapel and how "After prayers the President attended us to the balcony of the college, where we have a prospect of an horizon of about eighty miles diameter." The doctor visited the Massachusetts men at their lodgings and took "a dish of coffee. He is one of the committee of correspondence, and was upon the Provincial Congress for appointing delegates from this Province to the General Congress." On Sunday, Adams reported, "Heard Dr. Witherspoon all day; a clear, sensible preacher."

In the spring of 1776, the New Jersey Patriots were working feverishly to prevail in their own colony. On May 17, declared a day of Fasting by Congress, Witherspoon delivered at Princeton a sermon on "The Dominion of Providence over the Passions of Men." For the Colonies to depend on the legislature of Great Britain would be, he said, "injury to the master, and ruin to the slave . . . If on account of their distance and ignorance of our situation, they could not conduct their own quarrel with propriety for one year, how can they give direction and vigour to every department of our civil constitutions, from age to age? There are fixed bounds to every human thing. When the branches of a tree grow very large and weighty, they fall off from the trunk. The sharpest sword will not pierce when it cannot reach. And there is a certain distance from the seat of government where an attempt to rule will either produce tyranny and helpless subjection, or provoke resistance and effect a separation." Dedicated to John Hancock, this sermon was published in America. It was reprinted in Glasgow, with notes denouncing the author as a rebel and traitor.

A member of the Colony Convention which framed the new constitution overthrowing the royal governor, William Franklin, Witherspoon was elected by the Provincial Congress a delegate to the Continental Congress.

When a member of Congress said that they were "not yet ripe for a declaration of independence," Dr. Witherspoon replied, "In my judgment, sir, we are not only ripe but rotting."

On July 1, during the "greatest debate of all," as previously told, John Adams summed up the arguments on independence for the New Jersey delegates who had just come to Congress. After hearing the "violent" New Englander they were ready to vote and Dr. Witherspoon is said to have made a speech favoring the move. Lee's motion was then carried in the committee of the whole and independence voted by Congress on July 2.

Impatient of delay in passing the Declaration, Witherspoon asserted, "He that will not respond to its accents, and

strain every nerve to carry into effect its provisions, is unworthy the name of freeman." As for himself, he vowed,
"Although these gray hairs must soon descend into the sepulchre, I would infinitely rather that they should descend
thither by the hand of the public executioner than desert at
this crisis the sacred cause of my country." He was among
those present in Congress on August 2, to sign the Declaration on parchment.

At this time Witherspoon shared lodgings in Philadelphia
with two other New Jersey Signers, Abraham Clark and John
Hart. Clark wrote from that city to Colonel Dayton: "As to
my Title—I know not yet whether it will be honourable or
dishonourable, the issue of the War must Settle it—Perhaps
our Congress will be Exalted on a high Gallows. . . . Dr.
Witherspoon Mr. Hart and my Self quarter together . . . P.S.
You'l please to Accept this on Plain Paper, our dignity don't
afford Gilt, and our pay scarcely any."

As the British invaders approached Princeton in November, 1776, President Witherspoon announced on the twenty-
ninth that the college could no longer continue in peace, and
classes were suspended. Work was not resumed until August,
1777. On December 2, 1776, General Washington hurried
through the town and the British arrived five days later,
billeting themselves in Nassau Hall and in most of the
houses. They were driven out by Washington at the Battle
of Princeton, on January 3, 1777.

Thomas Nelson, Jr., wrote to Jefferson about the damage
wrought by the enemy: "Old Weatherspoon has not escap't
their fury. They have burnt his Library. It grieves him
much that he has lost his controversial Tracts." Also bringing grief to the Patriot minister was the damage done to the
college he had worked so hard to build up. The library of
two thousand books was scattered and the Rittenhouse orrery
or planetarium was broken up.

Witherspoon took an active and very creditable, part in Congress, in debates and on committees, serving until 1782, with one interval. He was appointed to the important Committee of Secret Correspondence (October, 1776) and to a committee to consult with General Washington on the military crisis in November.

John Adams' diary tells of dining in February, 1777, at a Mrs. Page's with Dr. Rush, Mr. Sergeant, the two Colonel Lees, and Dr. Witherspoon. . . The next day he "heard Dr. Witherspoon . . . an excellent sermon. I find that I understand the Doctor better since I have heard him so much in conversation, and in the Senate . . ."

The Doctor was a member of the Board of War, and in 1778 was appointed to the committee on finances. He served, too, on committees to procure supplies for the army, to negotiate with the Vermonters who wanted to establish a state on New Hampshire grants, and others. Many papers were written by him on currency and army supplying, as well as proclamations for fasting and prayer on days appointed by Congress.

His service in regard to the general war economy of the country while in Congress was extremely important. He advocated sound bookkeeping and control of military expenditures, and opposed regulation of prices. His *Essay on Money* (1786) reflects his speeches in Congress. A consistent advocate of sound money, he warned against debasement of public credit. His strong pleas for thrift and honest credit endangered his popularity when unsound monetary policies were being promoted, but experience proved that he was correct and those who sought to tamper with the monetary system were wrong.

When he retired from Congress for good in 1782, Dr. Witherspoon turned to the arduous task of rebuilding the college—Nassau Hall, also used by American troops, was not yet restored and enrollment had fallen way off. He lived then at his country house, "Tusculum," having installed his son-in-law, the Reverend Doctor Samuel S. Smith, in the house on the college grounds. Doctor Smith was given charge of the college curriculum.

In 1783, with Joseph Reed, Witherspoon made a tour in Britain in behalf of the college, which was not successful. Returning, he resumed his college duties and did some scientific farming at Tusculum. He was proud of his kitchen garden and on one occasion when a visitor observed that he had an excellent garden but no flowers, he replied, "No, madam, neither in my garden, nor in my discourse."

Owing to a sort of nervous dizziness, he kept his oratory well under restraint but his eloquence was described as having made blood "shiver along the arteries." His religious devotions were constant all his life and he was a firm believer in family prayer. Excepting Washington, he is said to have possessed more "presence" than any other man of his time.

His wife having died in 1789, he married less than two years later a Philadelphia widow much younger than he. They had two daughters, and shortly after the birth of the second girl, her father died suddenly, in November, 1794. His son-in-law, Doctor Smith, succeeded him as president of the college. Among the Smiths' descendants was Vice-President John C. Breckenridge.

One of Dr. Witherspoon's early biographers said: "It was a distinguished feature in the American Revolution that religious feeling was closely connected with political action." Although he was only in this country a little less than eight years before independence was declared, this man of God stood up to be counted as an American not long after his arrival—proud and unafraid, he signed the Declaration on oath, on August 2, 1776, risking irretrievably his cherished

literary possessions, his honor and his standing in the Church
to establish the American Republic under God.

Another New Jersey Signer, Abraham Clark (1726-1794)
was born in his father's farmhouse in Elizabethtown, New
Jersey. He became a farmer. Educated in mathematics and
civil law, he engaged in conveyancing or property title trans-
fer and surveying. Legal advice given gratuitously to his
neighbors earned him the title of "poor man's counsellor."
High sheriff of Essex County and clerk of the New Jersey
Assembly under the royal government, he became an active
Whig at the approach of the Revolution, serving on the committees of vigilance and public safety. Elected to the Continental Congress in June, 1776, he was re-elected eight times
in the following twelve years and was a member of the State
Legislature. Unable to serve in the Constitutional Convention in 1787 because of illness, he made the motion in Congress on July 2, 1788, by which the United States Constitution
became effective. He was chosen a representative in the
Second Congress under the Constitution.

On the fateful morning of July 4, 1776, Clark wrote from
Philadelphia: "At the Time our Forces in Canada were retreating before a Victorious Army, while Genel. Howe with
a Large Armament is Advancing towards N. York, Our Congress Resolved to Declare the United Colonies *Free and
independent States*. A Declaration for this Purpose, I expect,
will this Day pass Congress, it is nearly gone through, after
which it will be Proclaimed . . . we must now be a free independent State, or a Conquered Country . . . I assure you, Sir,
Our Congress is an August Assembly—and can they Support
the Declaration now on the Anvil, they will be the greatest
Assembly on Earth—"

Known in his community as "Honest John Hart," this
New Jersey Signer was baptised in Hopewell Township in

1714. He was the son of Edward Hart, who commanded the New Jersey Blues, a volunteer corps that served in the French-Canadian wars. John, a successful farmer, served several terms in the Colonial Assembly and promoted laws on road improvement, schools and administration of justice. Recognizing the danger in the Stamp Act of 1765, he assisted in the selection of delegates to the Stamp Act Congress in New York that year. Elected as a delegate to the Continental Congress in June, 1776, he voted and signed for independence.

When New Jersey was invaded by the British that fall, John Hart's stock, farm and mills were destroyed by the Hessians, and his family was forced to flee. Hart hid in the forest, suffering privation and great sorrow in the death of his wife, Deborah Scudder Hart, in October. After the Battles of Trenton and Princeton, he was able to return to his farm, passing the rest of his life in agricultural pursuits. In 1777-78 he was chairman of the New Jersey Council of Safety. He died in 1779.

Rush said of John Hart: "A plain, honest, well meaning Jersey farmer, with little education, but with good sense and virtue eno' to discover and pursue the true interests of his country."

And of John Witherspoon, for whose coming to America Rush was directly responsible, the doctor wrote: "A well informed statesman and remarkably luminous and correct in all his speeches. . . . He was a zealous Whig, but free from the illiberality which sometimes accompanies zeal."

Francis Hopkinson *1737–1791*

FRANCIS HOPKINSON's satirical ballad, *The Battle of the Kegs,* took off the British alarm at the kegs filled with gunpowder that were floated by the Americans down the Delaware River toward Philadelphia and the British ships anchored there in 1778, during the occupation of that city. Professor Moses Coit Tyler, in his *Literary History of the American Revolution,* said that to the cause of the Revolution this ballad "was worth perhaps as much just then as the winning of a considerable battle."

New Jersey's Signer Hopkinson was born in Philadelphia on October 2, 1737, one of the eight children of Thomas and Mary Johnson Hopkinson. Thomas emigrated to Pennsylvania from England about 1731. Trained as a lawyer, he worked hard for a successful career. He was clerk of the Orphans' Court, common councilman of Philadelphia, judge of the admiralty, member of the Provincial Council, one of the incorporators of the Library Company, an original trustee of the College of Philadelphia and first president of the Philosophical Society. To him Benjamin Franklin attributes his introduction to the study of electricity: "The power of points to throw off electrical fire was first communicated to me by my ingenious friend, Mr. Thomas Hopkinson."

When Francis was only fourteen, Thomas Hopkinson died and his widow assumed the responsibility of educating and raising the family. Francis entered the College of Philadelphia in the first class, graduating in 1757 and receiving a master's degree three years later. He studied law under Benjamin Chew and was admitted to the bar in 1761. That same year he acted as secretary at a treaty with the Indians, which he commemorated by a poem, *The Treaty*, written on the banks of the Lehigh River and published soon afterward.

In May, 1766, Hopkinson sailed for Europe and spent about a year in London. He met John Penn, Benjamin West, Lord North and other prominent people, endeavoring without success to secure an appointment as a commissioner of customs for North America. He also visited his mother's cousin, the Bishop of Worcester, and Benjamin Franklin.

Returning to the Colonies, Francis Hopkinson married Ann Borden of Bordentown, New Jersey, in September, 1768. He was a member of the two groups which merged in 1769 to form the American Philosophical Society and became a director of the Library Company in 1771. The following year he was collector of customs at New Castle, later losing this office because of his Patriot sympathies.

A resident of Bordentown for several years, he was a member of the Provincial Council of New Jersey in 1774. To support the Patriot cause, he wrote *The Pretty Story* that year, influencing public opinion to the colonists' side. It was an allegory which represented the grievances of the Colonies in a pleasing, humorous style and was widely read.

After the arduous preliminary work by Jonathan Sergeant and other Patriots, Francis Hopkinson was one of the five new delegates elected on June 22, 1776, to the Continental Congress from New Jersey. "Jersey has chosen five new Members, all independent Souls," wrote John Adams, "and instructed them to vote on the first of July for Independence."

Six days later, on June 28, the *Journal of Congress* records: "Francis Hopkinson Esquire one of the Delegates for New Jersey attended & produced the credentials of their appointment." He was added to the committee to prepare the Articles of Confederation. Concerning this new delegation, a contemporary commented: "Mr. William Livingston and all others, who had hitherto resisted independence, were left out." Later on, however, Livingston led his troops off in defence of his country.

Hopkinson voted for independence and signed the Declaration on August 2. On the twenty-first John Adams, writing to his wife Abigail, described him: "Yesterday morning I took a walk into Arch Street to see Mr. Peale's painter's room . . . At this shop I met Mr. Francis Hopkinson, late a Mandamus Counsellor of New Jersey . . . who, it seems, is a native of Philadelphia, a son of a prothonotary of this country, who was a person much respected. The son was liberally educated, and is a painter and a poet. I have a curiosity to penetrate a little deeper into the bosom of this curious gentleman, and may possibly give you some more particulars concerning him. He is one of your pretty, little, curious, ingenious men. His head is not bigger than a large apple . . . I have not met with anything in natural history more amusing and entertaining than his personal appearance; yet he is genteel and well bred, and is very social."

During the struggle for independence, Hopkinson's political writings were of great importance to the American cause. These included *The Prophecy* (1776), *Political Catechism* (1777), Letters to James Rivington, printer of the *Royal Gazette* at New York, *Epistle to Lord Howe, Two Letters by a Tory,* and others.

Best known was *The Battle of the Kegs,* which Hopkinson explained in this way: "N.B. This ballad was occasioned by a real incident. Certain machines, in the form of kegs, charg'd with gunpowder, were sent down the river to annoy the British shipping, then at Philadelphia. The danger of the machines being discovered, the British manned the wharfs and shipping, and discharged their small arms and cannons at everything they saw floating in the river during the ebb tide."

And here in part is his poetical version:

> The cannons roar from shore to shore.
>   The small arms make a rattle;
> Since wars began I'm sure no man
>   E'er saw so strange a battle. . . .
>
> An hundred men with each a pen,
>   Or more upon my word, sir.
> It is most true would be too few,
>   Their valour to record, sir.
>
> Such feats did they perform that day.
>   Against these wick'd kegs, sir,
> That years to come, if they get home,
>   They'll make their boasts and brags, sir.

Another song was *The New Roof, A Song for Federal Mechanics,* an allegory of the principal arguments at the Pennsylvania Convention which assembled in 1778 to consider the Articles of Confederation. Of this song, Rush observed that it *"must last as long as the citizens of the United States continue to admire, and to be happy under* the present national government of the United States."

In 1779 Hopkinson succeeded George Ross as judge of admiralty in Pennsylvania, serving for ten years. He was United States district judge for that state from 1790 until his death. He was impeached for alleged misdemeanors while judge of admiralty but was acquitted on all counts.

Dr. Rush recounted that "Newspaper scandal, frequently for months together, disappeared or languished, after the

publication of several of his irresistible satires upon that disgraceful species of writing. He gave a currency to a thought
or phrase . . . which never failed to bear down the spirit of
the times, and frequently to turn the divided tides of party-
rage, into one general channel of ridicule or contempt."

Hopkinson sometimes used his power of satire to expose
the formalities of technical science and education. His piece,
A Skit on College Examinations, published in the *American
Museum,* February, 1787, and later in his *Miscellaneous Essays* (three volumes 1792), was popular. Under "Logic" it
begins:

Prof. How many parts are there in a salt-box?
Stu. Three. *Bottom, top,* and *sides.*
Prof. How many modes are there in salt-boxes?
Stu. Four. The *formal,* the *substantial,* the *accidental,* and
      the *topsey-turvey.*
Prof. Define these several modes.
Stu. The *formal* respects the figure or shape of the box, such
      as round, square, oblong, and so forth; the *substantial*
      respects the work of the joiner; and the *accidental* de-
      pends upon the string by which the box is hung against
      the wall.
Prof. Very Well—And what are the consequences of the *ac-
      cidental* mode?
Stu. If the string should break the box would fall, the salt
      be spilt, the salt-box broken, and the cook in a bitter
      passion: and this is the accidental mode with its conse-
      quences.

Among Hopkinson's other pieces were *Essay on White-
washing, A Specimen of a Modern Lawsuit,* in which
Lawrence Landlord and Timothy Tenant "are sketched to
nature;" *The Typographical Mode of Conducting a Quarrel,*
and *The High Court of Honor.* A year after writing the latter, he composed an imaginary case which caused a scene in
a real courtroom. The manuscript was stolen from the house

of James Wilson, for whom it was intended. The thief thought that he had discovered a terrible plot and tried to have this "literary sport" read as evidence before Chief Justice Wilson!

Hopkinson "excelled in music and poetry, and had some knowledge in painting. But that these arts did not monopolize all the powers of his mind; further, he was well skilled in many practical and useful sciences, particularly mathematics and natural philosophy, and that he had a general acquaintance with the principles of anatomy, chemistry, and natural history. But his forte was humour and satire, in both of which he was not surpassed by Lucian, Swift, or Rabelais. These extraordinary powers were consecrated to the advancement of the interests of patriotism, virtue, and science." Rush continues: "He possessed uncommon talents for pleasing in a company. His wit was not of that coarse kind which sets 'a table in a roar.' It was mild—delicate and elegant, and infusing chearfulness rather than mirth in all who heard it. . . He shared largely in the friendship of Dr. Franklin. He was so agreable as neighbour that he constantly created friends in every part of the city in which he resided. . . . His domestic character was unsullied by any of the usual imperfections which sometimes cleave to genius. He was frugal—regular—faithful—and kind in his family. In public life he was active and just . . ."

Hopkinson's musical talents were directed not only to satire but to psalms. In 1764 the vestry of Christ Church in Philadelphia thanked him for teaching the choir the art of psalmody. He later served as rector's warden.

To Hopkinson has come the honor of being America's first native composer. His *My Days Have Been So Wondrous Free* is considered to be the earliest piece of music by an American.

As for his appearance, "His person was a little below the common size. His features were small, but extremely animated. His speech was quick, and all his motions seemed to partake of the unceasing activity and versatility of the powers of his mind."

Joseph Hopkinson, the Signer's son, had a distinguished career as a jurist and was the composer of the song, *Hail Columbia*. Francis Hopkinson Smith, a descendant of the Signer's daughter, Maria Hopkinson Smith, was distinguished as an author, engineer and artist. He supervised the construction of the foundation for the Statue of Liberty in upper New York Bay, symbol of our freedom. Secure and strong as this appears to be, it is only by looking back to the real foundations of our Republic, laid down at the cost of such extreme sacrifices by the Signers and their fellow Patriots, and by living up to their ideals that we can hope to keep Miss Liberty intact.

Of Francis Hopkinson there remains only this to say, in the words of Dr. Rush—that "the various causes which contributed to the history of the establishment of the Independance and the federal Gov:t of the United States will not be fully traced Unless much is ascribed to the irresistable influence of the Ridicule which he occasionally poured forth upon the enemies of those great political events—"

James Wilson *1742–1798*

JAMES WILSON is best known for his part in framing the United States Constitution at the Constitutional Convention held during the summer of 1787 in Philadelphia. A fellow delegate to the Convention, quoted in *Biography of the Signers to the Declaration of Independence* (Sanderson-Waln) Vol. VI, page 154, observes that "in his opinion, the most able and useful members of it, were James Wilson, and James Madison; that he is in doubt which of these deserved the preference, but was inclined to give it to the former."

Wilson served later in the Pennsylvania Convention which ratified the Constitution. He made a long speech in favor of its adoption and concluded his argument— "If there are errors, it should be remembered, that the seeds of reformation are sown in the work itself, and the concurrence of two-thirds of the congress, may, at any time, introduce alterations and amendments. . . . Regarding it, then, in every point of view, with a candid and disinterested mind, I am bold to assert, that it is the BEST FORM OF GOVERNMENT WHICH HAS EVER BEEN OFFERED TO THE WORLD."

James Wilson, who had lived in the New World only eleven years before signing the Declaration of Independence, was born at Carskerdo, near St. Andrews, Scotland, on September 14, 1742. He received an excellent classical education, studying at the Universities of St. Andrews, Glasgow and Edinburgh. Emigrating to the Colonies in 1765, he landed in New York, and the following year he went to Philadelphia with a letter of introduction to Dr. Richard Peters, an Episcopalian minister there. Dr. Peters, a member of the Provincial Council, helped him to become Latin tutor at the College of Philadelphia. A few months later, through the aid of Judge Peters and Bishop White, James Wilson entered the law office of John Dickinson as a student and he was admitted to the bar in 1767. After a start in Reading, he settled at Carlisle and built up a successful practice, having established his reputation by his argument in an important land case against the proprietary owners of Pennsylvania, the Penn family.

He early adopted the colonists' cause and was a member of the Pennsylvania provincial meeting of July, 1774, which chose Edward Biddle, Joseph Galloway, Charles Humphreys, Thomas Mifflin, John Morton, Samuel Rhoads and George Ross as delegates to the First Continental Congress. Published in August, Wilson's pamphlet, *Considerations on the Nature and Extent of the Legislative Authority of the British Parliament,* maintaining that Parliament had no constitutional power to legislate for the Colonies, had a strong influence on the members of the Continental Congress meeting in September.

The following January, 1775, Wilson was a delegate to the Pennsylvania Provincial Convention. He introduced a resolution declaring the Boston Port Act unconstitutional, but it did not pass. In May he was elected to the Continental Congress, along with the other new delegates, Benjamin Franklin and Thomas Willing. John Dickinson had been added to the delegation previously.

Wilson was chosen as colonel of the militia raised in Cumberland County, Pennsylvania, and later he was appointed by Congress as a commissioner of Indian affairs for the middle department.

Like John Dickinson, the "Farmer," whose famous letters of 1768 had aroused such feeling against British oppression on constitutional grounds, James Wilson was a "moderate," opposed to independence during the winter of 1775-1776. The diary of Richard Smith of New Jersey shows that on January 9 "Wilson moved and was strongly supported that the Congress may expressly declare to their Constituents and the World their present Intentions respecting an Independency, observing that the Kings Speech directly charged Us with that Design . . ."

This motion aimed against independence alarmed Samuel Adams. As he wrote to John, who was home on leave of absence, he was "apprehensive that we might get ourselves on Dangerous Ground . . . and I ought the rather to suspect it, because the Majority of your Colony as well as of the Congress were of a different Mind."

Smith's diary reveals that on February 13 "Wilson brought in the Draught of an Address to our Constituents which was very long, badly written and full against Independency." And later, Wilson is named as a "Principal Speaker" for the motion to publish Dr. Smith's oration, which declared the sentiments of Congress were to continue dependent on Great Britain.

On March 22, according to the same diary, Wilson opposed an amendment to the privateering preamble in which the King was made the author of the colonists' "Miseries" instead of the Ministry on the ground that this would alienate the King forever.

In the debates on the adoption of the preamble to the new government resolution Wilson argued: ". . . the people will be instantly in a state of nature. Why then precipitate this measure? Before we are prepared to build the new house, why should we pull down the old one, and expose ourselves to all the inclemencies of the season?" Thomas McKean had just declared: "I do think we shall lose our liberties, properties, and lives too, if we do not take this step."

Jefferson's notes of the debate on Lee's June 7 independence motions state: "It was argued by Wilson, Robert R. Livingston, E. Rutledge, Dickinson and others

"That tho' they were friends to the measures themselves, and saw the impossibility that we should ever again be united with Gr-Britain, yet they were against adopting them at this time . . ."

The "moderates" also declared that the people of the Middle Colonies were not yet ready for separation from Britain but that they were "fast ripening," as the notes reveal.

On July 1, in the committee of the whole, Pennsylvania voted against the Lee motion. Wilson is said to have spoken, but this time in favor of independence, for the colony's delegates, on June 24, had been authorized by the Conference of Committees to concur in a vote "declaring the United Colonies free and independent States." A later McKean letter gives the Pennsylvania vote as Morton, Franklin and Wilson for independence; with Dickinson, Morris, Willing and Humphreys against it at that time.

When the final vote on the independence motion was taken, on July 2, Wilson, with Franklin and Morton, voted as before, two members stayed away, so Pennsylvania voted aye—three to two.

Jefferson's notes say, as quoted in the Prologue: ". . . members of a different sentiment attending that morning from Pennsylvania also, their vote was changed, so that the whole 12. colonies, who were authorized to vote at all, gave their voices for it."

John Morton's vote has an interesting story behind it. He was born in Chester County (now Delaware County), Pennsylvania, in 1724. His great-grandfather had sailed from

Sweden in 1654 and settled near Philadelphia. Morton served for many years in the General Assembly of Pennsylvania and was speaker of the House. A delegate to the Stamp Act Congress in 1765, he was subsequently a judge of the Supreme Court of the province.

Morton was speaker of the Assembly in June when Pennsylvania's new instructions to the colony's delegates in the Continental Congress were approved. Signed by him as speaker, these read: "When, by our instructions of last November, we strictly enjoined you . . . to dissent from, and utterly reject any proposition, should such be made, that might cause or lead to a separation from Great Britain . . . our restrictions (arose) . . . from an earnest desire to serve the good people of Pennsylvania with fidelity . . . The situation of publick affairs is since so greatly altered, that we now think ourselves justifiable in removing the restrictions laid upon you . . ."

Morton's own vote is said to have been influenced by the speech made by Sam Adams during the June debate of Lee's motion. A man of deep religious conviction and conscience, he wrestled with his earlier feeling and changed his vote. According to the *Biography of the Signers to the Declaration of Independence* (Sanderson-Waln), Vol. VI, page 219, the change came dramatically on the final day, bringing Pennsylvania into the United States; but on the testimony of McKean's letter of 1817, the change took place earlier, as Morton had voted with Franklin and Wilson on July 1.

John Morton married Ann Justis of Delaware. Eight of their children were living at the time of their father's death in April, 1777. Many of his friends had abandoned him because of his vote for independence, and his last message for them was that they would live to see the hour when they would acknowledge his vote "to have been the most glorious service that I ever rendered my country."

Both Wilson and Morton signed on August 2, having been re-elected the previous month. Wilson had been appointed to the Board of War, of which John Adams was chairman for almost a year and a half, "in continual employment, not to say drudgery." In May, 1777, Wilson composed the address "To the Inhabitants of the United States," urging support of the American cause, and while in Congress, he served on many important committees.

James Wilson was left out of the delegate list at the September, 1777, elections, as Robert Morris had warned him he would be, because of his opposition to the new Pennsylvania State Constitution. After practicing law for about a year in Annapolis, Wilson moved permanently to Philadelphia. In June, 1779, he was appointed advocate-general for the French government in the United States, receiving letters-patent in confirmation from the King of France in February, 1781. He gave almost all of his time and attention to this, for him, uncharted field.

In 1779, during a period of rioting over food shortages and high prices in Philadelphia, Wilson and some friends were attacked in his house by those opposed to his acting as counsel for Tories. There was loss of life on both sides. The City Troop intervened but Wilson was obliged to leave the city for a while.

He was appointed by Congress as a director of the Bank of North America in December, 1781, and the following year he acted as counsel for Pennsylvania before the court of arbitration which decided against the claims of Connecticut to the Wyoming lands.

He was a member of Congress in 1783, and again two years later. At the Constitutional Convention in 1787, he supported popular suffrage and a single executive. His influence in this body was widely felt and he was appointed on the important Committee of Detail which prepared the draft of the Constitution passed upon by the delegates. With Gouverneur Morris, he wrote this draft which, as passed and with the addition of the Bill of Rights and succeeding amendments, is the present-day Constitution of the United States.

Instrumental in the proceedings of the Pennsylvania Convention which ratified the Constitution in 1787, James Wilson was chosen to deliver the oration on the fourth of July, 1788, at the celebration in Philadelphia of the adoption of the United States Constitution.

A delegate to the Pennsylvania State Constitutional Convention of 1789-1790, Wilson was a member of the committee which drafted the new State Constitution. He was appointed by George Washington an associate justice of the United States Supreme Court in 1789 and served until his death at Edenton, North Carolina, in August, 1798. In 1793 he wrote the decision in the case of Chisholm *vs*. Georgia, signifying that the United States was a sovereign nation and not a confederacy.

In appearance, Judge Wilson was about six feet tall and his features sometimes looked very stern, owing to his nearsightedness. His voice was powerful, "his eloquence as a speaker, singularly forcible and commanding." In 1771 James Wilson married Rachel Bird, daughter of William Bird of Berks County, proprietor of the Birdsboro Iron Works. Among their six children was the Reverend Bird Wilson, lawyer and Episcopal clergyman. During 1803 and 1804 he published his father's *Works* in three volumes. James Wilson was also the author, with Thomas McKean, of *Commentaries on the Constitution of the United States* (1792) and, with Bishop White, of some essays titled The Visitant (1767-1769).

James Wilson's son by a second marriage died in infancy and his only grandchild, Emily Hollingsworth, died unmarried, so no direct descendants of this Signer survive.

As we look today at the United States Constitution, in the formation of which James Wilson, styled by his opponents "The Caledonian," played so constructive a part, it bears out his fighting words to the Pennsylvania Convention—"that it is the BEST FORM OF GOVERNMENT WHICH HAS EVER BEEN OFFERED TO THE WORLD."

Robert Morris *1734–1806*

Robert morris, financier of the American Revolution, pledged his personal credit to the Republic, making possible the Yorktown Campaign in 1781, which ended the military operations of the war with the surrender of Lord Cornwallis.

Morris was born in Liverpool, England, on January 31, 1734. His father was an iron worker who later emigrated to the Colonies, leaving his son under the care of his grandmother. In 1747, when he was well established at Oxford, on Maryland's Eastern Shore, as a tobacco merchant, the elder Morris sent for his son, who arrived in America at the age of thirteen. After studying for a short while with the Reverend Gordon, Robert was placed in the counting house of Mr. Charles Willing, a successful merchant, to receive a commercial education. Left an orphan at fifteen, Morris worked hard and faithfully, gaining the confidence of "his master" through his interest and business acumen. Learning of a sudden advance in the price of flour in a foreign market, on one occasion, Morris, in Willing's absence, immediately contracted for all the local flour he could obtain, to the dismay of the rival merchants.

In 1754 he was taken into partnership with Thomas Willing, and the firm, Willing and Morris, was prominent in

Philadelphia for almost forty years. It was so extensive and lucrative that both men became wealthy long before the Revolution. Using their own vessels, they traded with Europe and the West Indies. Morris sometimes made voyages with his ship captains, and it is told that on one trip he was taken prisoner by the French. Put ashore in France without a shilling, he was in a precarious position, but by ingeniously mending a Frenchman's watch, he earned a small sum and made his way to a port and a ship for America.

Opposed to the Stamp Act, Morris signed the nonimportation agreement of November, 1765, to accept no merchandise from England until the repeal of the Act—at great sacrifice to Willing and Morris, which imported large quantities of goods of British manufacture and colonial produce.

In 1769 Morris married Mary White, daughter of Colonel Thomas White of Maryland and sister of William White, later the first Episcopal Bishop of Pennsylvania. They had three sons and a daughter when Morris, the active partner of the leading importing house in Philadelphia, was elected to the Second Continental Congress, in November, 1775, along with Andrew Allen. Soon after taking his seat, Morris was added—as chairman—to the Secret Committee, recently set up to contract for the importation of arms, ammunition and gunpowder. Later he was appointed to the committee to devise ways and means for furnishing the Colonies with a naval armament. He also served as vice-president of the Pennsylvania Committee of Safety.

Morris' career as a public financier began in April, 1776, when he was commissioned by Congress to negotiate bills of exchange and to provide ways and means of financing the war.

Regarding Pennsylvania, founded by William Penn in 1681 as a proprietary colony, a "violent" observed that the province was hampered by the Quaker and proprietary interests but these groups were losing their control. The majority of the Pennsylvania delegation, however, voted against the independence motion, on July 1, as told before. On the second of July Robert Morris, a confirmed "moderate," and John Dickinson, leader of the "dilatory system," stayed away and thereby turned the vote of their colony for independence.

Benjamin Rush, in his sketch of Morris, declared: "He was opposed to the *time* (not to the *act*) of the Declaration of Independance, but he yielded to no man in his exertions to support it, and a year after it took place he publickly acknowledged on the floor of Congress that he had been mistaken in his former opinion as to its time, and said that it would have been better for our country had it been declared sooner."

Morris, alone of those in the delegation who had voted against independence, was re-elected on July 20, as were the three who had voted in favor of the motion. George Ross, "left out" in November 1775, was again chosen, and four new delegates were added. Writing to Joseph Reed at this time, Morris stated that he had "opposed the Declaration of Independence," because in his "poor opinion" it was an improper time and, although prompted to decline the unexpected election, he could not go back on the conviction which first induced him to enter public life—his belief that it was "the duty of every individual to act his part in whatever station his country may call him to in hours of difficulty, danger, and distress." He served through 1778.

On August 2, Robert Morris signed the Declaration, as did George Ross and the seven other Pennsylvania delegates.

Ross, the son of an Episcopal minister (formerly Presbyterian), the Reverend George Ross, and his second wife, Catherine van Gezel, was born in New Castle, Delaware, on May 10, 1730. His sister Gertrude married the Delaware Signer, George Read, as her second husband, while his sister Mary married Mark Bird, brother of Rachel Bird Wilson.

A lawyer, Ross settled in Lancaster. He served in the Pennsylvania Assembly from 1768 to 1775 and in the First Continental Congress. Rush says of him: "A man of great wit, good humor and considerable eloquence. His manner in speaking was agreeable, and commanded attention. He disliked business, and hence he possessed but little influence in Congress." On his retirement from that body in 1777, because of failing health, the citizens of Lancaster voted him a piece of plate worth £150. He declined this, saying that it was the duty of every man, "especially of every representative of the people, to contribute by every means within his power to the welfare of his country without expecting pecuniary rewards."

Pennsylvania's internal fight over the 1776 State Constitution was interrupted, as was Congress itself, by the approach of the British armies. When Congress fled to Baltimore on December 12, Morris was left in charge of its affairs. He was authorized to borrow $10,000 for the use of the Marine Committee, to strengthen the defenses on the Delaware River. He was the acting member of a committee appointed from Baltimore to carry on "Continental business."

Mrs. Morris and the children had fled southward, taking refuge with Mrs. Hall, her stepsister, in Maryland. "Having got my family and books removed to a place of safety, my mind is more at ease," wrote Morris, "and my time is now given up to the public, although I have many thousand pounds' worth of effects here without any prospect of saving them." He said that he would be glad to finish the business of the Congress in the city, "with General Howe's permission."

Morris worked hard to remove stores of salt, provisions and clothing to Lancaster and other places in the interior and to save the Continental ships. Opposed to the issuing of inconvertible paper money, he warned Congress: "It is very mortifying for me when I am obliged to tell you disagreeable things; but I am compelled to inform Congress that the Continental currency keeps losing its credit. Many people refuse openly and avowedly to receive it." From the residents in the country districts he states that "nothing can be got for your money." Although he declared that "the game will be up" unless "this evil" was speedily remedied, even Morris probably did not foresee the disastrous collapse of the currency five years in the future, when one thousand paper dollars were required to buy one silver dollar!

Crossing the Delaware in a snowstorm on Christmas night, General Washington and his forces surprised and captured the Hessian garrison at Trenton. Then Washington retreated across the Delaware to Pennsylvania. Four days after the daring raid, the American Commander recrossed to Trenton but he lacked the financial means to follow up his victories. He had been sent a little more than four hundred Spanish dollars to procure needed intelligence of the enemy's movements. On December 31 he appealed to Robert Morris for the "needful," which was required immediately to make good his bounty promise to the troops for six more weeks of service. Morris, upon whom the money calls were "loud, large and constant," replied the next morning: "I am up very early this morning to despatch a supply of $50,000 to your Excellency. . . . but it will not be got away so early as I could wish, for none concerned in this movement except myself are up. . . . if further occasional supplies of money are necessary, you may depend on my exertions either in a public or private capacity."

It was on this occasion that Mr. Morris is said to have called on a Quaker friend, who asked him for the latest news. "The most important news is, that I require a certain sum in specie, and that you must let me have it," was the prompt reply. The Friend hesitated. "Your security is to be my note and honour," Morris continued.

"Robert, thou shalt have it," the Quaker replied.

The money went off to Washington an hour or two after sunrise, enabling the Commander-in-Chief to carry out his bold New Jersey campaign, including the Battle of Princeton, which brought new hope to the American cause.

Morris is said to have helped with the design of the American Flag. According to the story told by a grandson of Betsy Ross before the Historical Society of Pennsylvania, in 1870, General Washington, George Ross and Robert Morris called upon Betsy Griscom Ross, who had married John Ross, nephew of George, in her little upholstery shop in Arch Street, Philadelphia, one day in 1777. They asked if she could make a flag, showing her a tentative design. Her suggestion for using five-pointed stars was well received and soon afterward she completed her first flag—The Star-Spangled Banner—with a circle of thirteen white stars against a blue square set in the upper left corner of a field of red and white stripes. These stripes would be thirteen in number too, thus honoring the original Colonies which had joined in the Declaration of Independence. The design was approved by Congress on June 14, which is now celebrated as Flag Day.

When John Hancock determined to resign as president of Congress in October, 1777, Morris was offered the post but declined, due to the pressure of his private affairs.

A confusion of public and private accounts, when Morris' own credit was higher than the government's, brought on charges of dishonesty, and an investigation in Congress early in 1779. Morris was completely exonerated by Congress and his conduct was given "that express approbation which patriotism in the public, and integrity in every walk of life always merit and seldom fail ultimately to receive," as John Jay, President of Congress wrote to Robert Morris. But the latter continued to have trouble over price-fixing with Paine and the Constitutionalists and he was not re-elected to the State Legislature that year.

The financial situation of the United States had reached a low point and the King of England was expecting that this would bring about an early end to the rebellion when, as Sullivan expressed it, he found the eyes "of Congress turned upon Robert Morris as financier." On February 20, 1781, Morris was elected to the new office of Superintendent of Finance. After certain conditions were agreed to, he finally gave his consent to this appointment, which he termed "unsolicited, and dangerous to accept of" and felt would expose him to the "calumny and detraction of the envious and malicious." There were indeed critics. One wrote later: "Mr. Morris, who had been long pursuing a gainful traffic from which others were excluded by embargo and restrictions, naturally presented himself as combining the necessary qualities; but his terms were high, and at first blush inadmissible." Morris immediately entered upon his duties but did not take the official oath until the end of June, when the state credit was established on a firmer basis, due to his measures. At the end of July, Congress resolved that Morris, with Richard Peters of the Board of War and James Wilson, should visit army headquarters to bring about a better understanding between the military and the civil administrations. Leaving Gouverneur Morris, his able assistant who was no relation, in charge, Robert Morris and the two others traveled to General Washington's encampment near Dobbs Ferry, New York, by a circuitous route, to avoid capture. Morris conferred privately with Washington and Comte de Rochambeau on the questions of supplies and arrangements for the next campaign. Instead of moving against New York in 1781, as was generally expected, Washington decided to strike against Cornwallis in Virginia.

When Morris arrived back at Philadelphia on August 21, everything was put aside to aid the secret project of moving the American army several hundred miles to Yorktown. Nine days later, Washington appeared in Philadelphia with

his tattered regiments and de Rochambeau and the French
troops, and a dinner was given at Morris' town house on
High (now Market) Street, which became the headquarters
for Washington and his suite.

Morris was working hard to meet the Commander-in-
Chief's requirements for the army. "Should the operations
against Cornwallis fail for want of supplies," he told the
Commissary General, "the states must thank their own negli-
gence." Delaware and Maryland were asked for fresh beef,
salt, rum, salt beef and salt pork; Virginia for flour, beef
and pork (fresh and salted), tobacco, hay, Indian corn and
other forage for horses and cattle. Matthew Ridley was appointed agent in Baltimore for securing boats and supplies
there. Not enough transports were obtained, and some of the
army had to proceed on foot to the place of siege.

To meet Washington's request for "a douceur of a little
hard money" for the northern regiments, Morris approached
the French Commander. With the aid of Gouverneur Morris' fluent French, he was finally able to obtain a loan of
$20,000 in specie until October 1, on the news of the safe ar-
rival of Comte de Grasse and his squadron in Chesapeake Bay.

General Washington needed more money, and Morris was
compelled to send a sum from the Treasury. He had written
to the President of Pennsylvania: "The late movements of
the army have so entirely drained me of money that I have
been obliged to pledge my personal credit very deeply in a
variety of instances, besides borrowing money from my
friends and advancing to promote the public service every
shilling of my own."

In September, Morris had also accepted the post of Agent
of Marine, Congress having entrusted the affairs of the in-
fant navy, as Morris said, to one who "had already more to
do than either his time or abilities permitted him to execute
equal to his wishes."

On October 1, while the allies were besieging Yorktown,

Morris was unable to meet the French loan. Begging for a longer time, he explained that specie would be coming from Boston. This was French money, landed there and brought overland by a secret, heavily-guarded treasure train of wagons which arrived in Philadelphia in November.

On October 19, Cornwallis surrendered and, on the invitation of the Minister of France, Morris later attended a *Te Deum* sung in the Catholic Church in Philadelphia in honor of the great victory. The colors taken from the British were escorted through the city and presented to Congress in the State House—Independence Hall.

Specie from the treasure train helped Morris organize his National Bank, to which he subscribed $10,000, as did other private individuals. One of the subscribers was Haym Salomon, a financier of the Revolution, who advanced large sums to the Superintendent of Finance beginning in August, as shown by the entries in Morris' diary.

After Morris retired from the finance post in 1784, he served in the Constitutional Convention in 1787. Offered the Secretaryship of the Treasury under the new government, he declined, suggesting Alexander Hamilton instead. He was United States Senator from 1788 to 1795.

Morris speculated heavily in Western lands and failed for a large amount. He lost everything, including his favorite residence, his country seat, The Hills, on the Schuylkill River, and his town houses, and was sent for nonpayment of debt to the Prune Street jail in Philadelphia in 1798. Freed in 1801, after the passage of the national bankrupt act, he lived quietly in a small house his wife had acquired, until his death in 1806.

Mary Morris, who had presided beautifully over her husband's lavish entertaining, proved a strong support in these days of poverty and disgrace. Through Gouverneur Morris she had obtained an annuity from the Holland Land Company, which supported her.

In 1799, while visiting at Winchester, Virginia, she received a letter from George and Martha Washington which said: "We hope it is unnecessary to repeat in this place how happy we should be to see you and Miss Morris under our roof for so long a stay as you shall find convenient before you return to Philadelphia, for be assured we ever have and still do retain the most affectionate regard for you, Mr. Morris, and the family."

General Washington, who had written Morris that "My hand and my heart shall be with you" on his becoming Superintendent of Finance, even came to dine with Morris late in 1798 at the "hotel with grated doors," in Prune Street.

When Robert Morris retired as Superintendent, in a farewell message "to the inhabitants of the United States of America," he warned of the urgency of a sound economy. Observing that they were just emerging from a long and expensive war, he continued: "How soon we may be plunged into another, a longer or more expensive contest, is known only to Him from whom no secrets are hidden, but it has enabled us (by reasoning on past events) to conclude that the only moral surety for peace is a state of constant preparation for hostilities . . . May Heaven avert . . . evils and endue us with wisdom so to act, as may best promote the present and future peace, prosperity, and happiness of our country. This is the sincerest wish of your faithful servant and fellow-citizen,

Robert Morris"

Alexander Hamilton, in urging Robert Morris to accept the post of Superintendent of Finance, in which he might render no less a service than the establishment of American independence, wrote, " 'Tis by introducing order in our finances, by restoring public credit, not by winning battles, that we are finally to gain our object."

Benjamin Rush *1746–1813*

"HE AIMED WELL," Benjamin Rush writes of himself in his sketches of the Signers. His first ancestor in this country was John Rush, who had commanded a troop of horse in Cromwell's army. John Rush and his wife Susanna arrived in Pennsylvania from England in 1683, settling in Byberry. Benjamin belonged to the fifth generation. He was one of the six children of John and Susanna Hall Rush. His father, an Episcopalian, died in 1751 when only thirty-eight years old, and his widow was forced to keep a grocery store to bring up and educate her five surviving Rush children (she also had a daughter by a previous marriage).

About 1753, Benjamin was sent with his brother Jacob to West Nottingham Academy, then in the village of Rising Sun, Maryland. This was run by his uncle, the Reverend Doctor Samuel Finley. A memorial arch at the entrance of the present school commemorates its two alumni Signers, Benjamin Rush and Richard Stockton.

Dr. Finley, later president of the College of New Jersey, taught Latin, Greek, Arts, Sciences and Agriculture at the Academy. His teaching of religion made a deep impression upon young Benjamin Rush, who attributed to it his not having at any time of his life "ever entertained a doubt of the divine origin of the Bible." He wished that "this mode of fortifying the reason of young people in the principles of Christianity were more general." Manners were taught in allegory, through characters such as Thomas Broadbrim, Ned Short, Bill Slovenly and Johnny Courtly.

In the spring of 1759, Benjamin Rush, then only thirteen, was admitted to the junior class of the College of New Jersey (Princeton). He graduated in September, 1760. Acting on advice from Dr. Finley, Rush decided to take up "physic" instead of law and he became a pupil of Dr. John Redman in Philadelphia the following February.

Entering the University of Edinburgh in 1766, he graduated in June, 1768, a doctor of medicine. During his stay in Scotland, he alone of all who had tried finally persuaded Mrs. John Witherspoon that it was a good idea for her husband to go to America. Also during his stay in Scotland a chance meeting changed Rush's political principles. Influenced by a Mr. Bostock, Rush, who had opposed the Stamp Act, now felt "that no form of government can be rational but that which is derived from the Suffrages of the people who are the subjects of it," but he enjoyed "the new and elevating system of government" in theory only.

Rush visited London, where he was befriended by Benjamin Franklin, who gave a letter of credit for two hundred pounds to this "particular friend of mine" for use on Rush's trip to Paris. This kindness, said Rush, "attached me to him during the remainder of his life."

Returning to Philadelphia in July, 1769, Benjamin Rush began the practice of medicine, and two months later he was elected professor of chemistry in the College of Philadelphia. He was a pioneer in using the Suttonian method of smallpox inoculation. In the next few years he published essays on health, temperance and slavery. He led a life of "constant labor and self-denial," helping many charity patients as well as those who could pay.

Some newspaper pieces favoring the colonists' cause, published by Rush in 1773, brought him to the attention of Dickinson, Charles Thomson, Mifflin, and George Clymer, whose publications then "governed the public mind in Pennsylvania," aided by James Wilson's pamphlet.

George Clymer, a Pennsylvania Signer, was the son of an Englishman who had emigrated to Philadelphia. An orphan at one, George was brought up by his uncle, William Coleman, who took him into his counting-room and made him his heir. At a protest meeting in Philadelphia, on October 16, 1773, against the sale of taxed tea, he was made chairman of a committee to prevail upon those appointed to sell the tea to resign their appointments. Rush wrote of him: "A cool, firm, consistent Republican who loved liberty and government with an equal affection. Under the appearance of manners that were cold and indolent, he concealed a mind that was always warm and active towards the interests of his country. He was well informed in history ancient and modern, and frequently displayed flashes of wit and humor in conversation. His style in writing was simple, correct, and sometimes eloquent. . . ."

John Adams related that Benjamin Rush was one of those Philadelphia Sons of Liberty who rode out to Frankfort to meet the Massachusetts delegates in September, 1774. Rush returned to the city in the same carriage with John Adams and remarked that his "dress and manners were at that time plain, and his conversation cold and reserved."

Rush knew nearly all the members of this Congress and entertained most of them. He gave Patrick Henry an inoculation for smallpox, and the two Adamses were frequent visitors at his house.

In his *Travels Through Life,* Rush tells that after Lexington he felt separation from England was inevitable and that "the first gun that was fired at an American cut the cord that had tied the two countries together." From that time his publications were calculated to prepare the public mind for adopting independence.

He mixed freely with the members of the Second Congress, attended the party given George Washington on his appointment as Commander-in-Chief, and told of the thousands who thronged to see the General set off for Cambridge to take up his command.

Adams once described Rush in this way: "He is an elegant, ingenious body, a sprightly, pretty fellow. He is a Republican . . . says the Committee of Safety are not the representatives of the people. . . . But Rush, I think, is too much of a talker to be a deep thinker; elegant, not great."

Benjamin Rush was instrumental in the publication of the well-known pamphlet by Thomas Paine in January, 1776. As he tells the story, he called upon Paine and suggested to him the idea of writing this work, to which the latter readily agreed. "He read the sheets to me at my house as he composed them. When he had finished them, I advised him to put them into the hands" of Dr. Franklin, Samuel Adams, and Mr. Rittenhouse, who read the completed pamphlet. A title then was needed and "Mr. Paine proposed to call it 'plain truth.' I objected to it and suggested the title of 'Common Sense.'" This was adopted and Robert Bell consented to run the risk of printing it. "'Common Sense' bursted from the press of the latter in a few days with an effect which has rarely been produced by types and paper in any age or country."

As told, John Adams sensed the atheistic streak in the author which later discredited Paine, and was so upset at his proposed government that he wrote his own *Thoughts on Government, in a letter from a gentleman to his friend,* as an antidote.

Impressed by her "taste and understanding" and her good opinion of Dr. Witherspoon's preaching, Rush determined "to offer his hand" to Julia Stockton, eldest daughter of Richard Stockton, whom he had known in college days and in Scotland. On January 11, 1776, they were married.

Rush was a member of the Committee of Inspection (and Observation of the City and Liberties) which presented a memorial to the Continental Congress on May 25, signed by Thomas McKean, stating that the Assembly could not carry the May 15 new government resolution into effect and that a majority of the members did not "possess the confidence of the people."

Finally, on June 14, influenced by the meetings of the military, the Assembly paid the delegates and withdrew the instructions against separation, as has been told.

The Provincial Conference of Committees met four days later, with Rush, McKean and James Smith present, and McKean (Colonel of the Third Battalion) was chosen president. McKean, with Rush and Smith, prepared the draft of a Declaration, stating "our willingness to concur in a vote of Congress declaring the United Colonies free and independent States." This was read in Congress on June 25.

The elections to the July Provincial Convention were described by John Adams in a letter to his wife: "All the old members (of Philadelphia) left out . . . Dickinson, Morris, Allen, all fallen, like grass before the scythe . . . I am inclined to think, however, and to wish that these gentlemen may be restored at a fresh election, because, although mistaken in some points, they are good characters, and their great wealth and numerous connexions will contribute to strengthen America, and cement her Union."

At the Provincial Convention, held in the State House, Rush, Clymer, James Smith and George Taylor were the new delegates elected on July 20. They signed the Declaration later, with the other Pennsylvania representatives.

In Rush's sketches of the Signers, James Smith is described as: "A pleasant facetious lawyer. His speeches in Congress were in general declamatory, but from their humor, frequently entertaining. He was an early Whig, but wanted steadiness, it was said, in his political conduct." Smith, born in Ireland, had come to the Colonies with his family. Educated under the Reverend Francis Alison, he became a lawyer, settling in York and engaging in iron manufacture. He acquired a considerable fortune, which he lost in business and during the war. A supporter of the Patriot cause, he served in Congress until 1778, except for a few months. He was elected to the State Assembly in 1779, was appointed a judge the following year and a brigadier-general of the Pennsylvania militia in 1782.

George Taylor receives the following notation in the sketches: "A respectable country gentleman, but not much distinguished in any way in Congress." But the fact that Taylor worked his way up from the status of bond servant was in itself a distinction. A native of Ireland, he had come to the Colonies as a redemptioner, bound out to an iron manufacturer at Durham, Pennsylvania. He worked as a clerk, and several years after his employer's death he married the widow and successfully ran the iron works. Moving to Northampton County, he established a large iron mill and began to take part in public life, serving in the Pennsylvania Assembly. He was again elected to the Assembly in 1775 and was on the Committee of Safety. He later negotiated a treaty with the Indian tribes at the Susquehanna River border at Easton. He retired from Congress in March, 1777.

Rush took part in several debates in Congress and served on diverse committees including those on powder, medicine, the northern army and intelligence.

The first or second time he spoke, Rush records, was against a motion for a committee of Congress to meet Lord Howe at a peace conference in September, 1776, after the loss of Long Island. In the conclusion of his speech against humbling themselves he said: ". . . but I will go further: should this solitary state, the last repository of our freedom, be invaded, let her not survive her precious birthright, but in yielding to superior force, let her last breath be spent in uttering the word *Independance*."

When Congress adjourned to Baltimore, fearing capture by the enemy, Rush took his wife to a safe retreat at the home of his relative, Colonel Hall, in Cecil County, Maryland. Their first child was born there the following July. Part of Rush's furniture and books were left at Philip Price's, near Darby. "At his house," Rush relates, "Sir. Wm. Howe made his headquarters in one of his excursions from Philadelphia (during the occupation), and on one of my mahogany tea tables he wrote his dispatches to England. . . . This table bears the marks of his ink to this day."

Joining the Philadelphia militia, Rush visited General Washington with Colonel Joseph Reed probably the day before the famous crossing of the Delaware at his quarters about ten miles above Bristol and spent almost an hour with him the next morning in private. While assuring the worried commander of Congress's support, Rush "observed him to play with his pen and ink upon several small pieces of paper. One of them by accident fell upon the floor near my feet. I was struck with the inscription upon it. It was 'Victory or Death.' " On Christmas night Rush joined the militia at Dunk's Ferry and took part in General Cadwalader's unsuccessful attempt to cross the Delaware that night, in support of the attack on Trenton.

"Great bodies of floating ice rendered the passage of the river impracticable," records Rush. "We returned to Bristol in a heavy snow storm in the middle of the night. The next morning we heard that General Washington had been more successful in crossing the river above Trenton, and that he had surprised and taken 1000 Hessians at their posts." General Cadwalader finally succeeded in crossing and camped at Burlington on December 28. This force was at Crosswicks on December 30-31, and while there Rush discovered, as he explains it, "that in my interview with Genl. Washington, he had been meditating upon his attack upon the Hessians at their posts on the Jersey side of the Delaware, for I found that the countersign of his troops at the surprise of Trenton was 'Victory or Death.' "

While the militia lay at Crosswicks, Rush rode to Trenton, spending the day with Generals Mercer and St. Clair and Colonel Clement Biddle. In the evening it was learned that the enemy at Princeton intended to attack the American posts at Trenton and Crosswicks. A council of war was held at General Washington's quarters and Rush was called in to give an opinion on "whether the troops at Crosswicks should be drawn to Trenton, or left where they were to occasion a diversion of the British forces." General Washington asked his advice. "I said that I was not a judge of what was proper in the business before the council, but one thing I knew well, that all the Philadelphia militia would be very happy in being under his immediate command, and that I was sure they would instantly obey a summons to join his troops at Trenton." General Washington then requested Rush to take a letter to General Cadwalader, which he delivered about one o'clock in the morning to the General, who was in bed. "He instantly arose, and set his brigade in motion," wrote the bearer.

Rush reached Trenton about seven a. m. and begged the loan of General St. Clair's bed to get some sleep, but before he had a chance to enjoy his slumber the battle began. Riding to join the militia, he met them a little below Trenton and "rode slowly along with them towards the enemy. . . . General Knox was active and composed. In passing me he cried out 'Your opinion last night was very fortunate for us. You have—' I shall not conclude the sentence, for a man deserves no credit for an accident in which neither design nor judgement are discovered."

Rush ministered to the wounded and, losing touch with

the army, set off with Dr. Cochran and their patients to Bordentown, where they supposed the American army had retreated. The next morning they heard "that General
Washington had met a part of the British army at Princeton
on his way to the high lands of Morris County in New Jersey,
thro' a circuitous rout . . . and that he had defeated them."

Rush set off immediately for Princeton, to care for the
wounded there. One of these, General Mercer, died a week
later. At Princeton, Rush met his father-in-law, who was
finally permitted to return to his family on parole. Stockton
had been "plundered of all his household furniture and stock
by the British army."

At the election on February 5, 1777, Rush was left out of
the delegation to Congress. His joining in "public testimony" against the new State Constitution the preceding
autumn had "destroyed" his popularity with the Assembly.
In four long letters he had urged a revision, warning of the
dangers of a single legislative house.

Benjamin Rush accepted the commission of physician-
general for the middle department of the Continental Army
in April. His journal states: "I attended in the rear at the
battle of Brandywine on the (eleventh of September, 1777)
and had nearly fallen in the hands of the enemy by my delay in helping off the wounded."

Long distressed by the high rate of mortality among the
wounded soldiers and by the hospital system, he wrote a
letter of complaint on the state of the hospitals and the administration of the Director to General Washington. "I
loved my country and the brave men who had offered their
lives for its defense too well to shrink from what I conceived
to be my duty upon this occasion."

The hospital system was altered, saving many lives, but the
Director was continued in office. Since he foresaw only "dis-
cord," Rush resigned his commission in January, 1778. On
the evacuation of Philadelphia he returned to his practice

there. He was elected professor of the Institutes of Medicine of the University of Pennsylvania in 1792 and rendered valuable service during the yellow fever epidemic the following year, visiting from 100 to 120 patients daily.

Dr. Rush's activities during the epidemic brought him much animosity. Such strong attacks were made on him in a paper published by William Cobbett that he sued Cobbett for libel. In 1799 Rush was awarded $5,000 in damages.

In 1787 Rush was a member of the State Convention which ratified the Federal Constitution and of that for the formation of a state constitution two years later. He was a founder of Dickinson College, in Carlisle, and the Philadelphia Dispensary. He succeeded Benjamin Franklin as president of the Pennsylvania Society for the Abolition of Slavery, was the first president of the Philadelphia Medical Society, and a vice-president and a founder of the Philadelphia Bible Society, advocating the use of scriptures in the public schools. His teachings gave great impetus to the study of medicine in this country and his writings on medical and other subjects were extensive. From 1799 until his death, he was treasurer of the United States Mint, which helped out his earnings.

In 1813 Rush recorded in his journal the death of his fellow Signer, George Clymer, commenting that he was "long my patient and friend, and from whose conversation I derived more instruction than from any citizen in Philadelphia." Clymer had also been left out at the election in September, 1777. His house in Chester County was sacked by the enemy just after the Battle of Brandywine and an attempt was made to destroy his aunt's house in Philadelphia, which was thought to be Clymer's property. This year also he was one of three commissioners appointed to investigate the causes and extent of disaffection near Fort Pitt, and to deal with the Indians there. A member of the Constitutional Convention in 1787, he was elected to the First Congress held under its provisions. Rush ended his character sketch of Clymer, "The mould in which this man's mind was cast . . . was seldom used."

In a tribute to his wife, Julia Stockton Rush, Benjamin wrote: "Let me here bear testimony to the worth of this excellent woman. She fulfilled every duty as a wife, mother . . . with fidelity and integrity. To me she was always a sincere and honest friend. Had I yielded to her advice upon many occasions, I should have known less distress from various causes in my journey thro' life. . . . May God reward and bless her . . ." Among their thirteen children were Richard Rush, attorney-general of the United States, minister to Great Britain and later to France; and James Rush, a physician, who left the fortune of his wife, Phoebe Ann Ridgway Rush, to found the Ridgway Library, now a branch of the Free Library of Philadelphia.

In his *Travels Through Life,* written for the use of his children, Rush remarks: "I review the time I spent in the service of my country with pleasure and pain. . . . I was animated constantly by a belief that I was acting for the benefit of the whole world, and of future ages, by assisting in the formation of new means of political order and general happiness. Whether my belief as far as it relates to the last great object will be realized, or not, is yet a secret . . ."

Benjamin Rush achieved many of his aims but he acquired and received nothing from the world which he prized so highly, he once wrote to John Adams, as "the religious principles" inherited from his forebears who had lived in the simple Byberry farmhouse.

Benjamin Franklin *1706–1790*

Famous in europe for his electrical discoveries, Benjamin Franklin became the personification of the New World to eighteenth-century Europe, from Scotland to Italy. He was Mr. America to thousands of people abroad. In England in 1771, he first began to write of his amazing career in his *Autobiography:* "Having emerged from the poverty and obscurity in which I was born and bred, to a state of affluence and some degree of reputation in the world . . . with the blessing of God. . . ." This famous autobiography, interrupted by the "affairs of the Revolution," was continued later upon the urging of a friend who felt that it would "promote a greater spirit of industry and early attention to business, frugality and temperance with the American youth."

Scientist, moralist, philosopher, humanist, meteorologist, politician, author, statesman—Franklin was thinking in terms of a colonial union in 1751. And Franklin was presenting his ideas about American union to the royal governor of Massachusetts Bay in 1755—ideas which were woven into the fabric of American independence.

Benjamin Franklin was born in his father's house in Milk Street, Boston, on January 17, 1706, and baptized that same day in the Old South Church near by, of which his parents were members. His father, Josiah Franklin, had emigrated from England to enjoy his "mode of religion with freedom," and became a tallow chandler. Benjamin, the fifteenth of Josiah's children, was the eighth child of his second wife, Abiah Folger, daughter of Peter Folger of Nantucket—teacher, surveyor, miller, weaver and "a godly, learned Englishman."

At eight, Benjamin, intended by his father for the ministry as the tithe of his sons, was sent to the grammar school (now the Boston Latin School). About a year later his father found he could not afford a college education for him, with such a large family to maintain, so he was transferred to a school for writing and arithmetic.

When ten years old, Benjamin was taken out of school to assist his father in the tallow chandlery business, but the boy's continuing dislike of this trade caused his father to consider other occupations for him.

Athletically inclined and often a leader among boys, Benjamin also had "bookish" tastes. Fond of reading since childhood, he did not remember when he could not read. His few pennies were spent on books—*Pilgrim's Progress* was an early favorite. This bookish inclination at length determined his father to make him a printer and at twelve he was indentured to his brother James, to serve as an apprentice in his printing shop, until Benjamin was twenty-one years of age.

The boy worked hard and soon knew his trade well. He now had access to a wide range of books and spent most of his spare time reading and studying. His first poems were discouraged by his father and he turned to the study and practice of prose, rewriting material from a copy of Addison's *Spectator*. The literary ability he so laboriously developed later became, as he records in his *Autobiography*, "a principal means of my advancement."

Some of his reading led him to adopt vegetarianism for a time, and the money he saved "was an additional fund for buying books." Other writers he studied turned him temporarily to Deism, even to Freethinking, despite his pious upbringing.

In 1722 Benjamin started contributing prose to his brother's newspaper, *The New England Courant,* under the pen name of Silence Dogood. Later he edited the paper for a time when his brother ran into difficulties with the Massachusetts Council. But increasing differences and quarreling with his brother finally grew unbearable, and breaking his indenture agreement, Benjamin left Boston secretly in 1723, on a New York-bound sloop.

Reaching Philadelphia with one Dutch dollar, the young runaway apprentice secured work with a printer named Keimer and lodged with the Reads, whose daughter, Deborah, had seen him the day he arrived in the city, walking up Market Street with "three great puffy rolls," one under each arm and eating the other.

He attracted the notice of the Governor, Sir William Keith, who proposed to set him up in business with a printing-house of his own. Franklin went to London to choose the press and types. But the Governor's promises proved empty and Franklin went to work at a printing-house in London.

Returning to Philadelphia in October, 1726, Franklin, after a short time as a merchant's clerk, became manager of Keimer's printing-house, using new skills he had garnered in London. Soon after Benjamin had spent six intensive months breaking in Keimer's "raw, cheap hands," the printer fired him. One of Benjamin's pupils, Hugh Meredith, arranged for backing from his father and plans were made to set Franklin and Meredith up in the printing business as equal partners.

Benjamin Franklin made friends easily, very often among those who loved reading and conversing as he did. In the autumn of 1727, he formed a club called the Junto or

Leather Apron, composed of most of his "ingenious acquaintance" in Philadelphia. This "secret" brotherhood lasted for over thirty years.

Meeting on Friday evenings, the members introduced queries on Morals, Politics and Natural Philosophy to be discussed. Every three months an essay had to be produced and read.

Franklin formulated further rules for the Junto, which were adopted in 1728, following in part Cotton Mather's discussion plan for the Boston neighborhood benefit societies he had organized for the churches there. In the Junto's weekly ritual were questions such as these:

> Have you lately observed any encroachment on the just liberties of the people?
>
> Have you lately observed any defect in the laws of your country of which it would be proper to move the legislature for an amendment?
>
> Do you know of any deserving young beginner lately set up whom it lies in the power of the Junto any way to encourage?
>
> In what manner can the Junto, or any of them, assist you in any of your honorable designs?"

The members were helpful, too, in getting business for Franklin and Meredith, after the opening of their printing-house in 1728. A Junto friend brought the struggling young concern its first large order, "from the Quakers the printing forty sheets of their history, the rest to be done by Keimer." So anxious was Franklin to do "a sheet a day of the folio" that one night when, as he tells the story in his own words, "having impos'd my forms, I thought my day's work over, one of them by accident was broken, and two pages reduced to pi, I immediately distributed and compos'd it over again before I went to bed; and this industry, visible to our neighbors, began to give us character and credit." The general opinion at the Merchants' Every Night Club was that the new printing-house must fail, since there were already two printers in the city, Bradford and Keimer, but one member voiced a different opinion: "For the industry of that Franklin is superior to any thing I ever saw of the kind; I see him still at work when I go home from the club, and he is at work again before his neighbors are out of bed." This impressed the rest and soon brought offers from one merchant to supply the printers with stationery. When Benjamin was a boy, Josiah Franklin had often repeated to his son a proverb of Solomon: "Seest thou a man diligent in his calling, he shall stand before kings . . ." The son wrote in his *Autobiography,* "I from thence considered industry as a means of obtaining wealth and distinction, which encouraged me . . ."

In November, 1728, Benjamin Franklin composed his *Articles of Belief and Acts of Religion,* to serve as his creed and private religious service. In the Petition, asking for help in many ways, he prays—

> That I may be preserved from atheism and infidelity, impiety and profaneness . . . and in my addresses to Thee carefully avoid irreverence and ostentation, formality and odious hypocrisy, Help me, O Father!
>
> That I may be loyal to my prince and faithful to my country, careful for its good, valiant in its defence, and obedient to its laws, abhorring treason as much as tyranny, Help me, O Father!

Keimer, hearing that same year of Franklin's plans for starting a newspaper, announced one of his own, the first copy of which appeared in December. But Keimer failed and he was obliged to sell his paper to Franklin "for a trifle."

On October 2, 1729, the new owner issued the newspaper with a simplified title, *The Pennsylvania Gazette.* He describes the early numbers as follows: "Our first papers made quite a different appearance from any before in the province; a better type, and better printed; but some spirited remarks of my writing, on the dispute then going on between Governor Burnet and the Massachusetts Assembly, struck the principal people . . . and brought them all to be our subscribers. . . . This was one of the first good effects of my having learnt a little to scribble . . ."

Bradford was still the public printer for Pennsylvania. He had printed an address of the House to the Governor in what Franklin dubbed "a coarse, blundering manner," continuing rather smugly, "we reprinted it elegantly and correctly, and sent one to every member . . . they voted us their printers for the year ensuing."

The cry among the people of the province for more paper money was discussed fully in the Junto. Franklin wrote an anonymous pamphlet, backing the proposed issue of paper money against strong opposition. Entitled *A Modest Enquiry into the Nature and Necessity of a Paper Currency,* his booklet aroused more support for the measure, and it was carried in the House. This resulted in Franklin's being employed to print the money.

The partnership with Meredith did not work out and it was dissolved in July, 1730, when two of Franklin's Junto friends took over his indebtedness and backed him financially. Feeling the need to settle down, Franklin married Deborah Read on September first of that year and they lived in his printing-house. He describes her in the following way: "as much dispos'd to industry and frugality as myself. She assisted me cheerfully in my business. . . . We kept no idle servants, our table was plain and simple." But one day he found his breakfast of bread and milk served in a china bowl, with a spoon of silver, instead of the accustomed twopenny earthern porringer and pewter spoon. Deborah thought that *her* husband deserved these marks of luxury as well as any of his neighbors!

In addition to William Franklin, there were two other children in the household—Francis Folger, "Franky," who was mourned for years after his death of smallpox when he was only four, and Sarah, born in 1743.

Seeking a way in which the Junto members could pool their resources of books, Franklin proposed that the club organize a subscription library for its own group and other interested citizens. The Instrument of Association was signed in July, 1731, and later a charter was obtained for the Library Company, the first American subscription library.

Franklin formulated several plans of living, and about this time he conceived the project of striving toward moral perfection. He listed the necessary virtues in a little book, at first alloting a week's practice to each in rotation. To the original twelve virtues, which included Temperance, Resolution and Sincerity, he added a thirteenth, Humility, when a Quaker friend warned him of his pride. He credits the "constant felicity of his life, down to his 79th year" to his struggle for all these virtues—with the blessing of God.

1732—this year was very important to Franklin. *The Pennsylvania Gazette* was a success and he had a partnership in *The South Carolina Gazette*. He enjoyed a widening circle of friends and influence through the Library and the Masons. He could now see his way to paying off his debts—all his life he regarded debt as "a species of slavery." In December of that year, Franklin published the first of the famous *Poor Richard Almanacs*. The almanacs of those days were pocket-size booklets—sort of glorified calendars, with tide tables and weather forecasts. They also contained some astrology, recipes, jokes, maxims and varied facts. The page margins were often used for a diary. Very popular in colonial homes, almanacs were sure to sell. Franklin's creation, "Poor Richard," a homely, humorous character, quickly outstripped his rivals. Poor Richard wrote a homey column, enjoyed literary tiffs with his wife. Franklin "filled all the little spaces" in

the calendar "with proverbial sentences, chiefly such as in-
culcated industry and frugality." His almanac became an
American institution and was carried on for about twenty-
five years.

Among Poor Richard's wise and witty sayings, collected,
adapted and written by Franklin, were these gems:

> Men and melons are hard to know
> He that can have patience can have what he will
> The family of fools is ancient
> The rotten apple spoils his companions.

The essence of twenty-five years of Poor Richard's wisdom
was prefixed by Franklin to the almanac of 1758, called *Poor
Richard Improved*. This preface, "The Way To Wealth,"
was copied in all the newspapers of the Continent, reprinted
as a broadside in Britain and translated into French.

In 1733 Franklin began to study languages. He learned
how to speak and write French. His business successes increased. By the next year he was public printer for Delaware and New Jersey and through his appointment as clerk
of the Pennsylvania Assembly in 1736 he was assured of the
government printing. This connection lasted until 1751.
In 1737 he replaced Bradford as Philadelphia postmaster
which was of great advantage to the circulation of the *Gazette*.

Turning his thoughts more to the welfare of the public,
Franklin formed the Union Fire Company, planned a city
police force, invented the Pennsylvania fireplace or Franklin
stove and established the American Philosophical Society, an
intercolonial Junto.

In 1746 Franklin encountered a subject which completely
engrossed his attention—electricity—in which field he made
several fundamental contributions. His studies were interrupted the following year by the necessity of defending the
colony from the French. With the aid of a pamphlet, *Plain*

Truth, he organized an "Association" of volunteer militia which grew to more than ten thousand men in the province.

The end of King George's War in 1748 and his retirement from active business gave Franklin time to take an increasing part in public affairs, as well as to continue his scientific experiments. In 1749 he organized the Academy which is now the University of Pennsylvania, and two years later he was elected to the Assembly.

Franklin's theory that lightning was electricity and could be prevented from doing mischief by iron rods was proved first in France, in June, 1752. But Franklin, assisted by his son William, proved his theory independently that summer with the "Electrical Kite." Honors and fame came to Franklin in Europe as well as in America.

Degrees from Harvard, Yale and William and Mary, and a gold medal from the Royal Society in London were awarded Franklin. He was later elected to the latter august Society. Even the King of France joined in the applause.

In 1754, Benjamin Franklin, now joint deputy postmaster of North America, served as a commissioner to the Albany Congress. His Plan of Union, approved by the conference, was later rejected by the colonial assemblies. His *Gazette* had published the first known American cartoon before the Congress met. It was a picture of a snake divided into eight pieces, representing different colonies, and was captioned "Join or Die."

Three years later he was sent to England by the Pennsylvania Assembly to plead their case against the proprietors in the financing of the colony's defense against the French. After winning a compromise, he returned to America in 1762 as Dr. Franklin, having received the degree of LL.D. from the University of St. Andrews, in Scotland.

The following summer Franklin toured the northern colonies with his daughter, Sally, to inspect the post offices, continuing his reforms in the speed and safety of the mail service which had done so much to bring the Colonies into closer touch with each other. In 1764 he was defeated for re-election to the Pennsylvania Assembly, but his party, re-taining a majority, sent him to England in November as their agent, to present a petition to the King "to take the people of this province under his immediate protection . . ."

The great resentment aroused in America by the Stamp Act caused the Pennsylvania agent to battle with the British ministers over this new internal taxation of the Colonies.

Largely as a result of Franklin's famous examination before the House of Commons, in February, 1766, the Stamp Act was repealed. This success brought him added fame in Europe and America and he was appointed agent for Massa-chusetts, New Jersey and Georgia. Fighting tirelessly against further schemes and methods of taxing the Colonies, he was dismissed from his office of deputy postmaster general in 1774, soon after news of the Boston Tea Party reached Lon-don. Franklin returned to America, having sacrificed his high offices for the sake of the Colonies. He arrived in Phila-delphia on the fifth of May, 1775, and the very next day he was chosen by the Assembly to be a delegate to the Second Continental Congress, which was to meet in Philadelphia four days later. Mrs. Franklin had died in 1773 and the doctor lived with his daughter and son-in-law, Sarah and Richard Bache, in his new house.

Congress elected him postmaster general of the Colonies in July and, as a delegate, he served on many committees, in-cluding those to promote the manufacture of saltpetre for gunpowder, to draw up the declaration for George Washing-ton on taking command of the Continental Army and to arrange for the printing of paper money. He also served as president of the Pennsylvania Committee of Safety and in many other capacities. In October he was sent by Congress, with Thomas Lynch of South Carolina and Benjamin Har-rison of Virginia, to confer with Washington at Cambridge.

On meeting Franklin at dinner, Abigail Adams, wife of John Adams, wrote: "I thought I could read in his countenance the virtues of his heart; among which patriotism shone in its full lustre, and with that is blended every virtue of a Christian: for a true patriot must be a religious man."

In November Franklin was assigned to a most important committee, with Benjamin Harrison, Thomas Johnson of Maryland, John Dickinson of Pennsylvania and John Jay of New York. These five had "the sole purpose of corresponding with our friends in Great Britain, Ireland and other parts of the world." It was a secret committee, and was the beginning of American diplomacy abroad.

In the last week of March, 1776, Franklin and the other commissioners appointed by Congress, Samuel Chase, Charles Carroll of Carrollton and Father John Carroll, all of Maryland, set out for Canada to try to win over the French Canadians to the side of the rebellious Colonies. The mission met with no success and the complete disasters which had befallen the American forces sent to capture Canada were revealed.

Ill and tired, Franklin arrived back in Philadelphia the end of May. Later he wrote to Washington that his gout had kept him "from Congress & *Company*" almost ever since Washington had returned from Philadelphia to New York. And therefore he knew little of what was happening in Congress except that a Declaration of Independence was "preparing." He was promptly placed on the committee to draft this Declaration. Thomas Jefferson was to prepare the first draft. He submitted this to Franklin, who made some corrections.

Although Franklin does not appear to have taken a great part in the debates regarding the independence measures, there is no doubt that he was influential behind the scenes. On the first of July his vote for independence, along with those of John Morton and James Wilson, stood for only the minority of the Pennsylvania delegation, even though the Pennsylvania Assembly had voted to release their delegates to vote for independence. On the final day, Franklin, Morton and Wilson became the majority vote, with Dickinson and Morris abstaining, and Pennsylvania was carried for independence.

After the Declaration on July 4, Franklin worked on a committee to draw up treaties of alliance to be proposed to foreign powers. In September he was chosen as a commissioner to France. That country's sorely needed help had long been hoped for. He settled down at Passy and became extremely popular with the French people. Persuading the French to aid the Americans financially and materially, he led them into an alliance with the United States which was signed at Paris in February, 1778. Later that year, Franklin was appointed Minister Plenipotentiary to France.

In an effort to break up the French Alliance and force the young Republic to surrender, promises of pensions and possible peerages for American leaders were sent from England, through a go-between, in a letter to Benjamin Franklin in June, 1778. Besides Franklin, the offer included George Washington, John Hancock and John Adams. Franklin refused the lure, which he believed came straight from George III. He wrote scathingly that he doubted that the British conciliatory acts would hold good any longer after they had served their purpose of inducing the Americans to disarm. He refused to deliver his answer to this "tar-and-feather" honor to a stranger with a "rose in his hat" in the Cathedral of Notre Dame and it was never sent.

In 1781 he was chosen as a member of the commission to negotiate a treaty of peace between England and the United States and, after many difficulties, including disagreement among the American commissioners, on September 3, 1783, at Paris, he, along with John Adams and John Jay, signed the treaty which ended the War of the American Revolution.

After enjoying great prestige in France, Franklin sailed for home in 1785, with the permission of Congress. On his return to Philadelphia, he was elected three times to the Presidency of Pennsylvania and served as a delegate to the Constitutional Convention. In this body his wisdom and experience exerted a powerful influence, contributing greatly to the final draft of the Constitution of the United States, which he voted for in 1787.

The Saturday Evening Post, which Benjamin Franklin founded, recently quoted his timeless comment on the basic unanimity of Americans in the preservation of democracy's way, in spite of seeming dissensions: "Do not believe the reports you hear of our internal Divisions. We are, I believe, as much united as any people ever were, and as firmly."

Failing in health, he retired from public life but found time to write several papers on behalf of the abolition of slavery. He had still another plan, which he set forth in the concluding parts of his *Autobiography*. It was to establish a "United Party for Virtue, by forming the virtuous and good men of all nations into a regular body, to be governed by suitable good and wise rules . . . whoever attempts this aright, and is well qualified, can not fail of pleasing God . . ."

Benjamin Franklin died on April 17, 1790, and world-wide respects were paid to this second-generation American who had made the most of the opportunities offered in the New World, to the everlasting benefit of the United States of America.

In his will he designated himself: "I, Benjamin Franklin, Printer, late Minister Plenipotentiary from the United States to the Court of France, now President of Pennsylvania . . ." He never forgot what he owed to his trade. As an indentured printer's apprentice, little did he think that he "should ever literally *stand before kings* . . ." He continues with satisfaction to point out that this has since happened, for he has "stood before *five* . . ."

When Benjamin Franklin signed the Declaration of Independence he had helped as much as any man to establish the United States of America as a land of opportunity for all manner of patriotic citizens.

Thomas McKean *1734–1817*
Caesar Rodney *1728–1784*

CAESAR RODNEY AND THOMAS MCKEAN played a dramatic part in the vote for independence. When the unanimity of the United States was at stake, on July 1, 1776, Caesar Rodney, summoned by McKean, rode through a stormy night to bring Delaware into the independence column, as told in the Prologue.

The first Rodney of the Signer's line in America was William, who came to Kent County on the Delaware River to make his way after family reverses. Kent, one of the three Lower Counties on the Delaware, is now part of the state of Delaware. Originally settled by Swedes—with a Dutch interlude, then a merger with Pennsylvania—the Lower Counties had achieved a separate assembly in 1702, partly due to William Rodney's efforts. William Rodney's estate, which was considerable for those times, was inherited by his son, Caesar, named for Sir Thomas Caesar, a wealthy merchant ancestor. Caesar Rodney and his wife, a daughter of the Reverend Thomas Crawford, had eight children, of whom the eldest, another Caesar, was the Signer. He was born on October 7, 1728, at Dover, Delaware. By the law of entail, he succeeded to his father's lands.

In 1755 he became high sheriff of Kent County for three years, then was made a justice of the peace and a judge of all the lower courts. He was also a captain in the county militia.

In 1762 Rodney was elected to the Assembly (as he had been earlier), and with Thomas McKean prepared the answer to the Governor's opening address. The two also were selected to revise and print the colony laws passed since 1752. In 1765, Rodney, McKean and the speaker of the House were sent as delegates from the colony to the Stamp Act Congress in New York.

Through the efforts of Thomas McKean, each colony was given one vote only. He was selected, with Mr. Livingston and Mr. Rutledge, to revise the proceedings of the Congress and he was appointed, with Mr. Lynch and Mr. Otis, to prepare the address to the House of Commons. On the last day of the Congress, when the president, Timothy Ruggles, and some others declined to sign the petitions of rights and grievances, McKean rose and asked for an explanation, as the president had not indicated disapproval previously. Pressed by others, too, Ruggles said "it was against *his conscience.*" According to the *Biography of the Signers* (Sanderson-Waln), "Mr. McKean now rung the changes on the word conscience so long and loud" that a personal challenge was given by Ruggles and accepted by McKean, but no duel was fought, as the president left New York early the next day.

McKean was successively appointed chief notary for the Lower Counties, judge of the Court of Common Pleas and judge of the Orphans' Court of New Castle. During the November term in 1765, he ordered that all the proceedings of the court be recorded on unstamped paper. This is believed to be the first time that a court in the Colonies evaded the Stamp Act.

On the repeal of this hated Act the next year, Rodney, Mc-

Kean and George Read prepared the Legislature's address of gratitude to the King. But the Townshend Acts of 1767 alarmed the colonists, and the same three colleagues (later Delaware's three Signers) composed a petition of protest to the King— "We cannot think we shall have even the shadow of liberty left. We conceive it to be an inherent right in your majesty's subjects, derived to them from God and nature . . . in person, or by their representatives, to give and grant to their sovereign, those things which their own labours and their own cares have acquired and saved, and in such proportions, and at such times" as may be required.

About this time Rodney's health was seriously affected, due to a malignancy on his face, and he was forced to leave his duties in order to obtain medical aid at Philadelphia. It was urgently felt that he should go to England for further treatment, but, owing to temporary relief and the pressure of political events, the trip was postponed. When the Assembly met in 1769, Rodney was elected speaker. Later he became chairman of the Committee of Correspondence.

In the summer of 1774, acting on a New Castle request, Rodney, as speaker, organized a convention to protest British aggression. This convention elected Thomas McKean, George Read and Caesar Rodney, its chairman, to be delegates at the First Continental Congress, to determine upon prudent and lawful measures for the relief of an oppressed people.

As the delegates were assembling for Congress, Thomas McKean was one of those who rode out from Philadelphia to meet the Massachusetts delegates at Frankfort. Rodney was introduced to John Adams on September 3, and the latter's diary entry for that day describes him as "the oddest looking man in the world; he is tall, thin and slender as a reed, pale; his face is not bigger than a large apple, yet there is sense and fire, spirit, wit, and humor in his countenance." A later account states: "In 1774 I became acquainted with McKean,

Rodney and Henry (Patrick). Those three appeared to me to see more clearly to the end of the business than any others of the whole body. At least they were more candid and explicit with me than any others. . . ."

McKean and Rodney were appointed on the committee to state the rights of the colonists. Delaware's instructions for the Second Congress, passed in March, 1775, were to "avoid, as you have heretofore done, everything disrespectful or offensive to our most gracious Sovereign, or in any way invasive of his just rights and prerogative."

Rodney was much impressed by John Adams' speech on the "unquestionable" interest of France in having the British Colonies independent and also on the negotiation of treaties of commerce while remaining strictly neutral, lest "we should be little better than puppets, danced on the wires of the cabinets of Europe." He said that Adams "had considered the subject of foreign connections more maturely than any man they had ever heard in America," and that all of his objections to foreign relations were removed by Adams' reasoning.

The February, 1776, "moderate" letter, quoted before, listed the Lower Counties (Delaware) among the majority for reconciliation except when their delegation was divided on the issue owing to "the absence of Rodney or Read." Colonel McKean, it stated, was one of the "violents." As the tide for independence rose that spring, according to a manuscript of Thomas Rodney, the delegate's younger brother, "General Rodney . . . came home to consult his friends and constituents on that important question. He communicated the matter to his brother, Colonel Rodney, and observed that he had a great deal at stake, and that almost all of his old friends in Congress were against it. . . ."

Thomas McKean, although then living in Philadelphia and taking a leading role in the change of government and struggle for freedom there, was instrumental in putting Delaware in the independence column.

Thomas Jefferson's notes of the debates of June 8 and 10 on the independence resolutions show the opposition claiming that Delaware was "not yet ripe for bidding adieu to the British connection," while Adams, Lee, Wythe and others maintained that the delegates from the Delaware Counties had declared their constituents ready to join. But on the postponement of the resolutions, the notes disclose Delaware as "not yet matured for falling from the parent stem."

The Delaware Assembly met on June 10, at New Castle, and on June 13 McKean wrote to Congress in Philadelphia, at 2:30 A.M.: "The Assembly here have information this moment by express that there are a thousand Tories under arms in Sussex county . . . but we expect soon to give a good Account of these misguided people." The same day, at seven in the evening, he reported that "the Insurgents in Sussex county have dispersed . . ."

The following day he delivered to the Assembly at New Castle a certified copy of the May 15 resolution of Congress on new governments. By the seventeenth he returned to Philadelphia "with Full Powers."

On July 1, as described in the Prologue, Jefferson's notes indicate that the Lee independence motion was carried in the committee of the whole— "Delaware having but two members present, they were divided—" On the request of Edward Rutledge of South Carolina the final vote was put off to the next day, since he thought his colleagues, though disapproving the measure, would join in it then for the sake of unanimity.

Thomas McKean described what followed in a letter that he wrote to a nephew of Rodney in 1813: "Whereupon, without delay I sent an Express (at my private expence) for your honored Uncle Caesar Rodney Esquire, the remaining member for Delaware, whom I met at the State-house door in his boots & spurs, as the members were assembling; after a friendly salutation (without a word on the business) we went into the Hall of Congress together, and found we were among the latest: proceedings immediately commenced, and after a few minutes the great question was put; when the vote for Delaware was called, your uncle arose and said: 'As I believe the voice of my constituents and of all sensible & honest men is in favor of Independence & my own judgment concurs with them, I vote for Independence,' or in words to the same effect."

Caesar Rodney, who had ridden from Dover all through a stormy night to turn the vote of Delaware to independence, selflessly relinquished any chance left to him of going to England for treatment of the ailment said to have eventually caused his death.

On the fifth of July, President Hancock sent a copy of the Declaration to Colonel Haslet, to be read at the head of his battalion in Dover. On August 2, Rodney and Read signed the Declaration on parchment. Thomas McKean was a post-signer. And it was he who, discovering that his name had been omitted from the list of Signers in the printed *Journals of Congress* for 1776, Vol. 2, found also that the date of the Signing on parchment was erroneously given as July 4. In the secret journal, on July 19, Congress directed that the Declaration should be engrossed on parchment, and signed by every member. Later this journal recorded the Signing of August 2. McKean told of hearing that a resolve had been passed that no person should have a seat in Congress during that year until he had signed the Declaration, even if he had been elected after July 4. This, he said, was in order to prevent traitors or spies from "worming themselves amongst us."

Because of Caesar Rodney's independence vote, the many Royalists in the Lower Counties prevented his re-election to Congress in the September, 1776, state convention. Defeated by this "tory strategem," he continued to serve on the Council of Safety and the committee of inspection, collecting supplies for the army. In the beginning of 1777 he served actively with the army. In June, 1777, he was chosen judge of admiralty but retained his military office, suppressing an insurrection against the government in Sussex County. In September, when the British advanced into Delaware, General Rodney collected troops and, by direction of General Washington, placed his forces south of the main army to observe the movements of the British at the head of Elk River, Maryland, and, if possible, to cut the enemy off from their fleet. He wrote to General Washington, telling of his difficulties in getting the militia to turn out, and saying that, "As soon as I can set forward I shall advise you. God send you a complete victory."

In December he was again elected to Congress but did not attend, as he was chosen president or governor of Delaware, serving in this office until 1781, when he declined re-election. He wrote to McKean that he hoped the political changes would "rouse this little branch of the union from its heretofore torpid state, which God of his infinite mercy grant."

As president, General Rodney encountered much difficulty. He wrote again to McKean on June 11, 1778: "You and I both have had our disagreeable moments, with respect to the complexion of the Delaware state. However, those who dare persevere in such days of trial cannot now be doubted. He that dare acknowledge himself a whig, near the waters of the Delaware, where not only his property, but his person is every hour in danger of being carried off, is more in my opinion to be counted upon than a dozen whigs in security . . . you know how precarious their situation, and you also know their firmness; they did not bear that proportion to the disaffected that I could have wished, yet while they dared contend, I hoped congress would not have supposed the state lost. I thank God! affairs now wear a different complexion, and can I but have the countenance and support of congress, which no doubt I shall, civil government . . . will soon be in such force, as to cause those who have offended to tremble."

As president of the state, Caesar Rodney received alarming appeals from General Washington for relief of the army's desperate need for supplies. In the spring of 1780 the General informed him that, ". . . the army is again reduced to an extremity of distress, for want of provision . . . we have *this* day but *one* day's supply (of flour) in camp." Rodney worked constantly to help. In a letter to John Dickinson (elected a Delaware delegate in November, 1776), he asked his colleague to assure the committee appointed to procure flour that he would do everything in his power, but he feared the flour would "come high; as those termed speculators are as thick, and as industrious as bees, and as active and wicked as the devil himself."

Chosen a delegate to Congress again in 1782, Rodney did not serve. The malignancy on his face, which caused him to wear a green silk veil for many years, grew worse and he died in the middle of 1784, while serving in the State Council.

His brother, Thomas, speaker of the Delaware Assembly, in 1803 was appointed a United States judge for the territory of Mississippi, where the town of Rodney was named in his honor. A son and a cousin served as United States Senators.

Of King George III and the Lord North Ministry, Caesar Rodney wrote to his friend, Thomas McKean, in May, 1778: ". . . they are trying to divide us— However, virtue and firmness will, with the blessing of God, as well frustrate them in this, as in all their other . . . projects to cajole and enslave."

Although not voting for independence in July, George Read, the third member of the Delaware delegation, signed and supported the Republic at the risk of his life.

George Read was born at the family estate in Cecil County, Maryland, September 18, 1733. His father, John, son of a wealthy English gentleman, had come to this country to seek a change after the sudden death of a young lady he loved. In America John Read discovered a new love, Mary Howell, daughter of a planter, whom he married. A founder of Charlestown, he moved to New Castle County, on the Delaware River, with his wife soon after the birth of George, who was the first of six sons. George received a classical education at a school in Chester, Pennsylvania, and then under the Reverend Doctor Alison at New London. After studying law with John Moland in Philadelphia, he was admitted to the bar at the age of nineteen. In 1754 he established himself at New Castle, where his father had a large plantation. He was appointed attorney-general of the three Lower Counties in 1763 and two years later was elected to the Delaware Legislature, in which he served for twelve years.

On hearing of the suffering of Boston under the Boston Port Bill, the inhabitants of New Castle County appointed a committee, including Read, to raise subscriptions for relief. In February, 1775, nine hundred dollars was remitted, and Samuel Adams thanked Read for this gift. His letter states that "with the exception of a contemptible few," the people of Boston "appear to be animated with *an inextinguishable love of liberty.*"

On being elected to the First Continental Congress of 1774, Read resigned as attorney-general, declaring he would not serve in that body while encumbered by an office under the King.

In late 1776, he was president of the Delaware Constitutional Convention and he served on the committee which drafted the state's first constitution. Under the new government Read became speaker of the Council and vice-president. When President McKinly was captured by the British at the fall of Wilmington, in 1777, Read was summoned to

assume the presidency of the state. He was in Philadelphia with Congress at the time and had trouble avoiding
capture when returning to Delaware. With his family, he
proceeded along the Jersey shore of the Delaware River,
finally arriving at Salem. Procuring a boat, they started
across the river in sight of several British men-of-war. An
armed barge was sent in pursuit of them. Their boat
grounded well off the Delaware shore, due to the low tide.
Hastily effacing all marks on the baggage aboard, Mr. Read
represented himself to the officers of the barge as a country
gentleman returning home. The story worked and the British sailors helped to carry his mother, wife and small children
ashore.

In 1786, Mr. Read was a delegate to the Annapolis convention which led to the Constitutional Convention in Philadelphia the following year. At the latter, he ably promoted
the rights of the small states to equal representation in the
United States Senate. Twice a United States senator, he later
became Chief Justice of Delaware, holding this post until
his death in 1798. His wife, Gertrude Ross Till Read, a
widow, was the sister of George Ross, a Pennsylvania Signer.
Two of his brothers, Thomas and James Read, had distinguished records in the war and his son, grandson and great-
grandson all rose to prominent places in the service of their
country.

Thomas McKean was born on March 19, 1734, in New
London, Chester County, Pennsylvania, the son of William
and Laetitia Finney McKean, both of Scotch-Irish families.
His brothers and sister were Robert, William and Dorothea.

After an elementary education, Robert and Thomas (then
nine years old) were placed under the tuition of the Reverend Doctor Francis Alison, to study languages, mathematics,
rhetoric, logic and moral philosophy. After acquiring a
knowledge of these subjects, Thomas entered the law office

of his relative, David Finney, at New Castle, as a student. In about two years he became register of probate of New Castle County. Admitted to the bar before he was twenty-one, he was appointed deputy attorney-general for Sussex County two years later and clerk of the Assembly, 1757-59. He was extremely successful in his law practice. In 1762 he was elected to the Assembly and he continued to be re-elected for seventeen years.

McKean bore the brunt of the battle to carry Delaware for independence, and he served on the committee appointed to prepare the Articles of Confederation which he signed for Delaware on February 12, 1779.

Though he represented Delaware in Congress until 1783 (except for one year) and was President of Congress in 1781, McKean was also Chief Justice of Pennsylvania from July, 1777, to 1799. Both states claimed this Patriot who retained his seat in the Delaware Legislature until 1779, serving briefly as acting governor in 1777.

In 1779 he described himself in a letter to his friend, John Adams, as being "hunted like a fox by the enemy . . . compelled to remove my family five times in a few months, and at last fixed them in a little log-house on the banks of the Susquehanna . . . they were soon obliged to move again on account of the incursions of the Indians."

As president of Congress in 1781, he received the dispatches of General Washington announcing the surrender of Cornwallis at Yorktown. He was a member of the Pennsylvania constitutional convention of 1790 and he served as governor of that state from 1799 to 1808. A movement to impeach him in 1807 and 1808 was unsuccessful.

Thomas McKean's first wife was Mary Borden, eldest daughter of Joseph Borden of Bordentown, New Jersey. She died in 1773, leaving two sons and four daughters, the youngest only two weeks old. On September 3, 1774, McKean married Sarah Armitage of New Castle, by whom he had five children.

In his opening address as Governor of Pennsylvania, he told the Assembly he trusted that "under his administration, their happy system of government, raised on the sole authority of the people, would, by the favour of God, be continued inviolate; and that neither foreign nor domestic enemies, neither intrigue, menace, nor seductions, should prevail against it." He added that "the security of persons, property, liberty, and reputation" would be his "chiefest care."

His administration also came under criticism for removing from office those of opposite political views. A letter from John Adams (his friend of many years) to McKean's son, also concerned in the charges, ends with this tribute: "P.S. Your father and Caesar Rodney, were among the Patrick Henrys, the Christopher Gadsdens, the Thomas Jeffersons, the Samuel Adamses, the Roger Shermans—the best tried and firmest pillars of the revolution."

Samuel Chase *1741–1811*
William Paca *1740–1799*

Of one man who participated in the long weary struggle of the "violent" minority in Congress, John Adams wrote, as quoted in the Prologue: "Mr. Chase, of Maryland, when he did speak at all, was always powerful, and generally with us." It was especially important to have Chase "with us," as politically he had not one vote but two. William Paca, Chase's friend from law student days in Annapolis until Paca's death in 1799, was described by Dr. Rush as ". . . a good tempered worthy Man, with a sound Understanding which he was too indolent to exercise. He therefore gave himself up to be directed both in his political Opinions & conduct by Sam¹ Chase who had been the friend of his youth, & for whom he retained a regard in every Stage of his life."

Samuel Chase was born in Somerset County, Maryland, on April 17, 1741. He was the son of an Episcopal clergyman of English birth, the Reverend Thomas Chase, and his wife Matilda Walker Chase, daughter of a Maryland farmer. Mrs. Chase died a short while later, and the Reverend Chase moved to Baltimore with Samuel in 1743, to become the rector of St. Paul's Church. Thomas Chase, a fine classical scholar, took charge of his son's early education and sent him to study law at Annapolis at eighteen. Samuel was admitted to the bar in 1761. He began practice in Annapolis, achieving success early. In 1762 he married Anne Baldwin of Annapolis, and they had a family of two sons and two daughters.

Samuel Chase was elected to the Maryland Assembly in 1764, and William Paca joined him four years later. This was the start of their long political and patriotic association in resisting oppressive measures of the Proprietary government and of Parliament. Chase, who served for twenty years in the Maryland Legislature, became known in the Colonial Assembly for his independent attitude and "his uncourtly bearing towards the royal governor and the court party."

At twenty-four, he openly disputed the parliamentary right to tax the Colonies without their consent. In violent reaction to the Stamp Act, a group of the Sons of Liberty, who had assembled at Annapolis in 1765, forcibly entered the public offices and seized and destroyed the stamps they found there. The stamp officer was also burned in effigy. Mr. Chase took part in both of these events and was designated as a "busy, restless incendiary" by the city authorities. In a printed reply, he admitted his participation but maintained that the so-called "mob" was composed of "men of reputation and merit" superior to "tools of power, emerged from obscurity and basking in proprietary sunshine."

In 1770 Chase voted for a new bill passed by the lower house of the Assembly which reduced the salaries of the government officials and the clergy stipends of the established Church of England, although his own father's income was affected. The Council, some of whom benefited by the higher fees, opposed the measure. Governor Eden dissolved the Assembly and issued a proclamation, continuing the former high salary and stipend rates, which aroused a great deal of feeling against the Proprietary government.

This resentment grew into a heated exchange of letters between "First Citizen" (Charles Carroll of Carrollton) and "Antilon" of the Governor's Council over the regulation of fees. These letters brought victory to the Patriot party in the May, 1773, elections. William Paca and Matthias Hammond were chosen to represent Annapolis by a "very great majority of freemen" over a candidate of whom "a strong suspicion was entertained of his political principles and Court connexions." The new representatives promptly signed an open letter publicly thanking Carroll for his patriotic part in the controversy.

When news of the Boston Port Bill reached Annapolis in May, 1774, great indignation was aroused. A Maryland patriotic convention met and agreed to join in a general congress in September. Samuel Chase, Robert Goldsborough, Thomas Johnson, Matthew Tilghman and William Paca were chosen as delegates "to effect one general plan of conduct, operating on the commercial connexion of the colonies with the mother country, for the relief of Boston, and preservation of American liberty." Paca was also serving on the Committee of Correspondence at that time.

On the first day of the Congress, at Philadelphia in September, 1774, William Paca, Robert Goldsborough and Samuel Chase were present in Carpenters' Hall for their colony. Chase was active in the debates on nonimportation and was described by Rush as "a bold declaimer with slender reasoning powers. His person & manner were very acceptable . . . and to these, he owned much of his success in political life."

The deliberations of Congress, according to one participant, were "spun out to an immeasurable length. There is so much wit, sense, learning, acuteness, subtlety, eloquence, &c. among fifty gentlemen, each of whom has been habituated to lead and guide in his own Province, that an immensity of time is spent unnecessarily. Johnson of Maryland has a clear and a cool head, an extensive knowledge of trade as well as law. He is a deliberating man, but not a shining orator . . . Paca is a deliberator too; Chase speaks warmly . . ."

In those first days as it was necessary to act with great delicacy and caution, "to feel pulses, and to sound the depths, . . ." the meetings and social gatherings after the official business of the day was concluded were of paramount importance. A contemporary diary records that on October 11, Paca, John Adams, Reed, Rodney, Johnson, and Mr. R. Penn were among those dining with Mr. McKean in Market Street, and two days later Mr. Dickinson entertained Chase, Paca, Low, Mifflin, Penn and General Lee at dinner at six o'clock.

Maryland's delegation to the Second Continental Congress consisted of the previous representatives, with the addition of Thomas Stone and John Hall. When this Congress reconvened in September, 1775, after the short summer adjournment, Chase is described in John Adams' diary as being "violent and boisterous, asking his pardon; he is tedious upon frivolous points." In consequence of many talks and consultations with Adams, Samuel Chase made a motion for sending ambassadors to France. It was seconded by Mr. Adams, who commented: "Whether the effect of the motion resembled the shock of electricity, of mesmerism, or of galvanism, the most exactly, I leave you philosophers to determine; but the grimaces, the agitations and convulsions were very great." It was in defending this motion that Adams made such an impression on Congress, but the motion was "murdered." After twenty subtle projects to get rid of it, the debate on the Chase motion resulted in the creation of a committee of secret correspondence which had the sole purpose of corresponding with "our friends in Great Britain, Ireland, and other parts of the world."

Appealing to Judge Chase in later years to verify his long

stand on neutrality, Adams acknowledged with pride his close association with Chase at the time when the Marylander made the first motion for entering into foreign relations. "We flickered, disputed, and wrangled in public and private, but always with a species of good humor that never was suffered to diminish the confidence, esteem, or affection of each in the other."

In evaluating the choice of Chase to make the motion for diplomatic relations with France, it must be remembered that the New England delegates were "interdicted from taking the lead in any great measures . . . Because they had been suspected from the beginning of having independence in contemplation."

The idea of independence was still unpalatable in Maryland and the Maryland Convention, meeting in December, added Robert Alexander and John Rogers to the delegates and passed binding instructions, wishing ardently "for a reconciliation with the mother country" on terms that might ensure freedom to the Colonies. Without the approval of the Convention, the delegates were not to vote for independence, any foreign alliance, or confederation of the Colonies, unless absolutely necessary. If any such measure passed Congress against the judgment of Maryland, the province would not consider itself bound. Another instruction was to obtain a resolution that would bar a person holding military or civil office under the new army or government from serving in Congress.

On January 18 a declaration of the Maryland Convention avowed that the members "never did, nor do entertain any views or desires of independency." Samuel Chase, though, spoke strongly against publicizing an oration which declared that Congress wished to continue dependent on Great Britain.

Samuel Chase and Benjamin Franklin were appointed commissioners to travel to Canada, and try to enlist the support of that province. With Charles Carroll of Carrollton, and his cousin, John Carroll, they set out in March.

". . . my friend Chase . . . has promised me to call on you at Clermont," James Duane wrote to Robert R. Livingston from Philadelphia. "You will find that his usual warmth is not abated and that though closely attached to his friends he still keeps the start of them in his political system." But Chase wrote to John Adams, from St. Johns, that in his judgment there was no alternative between independence and slavery and that no American could hesitate in the choice. Another delegate was not so determined in his letter, written four days later. Stone prophesied to Daniel Jenifer that a separation would take place if peace commissioners did not arrive shortly from Britain. He wished to arrange matters so that a just reconciliation would take place, or else there would be a fairly unanimous choice of independence.

Maryland instructions of May reiterated the previous restrictions. The instruction to bar holders of military or civil office under the new government from serving in Congress caused John Adams some anxious and unpleasant moments. He was then Chief Justice of Massachusetts under the new regime and the opposition in Congress had spread the rumor that he wanted independence in order to keep this post. In his *Autobiography* he recounts that one day when he was speaking on independence, or new governments, a Maryland delegate of "high rank rose and said, he should move, that no person who held any office under a new government should be admitted to vote on any such question, as they were interested persons . . ." Adams thereupon rose from his seat with great coolness and deliberation and, feeling quite gay rather than resentful, seconded this motion and immediately moved another motion that no person holding an office under the old or present government be permitted to vote on such questions, being themselves also interested. This move, Adams continues, "flew like an electric stroke through every countenance in the room," as the delegate who had tried to unseat Adams held as high an office under the old regime as Adams under the new. His name is not disclosed by Adams. However, no further word was heard in Congress about the motion "levelled" at the New Englander's head!

On June 11, the day following the postponement of Lee's independence move, Chase and Carroll, who were so instrumental in bringing Maryland into the independence system, appeared in Congress, just returned from their futile mission to Canada. They were not a moment too soon to take part in the desperate struggle for freedom.

Chase wrote to Adams: "Mr. Chase will excuse the late Neglects and Inattention of Mr. John Adams to him, upon the express Condition, that in future he constantly communicate to Mr. Chase every Matter relative to persons or Things. Mr. Chase flatters himself with seeing Mr. Adams on Monday or Tuesday fortnight with the Voice of Maryland in favor of Independance and a foreign Alliance, which are, in Mr. Chases Opinion, the only and best Measures to preserve the Liberties of America—direct to Annapolis."

Adams replied that he would write "Facts," but would not "medelle with Characters, for the World." Mr. Adams "ever was and ever will be glad to see Mr. Chase, but Mr. Chase never was nor will be more welcome than, if he should come next Monday or Tuesday fortnight with the Voice of Maryland in Favour of Independence." Adams, who had had encouraging news from Delaware and Pennsylvania, added— "Maryland now stands alone. I presume she will join Company—if not she must be left alone."

Before this letter was received, the Maryland Convention, meeting at Annapolis, directed that their delegates obtain leave from Congress to attend the Convention and also—most important—a resolution in Congress postponing consideration of independence until their return to Philadelphia.

Chase, whose wife was very ill, wrote again to Adams from

Annapolis, reminding him of his neglect: "I am almost resolved not to inform You, that a general Dissatisfaction prevails here with our Convention. read the papers, & be assured Frederick speaks the Sense of many Counties. I have not been idle. I have appealed *in Writing* to the People. County after County is instructing."

Three days later, Adams answered that Congress had voted against the Maryland proposal to put off "those great Questions." He said it was felt that to postpone consideration again "would hazard Convulsions, and dangerous Conspiracies—" He added an urgent, "I hope that before Monday Morning next, we shall receive from Maryland, Instructions to do right."

On June 28 the Maryland Convention authorized the delegates to declare the United Colonies free and independent States, and Chase wrote Adams of this: "I shall offer no other Apology for Concluding, than that I am this Moment from the House to procure an Express to follow the Post with an Unan: Vote of our Convention for *Independence* e^t e^t— See the glorious Effects of County Instructions—our people have fire if not smothered . . ."

This unanimous vote of the Maryland Convention, as recorded by the *Journal,* was "laid before Congress & read" on the morning of July 1. It was a great boost toward independence. Chase had kept his word.

Paca, Stone and probably Rogers were present on July 2 and 4 to cast their colony's vote for independence. Samuel Chase answered Adams' letter of July 1 about the Maryland Convention vote four days later: "I hope ere this Time the decisive blow is struck. Oppression, Inhumanity and Perfidy have compelled Us to it. blessed be Men who effect the Work, I envy You! how shall I transmit to posterity that I gave my assent? . . . I have sent You our Paper and some Resolves of our Convention—do they not do Us Honor . . . I cannot conclude without requesting my most respectful

Compliments to Mr. (Samuel) Adams Col^e Hancock eṭ eṭ and all independent Americans."

Chase's chance to "transmit to posterity" his vote for independence came on August 2 when he, William Paca, Thomas Stone and Charles Carroll of Carrollton signed the Declaration on parchment for Maryland in the State House at Philadelphia.

Chosen a member of many important committees, Chase did not hesitate to return to Congress if it was necessary, even when he was off on leave of absence. Not long after the adoption of independence, in a letter to Richard Henry Lee, he wrote: "I hurried to congress to give my little assistance to the framing of a confederacy and a plan for a foreign alliance; both of them subjects of the utmost importance . . . demand immediate dispatch. The confederation has engaged our close attention for a week. Three great difficulties occur; representation, the mode of voting, and the claims to the south sea. . . . We do not all see the importance, nay, the necessity, of a confederacy." He warns that the country will remain weak and divided, and exposed to all the arts of the "insidious court" of Britain before confederation is achieved. Chase was appointed to the committee for suppressing the internal enemies of the country.

In 1778 Chase had an opportunity to fight the arts of the "insidious court." Bills proposed by Parliament to send peace commissioners to America were secretly circulated by Tories. Congress had drafts of these bills printed, along with a counteracting address prepared by Chase, Lee and Gouverneur Morris, which reviewed three years of war: "At length that God of battles, in whom was our trust, has conducted us through the paths of danger and distress to the thresholds of security. . . ."

Chase was left out of the Maryland delegation the following year because of alleged speculation based on knowledge gained from his membership in Congress.

In 1783, he was sent by Maryland to England to recover bank stock belonging to the former colony, which was completed by William Pinkney. While abroad, Chase married his second wife, Hannah Giles of Kentbury. He met Fox and Pitt, and visited Edmund Burke for a week. For the interest of his relatives, he described in his journal the appearance of the royal family at the theater. King George III was dressed in a "plain suit of clothes with gold buttons, with a large black ribbon across his breast," and Queen Charlotte in "white satin, her head dress ornamented with a great number of diamonds."

Samuel Chase moved to Baltimore in 1786 and in 1791 he became chief justice of the Maryland General Court. President Washington appointed him to the United States Supreme Court in 1796, and in 1804 his political opponents, led by John Randolph of Virginia, secured his impeachment on misdemeanor charges. Not convicted, he resumed his seat and held it until his death in 1811. His fellow Federalist and old friend, President John Adams, wrote of the effort required "to save a great and upright judge from unmerited ignominy."

Rather better fitted to be an advocate than a judge, forceful speaking earned for Samuel Chase the title "Demosthenes of Maryland." This Signer was effectively instrumental in bringing about the unanimity of the Declaration of Independence by delivering, as promised, the "Voice of Maryland in favor of Independance."

Thomas Stone served on the committee to prepare the Articles of Confederation and in 1784 acted as president pro tempore of Congress. This Maryland Signer was described as "An able lawyer, and a friend to universal liberty."

William Paca was born on a farm near Abingdon, Harford County, Maryland, on October 31, 1740. His family were successful planters during the late seventeenth century. William was educated in the customary branches of classical instruction and "in the principles of morality and honour." He was graduated from the College of Philadelphia in 1759 and began to study law at Annapolis, where he met Samuel Chase. Two years later he was admitted to practice in that city, and completed his law training at the Inner Temple in London. William Paca married Mary Chew of Annapolis, who had a very "considerable fortune."

In addition to Paca's valuable service to the American cause in the colony and in Congress, he and Samuel Chase supplied a volunteer corps with rifles at a personal expense of nearly a thousand dollars. On the adoption of the state constitution, he was made state senator, serving 1777-79. Chief judge of the Superior Court of Maryland, 1778-1780, he later officiated as governor of Maryland for three years. Nominated by President Washington for United States district judge in 1789, he held this office until his death ten years afterward. In public office his "graceful address," fine appearance and manner were of great benefit to him.

"Beloved and respected" by all who knew him, this Maryland Signer was considered at all times a "sincere patriot and honest man."

Charles Carroll of Carrollton
1737–1832

Dᴇsᴄᴇɴᴅᴇᴅ ғʀᴏᴍ ɪʀɪsʜ ᴋɪɴɢs, Signer Charles Carroll's grandfather, also Charles Carroll, emigrated to Maryland in October, 1688, bringing with him Lord Baltimore's commission as attorney-general of the Province of Maryland. Seeking religious freedom, he had chosen Maryland, founded in 1634 by Lord Baltimore, as his goal. This was planned as a province where Roman Catholics and members of other persecuted sects might worship freely. The second Lord Baltimore issued the famous Toleration Act in 1649, which read, "noe person or psons whatsoever within this Province . . . professing to believe in Jesus Christ, shall from henceforth bee any waies troubled, Molested or discountenanced for in respect to his or her religion."

As Charles Carroll embarked for the New World, he altered his family coat-of-arms, substituting "an Hawk uprising" for the passive bird that had topped the crest. He also adopted a new motto—*Ubicumque cum Libertate*—Anywhere so long as it be free. He landed in Maryland just a month before the Protestant Revolution took place in England and William and Mary gained the throne.

[212]

He and his son, Charles Carroll of Annapolis, earned great fortunes in Maryland—but not religious freedom. After the double tax on Catholics was passed, Charles Carroll of Annapolis planned, in 1757, to sell all his holdings and found a new colony in French Louisiana, but he did not get a grant there. When it became the choice of his son, the Signer, known as Charles Carroll of Carrollton, he preferred to stay in Maryland and enjoy the life there, although he was barred from becoming a lawyer or holding political office. A Roman Catholic in strongly Protestant surroundings, he held to his religious and his political principles, even though this was not convenient, comfortable or expedient.

The only son of Charles and Elizabeth Brooke Carroll, the Signer was born on September 19, 1737, at Annapolis, in the massive severely beautiful red-brick house that Carroll had built on Spa Creek, with space for "green Gardens." Elizabeth Brooke Carroll was the daughter of Clement and Jane Sewall Brooke of Maryland. A cousin of her husband, she was one of the beauties of her day.

The young Charles grew up in "Doughoregan," House of Kings, favorite country seat of the first two Charles Carrolls, and in the Annapolis town house. He was taught by his mother until he was ten since, owing to the Disenfranchisement Act, Catholic schools were not permitted. As Maryland schools of the day were mostly inadequate and were anti-Catholic, the Carrolls sent their young heir to one of the sub-rosa schools, Bohemia Manor Academy, conducted by the Society of Jesus, on Augustine Herman's old plantation. One of his classmates was his cousin "Jacky" Carroll, and the two boys went on from there to France, to study at the College of St. Omer, where the second Charles had been educated. The third Charles was a good student in "greek latin and the maps," but not so expert in "little figures." "I can easily see the great affection you have for Me," he wrote to his father in 1750 or 1751, "by sending me hear to a Colege, where I may not only be a learned man, but also be advanced in piety and devotion."

Jacky Carroll decided to become a priest, while Charles continued his education at the French Jesuit College at Rheims, and the College of Louis-le-Grand in Paris, then studied civil or Roman law at Bourges and English common law in the Temple at London. After five years in London, Charles sailed for home. As announced in the *Maryland Gazette* of February 14, 1765, "Tuesday last arrived at his Father's House in Town, Charles Carroll Jun'r. Esq. . . . after about sixteen years absence." Small and slight in stature, Charles was well made, with fine hands and regular features, and he moved with the smooth grace of the expert swordsman. In a few months he had become an ardent Marylander, speaking of "our Weather," "our Races," and even "our oppresive Laws."

His father made over to him Carrollton Manor, a large tract of land in Frederick County. Almost from the day of arrival, he signed himself as "Charles Carroll of Carrollton," to distinguish him from other Charles Carrolls, but he continued to live with his father.

Aroused by the Stamp Act, certain residents of Annapolis hanged the stamp collector in effigy in late August, 1765. Protesting the Act, Charles Carroll wrote to a friend in England, William Graves, master in chancery, asserting that neither threats nor force would make Americans "depart from the essential right of internal taxation without which our property would be at ye mercy of every rapacious minister." He felt also that "in these times of necessity and oppression it is a duty every man of fortune owes his country to set an example of frugality and industry . . ." He continued that the colonists would have to manufacture for themselves, "the worst of evils this, that can possibly befall England, the loss of liberty excepted." The letter then describes the violence aroused by the Act.

Carroll followed the political developments with intense interest but could not take any part in public life because of his religious beliefs. Opposed to the Townshend Acts, he wrote to Graves on August 27, 1767, saying they would give "great disgust" in America and promote colonial manufacture, though he expected to hear soon "of some act to restrain us from manufacturing altogether." If Americans are forced to go naked, he continued with sarcasm, their numbers will be reduced and "If England forces her colonies to rebellion, she must take ye proper steps to make that rebellion ineffectual by reducing their strength . . . putting a stop to ye increase of our people." Prophesying armed rebellion in a private letter to a friend abroad, at home he wisely said nothing and waited.

On June 5, 1768, Charles Carroll married his cousin, Molly Darnall, at the Carroll house in Annapolis. Molly was very social and the young Carrolls began going everywhere and entertaining a great deal. Charles was even invited to join the Homony Club, and among the young gentlemen who met there "in homony" were Samuel Chase and William Paca—great friends of Carroll's in Annapolis. The royal governor, Robert Eden, who had married the sister of the sixth Lord Baltimore, prominent lawyers and merchants also belonged, and a struggling young portrait painter, Charles Willson Peale, was a member too.

Charles Carroll of Carrollton now managed all the business affairs of the family. He kept an account book of the loans and mortgages, superintended the plantations and the sale of the tobacco. His annual income was a staggering sum for those days.

At the time of the Boston Massacre, Maryland was involved in a political fight which stirred the colony. On November 26, 1770, Governor Eden arbitrarily raised the salaries of government officials by proclamation, having dissolved the Assembly because the Lower House had passed a bill lowering the amounts. The bitter quarrel between the Governor and the Lower House grew and in January, 1773, an unsigned dialogue was printed in the *Maryland Gazette* between "First Citizen" and "Second Citizen," in which "First Citizen," a supporter of the Patriot cause, served as a "stooge" in asking questions that would bring out the favorable points of "Second Citizen," an adherent of the Governor.

The author was Daniel Dulany, a well-known lawyer, member of the Governor's Council and secretary of the colony. Nearly a month passed and no one in public life came forward to answer Dulany, so Charles Carroll took up the challenge for the Patriot party. At last he had a chance to take part in public affairs.

On February 4, 1773, came his answer, another unsigned dialogue, in which "First Citizen," protesting that the original dialogue had been incorrectly reported, submitted his own version. The journalistic battle turned into a series of letters, signed "Antilon" by Dulany and "First Citizen" by Carroll. These were widely read. There had been animosity between the families of the two writers before, and in 1769 Dulany's half brother had challenged Charles Carroll of Carrollton to a duel, which was accepted but not fought.

On April 8, 1773, Antilon inquired in the *Gazette*, "After all, who is this man that calls himself a citizen . . . has charged the members of one of the legislative branches with insolence . . . ?" And he went on to attack Carroll because of his religion. But this proved a boomerang and the honors of the argument, which continued a while longer, went to First Citizen.

Charles and Molly Carroll went about as usual but the Governor looked "very cool" upon his ex-fellow clubman, for the Homony Club had broken up. Among its former members were the outstanding leaders of the opposing political parties.

The local election of May, 1773, was determined by the

First Citizen letters and it was a landslide for the Patriot party. The first official act of the newly-elected Annapolis representatives was an open letter, printed in the *Gazette,* and signed by William Paca and Matthias Hammond, thanking First Citizen, Charles Carroll of Carrollton:

"Your manly and spirited opposition to the arbitrary attempt of government to establish the fees of office by proclamation, justly entitles you to the exalted character of a distinguished advocate for the rights of your country . . . Public gratitude, sir, for public services, is the patriot's dues . . ."

Notes of appreciation to First Citizen filled the pages of the *Gazette*—and must have been heavy going for the court party! On July 2, 1773, the Lower House declared the salary proclamation illegal. Adjourning, they marched in a body, with the townspeople following, to the Carroll house on Spa Creek and thanked Charles in person.

In May, 1774, a large crowd gathered in Annapolis on receipt of the news of the Boston Port Bill, to adopt measures for redress. A committee of correspondence was appointed: John Hall, Thomas Johnson, Jr., William Paca, Matthias Hammond—and Charles Carroll of Carrollton—his first post in public life.

It is said that a second assignment, as delegate to the First Continental Congress, was offered him but that he felt it would not be politic to accept. He accompanied the delegates to Philadelphia as an unofficial adviser, however. "When I see you," he wrote his father on September 12, "I shall be able to give you a full account of their (the delegates') deliberations. . . ." Feeling that the controversy would be decided by arms, he had written his father on the seventh, "I will either endeavour to defend the liberties of my country, or die with them . . ."

Some Maryland delegates "together with Mr. Carroll of Carrollton," hurried back to Annapolis before Congress adjourned. On October 14 the brig *Peggy Stewart* had arrived with *more than a ton of English tea,* and an Annapolitan tea party was brewing. Stewart is said to have consulted Charles Carroll before deciding to burn the ship and its incendiary cargo, and the painting by Turner in the Maryland State House depicts the scene with Charles Carroll included. A party was given a few evenings later, at which the host displayed a new silver punch bowl which he admitted had come over on the *Peggy,* in charge of the captain. It had been sent by a friend in England. An awkward silence followed and the guests looked at Carroll, of the Committee of Correspondence, who smiled and said, "We accept your explanation, provided the bowl is used to draw always this same kind of 'tea.' "

In August, 1774, Carroll was chosen on the Committee of Safety, and in November he was placed on the committee to carry into execution the association agreed on by the Continental Congress. There were other committee memberships, too, and provincial conventions to attend and Charles Carroll of Carrollton faithfully undertook his responsibilities as First Citizen, which he was often called. His devoted father was enjoying his son's career thoroughly and in the spring of 1775 was delighted at the birth of Charles Carroll IV.

The baby's father was not a delegate to the Second Continental Congress but he again went to Philadelphia as an adviser. He did not stay long however, owing to committee duties in Annapolis and his wife's poor health.

The military campaign to win Canada having failed utterly, Congress decided to send a diplomatic mission. On February 15, Dr. Franklin, Samuel Chase and Charles Carroll of Carrollton were appointed commissioners to go to Canada. As John Adams explained the choice of the latter in a letter to James Warren, "He speaks their Language as easily as ours; and what is perhaps of more Consequence than all the rest, he was educated in the Roman Catholic Religion . . .

In the Cause of American Liberty his Zeal Fortitude and Perseverance have been so conspicuous that he is said to be marked out for peculiar Vengeance by the Friends of Administration; But he continues to hazard his all, his immense Fortune, the largest in America, and his life. This Gentleman's Character, if I foresee aright, will hereafter make a greater Figure in America . . ." Father John Carroll, Carroll's cousin, also went to Canada. The four commissioners left Philadelphia the end of March.

Carroll's Journal of the trip, starting April 2, when he sailed up the Hudson from New York, gives an interesting and detailed account of the travels. Descriptions of the "wild and romantic appearance" of the Hudson River country, the Schuylers' hospitality at Albany and Saratoga and then of his rapidly acquired military knowledge were graphically written down.

The mission had no chance of success. Dr. Franklin, feeling ill, left Montreal and was joined by Father Carroll, who was later to be the first American Bishop of his Church. Carroll and Chase returned from Canada later, reaching Philadelphia on June 10, the date of the last journal entry. On June 11, the day after the postponement of the independence motion, Carroll wrote his father that the "desire of Independence is gaining ground rapidly."

But during the absence of such firm Patriots as Chase and Carroll, the May Convention in Annapolis had instructed the Maryland delegates in Congress to follow the December instructions—*against* independence! On June 20, when a new convention met, Chase was present and Carroll took his seat four days later. On June 28, the previous instructions were rescinded and Maryland's delegates were empowered to join with a majority in declaring independence.

The influence of Samuel Chase has been shown. James McSherry in his *History of Maryland,* says, "Principally instrumental in obtaining the passage of this resolution was Charles Carroll of Carrollton."

On July 4, Charles Carroll was elected by the Maryland Convention a delegate to the Continental Congress and he took his seat on July 18. On that same day he was added to the Board of War and the Chairman, John Adams, described him later in his *Autobiography* as, "an excellent member, whose education, manners, and application to business and to study, did honor to his fortune, the first in America."

Two traditional stories are told of Charles Carroll at the Signing of the Declaration on August 2. One is that Mr. Hancock asked if he would sign it. "Most willingly," was the reply, and taking a pen, Carroll wrote his name on the parchment, just under that of Stone. "There go a few millions," said one of the delegates near by, and all present agreed.

The second tale tells that one delegate answered, "Oh, no, he will get off! There are so many Charles Carrolls." Whereupon Carroll added "of Carrollton," to make sure that George III in particular might make no mistake as to his identity. But the signature on the document flows so smoothly together that this anecdote is probably founded on the fact that someone did not realize he had been accustomed to sign the distinguishing "of Carrollton" much earlier.

In August Carroll was chosen by the Maryland Convention as one of seven to prepare a Maryland Declaration of Rights and Constitution. Another of the Committee was his cousin, Charles Carroll "the Barrister," and to him is generally attributed the Maryland Bill of Rights. Of the State Constitution, Carroll of Carrollton wrote in 1817 to Virgil Maxcy: "I was one of the Committee, that framed the Constitution of this State, and the mode of chusing the Senate was suggested by me."

Carroll was elected to the first Maryland Senate and divided his time between state affairs and business of Congress. Left off the newly reorganized Board of War in November, 1777, by those opposed to Washington, Carroll was an uncompromising supporter of the Commander-in-Chief during the Conway Cabal to supersede him. The anti-Washington Board of War urged that a committee be sent to investigate the military situation at Valley Forge. The opposition group managed to control this committee and Washington's friends barely succeeded in having Charles Carroll and Gouverneur Morris appointed as minority members.

On the eve of the committee's departure, Carroll was called to Maryland because of his wife's illness, but her fortunate improvement allowed him to rush to Valley Forge. Carroll is said to have felt that Washington's destiny was the destiny of America, and he, with Morris, went to work on Francis Dana, the chairman of the committee. Dana was fearless in changing his mind when he became aware of the true picture and began to admire Washington's conduct and abilities. The committee placed the blame for the conditions at Valley Forge on Mifflin, the quartermaster-general, exonerating Washington, and the Conway Cabal lost its standing and soon collapsed.

In 1788 First Citizen Carroll was elected first Senator from Maryland under the United States Constitution and later he served again in the state Senate. On July 4, 1828, as a Director of the Baltimore and Ohio Railroad, he broke ground for the railroad that would unite the East and West "for the commencement of this great work which will commemorate an epoch in the history of the internal improvements of our beloved country."

As he broke the ground, with two pages dressed as Mercuries in attendance, Carroll is said to have remarked that it seemed to him an occasion second in importance only to his signing of the Declaration of Independence. At ninety-one, he was the last surviving Signer—a firm link between the

United States of America in 1776 and the Republic rapidly expanding to the Pacific.

Carroll spent his last years quietly among his children and grandchildren. He died in 1832.

"An inflexible patriot," Rush described him, "and an honest, independant friend to his country. He had been educated at St. Omer's, and possessed considerable learning. He seldom spoke, but his speeches were sensible and correct, and delivered in an oratorical manner."

In his long life perhaps his greatest devotion had been to his father. How often had he remembered those wise words of advice offered the first time he was completely on his own, ". . . now you can only rely on God's grace, your own prudence and ye good principles instilled into you by a virtuous Education: I beg you will never fail daily and sincerely to implore ye first, without which ye other two can be of no Service."

Thomas Nelson, Jr. *1738–1789*
George Wythe *1726–1806*

ON MAY 14, 1776, in the new General Convention of Virginia, Thomas Nelson, Jr., *moved for independence.* His motion was passed in the final form on May 15—a memorable day celebrated annually in Virginia.

Colonel Nelson himself took the famous resolution to Philadelphia, where he laid it before Congress. To his colony, Virginia, went the honor—and the daring—of being the first to instruct its delegates, of which he was one, *to propose to Congress* "to declare the United Colonies free and independent States. . . ."

Thomas Nelson, grandfather of the Signer, emigrated to the Colonies from Scotland about 1690 and founded the town of York in Virginia—later Yorktown, where Cornwallis surrendered in 1781. Nelson built the first custom house of the Colonies and accumulated a large fortune in merchandise. His son, William Nelson, added to his inherited property and purchased large estates. President of the Council and acting governor, he also presided as judge of the general or Supreme Court of the province. His lavish mode of living is indicated in a letter he wrote to a friend. It seems that he bought Lord Baltimore's six white coach horses just to give his own six black ones a rest in his Hanover meadows!

The Signer, Thomas Nelson, Jr., was born in Yorktown, December 26, 1738. He was the eldest of the five sons of William and Elizabeth Burwell Nelson, as indicated by the "Jr." though he was not given his father's first name. Sent to school at Hackney in England at fourteen, he later attended Cambridge, where he studied under Dr. Beilby Porteous, afterward Bishop of London. Rush's sketch of Nelson is illuminating: "A respectable country gentleman, with excellent dispositions in public and private life. He was educated in England. He informed me that he was the only person out of nine or ten Virginians that were sent with him to England for education that had taken a part in the American Revolution. The rest were all Tories."

Nelson returned to Virginia in 1761, and the following year he married Lucy Grymes, daughter of Colonel Philip Grymes of Middlesex County. Provided for by Nelson's father, the young couple lived in a spacious house at York, nearly opposite his father's, and entertained a great deal. On his daily rides to his plantation, Nelson practiced shooting game and he kept a pack of hounds at a small farm near the town. During the winter he went foxhunting once or twice a week with his friends and neighbors.

In 1774, Nelson represented York in the House of Burgesses. This House passed strong resolutions against the Boston Port Bill and was dissolved by the Royal Governor, Lord Dunmore. Nelson was one of the eighty-nine members who met the following day at Raleigh Tavern in Williamsburg, to protest the unwarranted invasion of their rights and recommend the appointment of deputies to meet in a general congress. Re-elected to the next House of Burgesses, Nelson was a member of the first general Virginia convention which met at Williamsburg on August 1, 1774, and chose seven delegates to attend the First Continental Congress—Richard Bland, Benjamin Harrison, Edmund Pendleton, Patrick Henry, Richard Henry Lee, George Washington and Peyton Randolph. The latter was elected president of Congress.

A member of the second convention of March, 1775, held in the old church in Richmond, Nelson supported Patrick Henry's resolution that Virginia "be immediately put into a state of defence," and a military force be organized. This was the occasion of Henry's famous and prophetic words, quoted in the Prologue: "The war has actually begun. The next gale that sweeps from the north will bring to our ears the clash of resounding arms. Why stand we here idle? . . . Is life so dear or peace so sweet as to be purchased at the price of chains and slavery? Forbid it, Almighty God! I know not what course others may take, but as for me, give me liberty or give me death!"

Less than a month later, the Battles of Lexington and Concord took place, and on April 20, before news of the "shot heard round the world" reached Virginia, the Governor seized the powder in the Williamsburg magazine. The militia, under Patrick Henry, quickly marched on the capitol, and while Nelson tried to protect Governor Dunmore, who had promised satisfaction, a party of British landed at York from the *Fowey,* a man-of-war, and threatened Nelson's uncle, who was secretary of the Council. They delivered a letter from the captain which stated that the town would be fired upon if harm came to the Governor. The same day, in Williamsburg, three hundred and twenty pounds was paid for the powder, and soon afterward the Governor and his family took refuge on board the *Fowey.*

At the convention at Richmond in July, Patrick Henry was elected colonel of the first regiment and Thomas Nelson, Jr., colonel of the second. On August 11, Nelson and George Wythe were elected delegates to Congress in place of Patrick

Henry and General George Washington, now Commander-in-Chief of the American army.

Thomas Nelson, Jr., and George Wythe took their seats in Congress on September 13, and John Adams sizes them up in his diary entry of the fifteenth as follows: "Nelson is a fat man, like the late Colonel Lee of Marblehead. He is a speaker, and alert and lively for his weight. Wythe is a lawyer, it is said, of the first eminence." And to his Abigail, Adams wrote that Nelson, Wythe and also Lee (Francis Lightfoot) were the new delegates from Virginia: "Wythe and Lee are inoculated. You shall hear more about them. Although they come in the room of very good men, we have lost nothing by the change, I believe."

In early 1776 Nelson expressed his views in a letter to John Page, wishing he knew the sentiments of his constituents "upon the grand points of confederation and foreign alliance, or in other words, independence," and commented on the absurdity of supposing that "we can have any affection for a people who are carrying on the most savage war against us." To the same correspondent, he wrote: "Independence, confederation and foreign alliance are as formidable to some of the congress, I fear a majority, as an apparition to a weak, enervated woman. . . ."

Nelson was present when, on May 6, forty-five members of the House of Burgesses reconvened in Williamsburg and unanimously dissolved the Assembly. The same day the general convention of delegates assumed authority, meeting at the capitol. On the fourteenth, the Convention took into consideration the state of the colony, and Nelson moved for independence.

Edmund Randolph wrote that, when the feeling of the people could not be mistaken, "(Patrick) Henry had full indulgence of his own private judgment, and he concerted with Nelson that he (Nelson) should introduce the question of independence, and that Henry should enforce it. Nelson affected nothing of oratory, except what ardent feelings might inspire, and characteristic of himself, he had no fears of his own with which to temporize . . ." Supposing others to have none either, Nelson passed over the questions of foreign aid, procurement of military supplies and inexperience of the army and pressed for independence on what were to him "incontrovertible grounds." At first Henry did not commit himself, apparently not wanting to put responsibility for the act on his eloquence. Then, "aroused by the now apparent spirit of the people," he began to speak for the motion. "As a pillar of fire, which notwithstanding the darkness of the prospect which would conduct to the promised land, he inflamed, and was followed by the convention."

Nelson's "rough resolution," considered to be the first one in Henry's handwriting, was changed and then passed the next day.

Colonel Nelson rode off, bearing the independence instructions to Congress—as Patrick Henry wrote to John Adams (from whom he had received a copy of *Thoughts on Government*)— "Before this reaches you, the resolution for finally separating from Britain will be handed to Congress by Colonel Nelson. I put up with it in the present form for the sake of unanimity. 'Tis not quite so pointed as I could wish . . . Our Convention is now employed in the great work of forming a constitution." Wishing that John and Samuel Adams were there, Henry concludes, ". . . may God preserve you, and give you every good thing," and then adds a postscript, "Will you and S. A. now and then write?"

When the resolution was laid before Congress by Colonel Nelson, General Washington was in Philadelphia, having been summoned by Congress to consult over the impending military crisis. He was delighted with the action of his colony and wrote to his brother, John Augustine, enthusiastically about it, as quoted in the Prologue.

Following the instructions of the Virginia Convention,

Richard Henry Lee moved for independence in Congress on June 7. Thomas Nelson, Jr., with the other Virginia delegates present in Philadelphia, voted for independence on July 2, and for their fellow delegate's Declaration on the fourth.

John Page, president of the Council of Virginia, wrote to Hancock on July 20, acknowledging receipt of the copy of the Declaration sent to Virginia and saying that the people "have been impatiently expecting it, and will receive it with joy." And it was proclaimed in Williamsburg on July 25, to the cheers of the people and firing of cannon and musketry.

Nelson signed the Declaration on August 2 and served on the committee to prepare the plan for confederation. He was forced to withdraw from Congress in May, 1777, because of illness. In August, on the approach of the British fleet, he was appointed a brigadier-general and commander-in-chief of the state forces, but Virginia was spared this possible invasion, as Howe's fleet sailed on up Chesapeake Bay to take Philadelphia.

The following spring, in response to an appeal of Congress for volunteer troops of light cavalry, "to serve at their own expense," except for provisions and forage, General Nelson raised a company of about seventy men. This company marched to Philadelphia, with General Nelson serving as their commanding officer—and their banker too, advancing substantial sums of money. On August 8, as recorded in the *Journal of Congress,* the company was disbanded, owing to the enemy withdrawal, and the thanks of Congress were given to General Nelson and his volunteers for "their brave, generous and patriotic efforts in the cause of their country."

In 1779, while he was again in Congress, illness forced Nelson to retire for a second time, but he worked to organize the militia to repel a British marauding expedition. Early in June, 1780, the Virginia Assembly called for $2,000,000, to be placed in the Continental treasury, to provide for the

French fleet. General Nelson personally attempted to raise the money but the constant reply to his appeals was, "We will not lend the government a shilling—but we will lend you, Thomas Nelson, all we can possibly raise." On his personal security he raised the larger part of the loan. He was subsequently forced to redeem this at a very great sacrifice, and the government never recompensed him for his loss. On another occasion he advanced his own funds to pay two regiments which had been ordered to the south and refused to march until their arrears were discharged.

In June, 1781, Nelson was elected Governor of Virginia, whose lands were exposed that year to coastal raids by Arnold and Phillips and overrun from the south by Cornwallis' troops. At the siege of Yorktown, Nelson commanded the Virginia militia under General Lafayette. Observing that his own house was unharmed, he asked the cause. On being advised that it was because the mansion was his property, he immediately had the fire directed on it, as he knew it to be occupied by important British officers. The first cannon shot went right through the house.

General Nelson did everything in his power, personal and public, to aid the allied armies and following the surrender of Cornwallis, General Washington, in the orders of the day for October 20, stated:

"The general would be guilty of the highest ingratitude . . . if he forgot to return his sincere acknowledgments to his excellency governor Nelson, for the succours which he received from him and the militia under his command, to whose activity, emulation and bravery, the highest praises are due."

Nelson resigned as Governor of Virginia in November, owing to his poor health. His fortune spent for his country, he lived at "Offly," in Hanover County, in moderate circumstances until his death in 1789. In his *Travels Through America,* the Marquis de Chastellux writes of visiting General Nelson, whom he had known during the Yorktown campaign. This great American Patriot was described by his French ally as conducting himself at that critical moment "with the courage of a brave soldier, and the zeal of a good citizen." He was buried in an unmarked grave at Yorktown.

A sketch of Nelson by Colonel Innis tells of his distinguished career, strongly marked by "true religion," and quotes Shakespeare, in concluding, "This was a man."

George Wythe, who became "one of our best men," was born in 1726, in the county of Elizabeth City, Virginia. His father was a prosperous planter and his mother was extremely well educated. With her teaching and assistance, George became an accomplished Latin and Greek scholar, and also studied grammar, rhetoric and logic.

After a brief attendance at the College of William and Mary, he took up law with Stephen Dewey in Prince George County. At twenty George was admitted to the bar and began to practice as an associate of John Lewis, an attorney of Spotsylvania County. He married Lewis' sister Ann in 1747 but she died the following year.

Wythe, in his sorrow, turned to dissipation and wasted his time for a few years. In his thirtieth year he reformed and lived an exemplary life for his remaining fifty years. His older brother died in 1755 and from him George inherited a large estate.

Wythe was early elected to the House of Burgesses and served until after the Revolution began. In November, 1764, he was on the committee which prepared a petition to the King, a memorial to the House of Lords and a remonstrance to the House of Commons on the proposed Stamp Act. Wythe drew up the last paper, which was so bold that it was viewed as bordering on treason and was accepted only after much modification. The following spring, Henry's famous resolutions protesting the Act, now passed by Parliament, were published throughout the Colonies. During the debates, when accused of being too daring, Henry spoke out: "If this be treason—then make the most of it." Wythe and others had opposed the resolutions as being too advanced. They felt that the papers of the preceding session had already expressed their views and that an answer to them could still be expected.

Resolutions passed in 1769 by the House of Burgesses, asserting Virginia's rights, caused the Governor to dissolve the House, but the same members, including Wythe, were re-elected with very few exceptions.

When Wythe came to the Continental Congress in September, 1775, he joined a famous pupil—Thomas Jefferson, elected on March 27, had been his law student and was introduced to the bar under his auspices.

In the debates on the resolution of October 6, recommending the arrest of those persons who endangered the "liberties of America," Wythe argued that such a step (including attempted seizure of Lord Dunmore, who had been terrorizing the coast of Virginia) would not affect friends in England. Every man in Great Britain, he said, would already be convinced that the colonists aimed at independence, by hearing of the Battle of Lexington and other events from the ministry and parliament.

John Adams tells that, in January, 1776, "Mr. Wythe, of Virginia, passed an evening with me, at my chambers. In the course of conversation upon the necessity of independence, Mr. Wythe, observing that the greatest obstacle, in the way of a declaration of it, was the difficulty of agreeing upon a government for our future regulation, I replied that each colony should form a government for itself, as a free and independent State. 'Well,' said Mr. Wythe, 'what plan would you institute or advise for any one of the States?'" Adams explained his ideas (he had written a letter on this subject to Richard Henry Lee on November 15, 1775) and Wythe re-

quested him to put all this down in writing, which Adams
did, sending it to Wythe in the form of a letter. Lee, on
reading this, asked that it be published, which it was under
the title of *Thoughts on Government, in a letter from a
gentleman to his Friend.*

As shown by the diary of Richard Smith, Wythe "also offered Propositions whereof the first was that the Colonies
have a Right to contract Alliances with Foreign Powers, an
objection being offered that this was Independency there
ensued much argument upon that Ground." In the debates
on opening the ports, Wythe declared: "If we should offer
our trade to the Court of France, would they take any notice
of it any more than if Bristol or Liverpool should offer theirs,
while we profess to be subjects? No. We must declare ourselves a free people."

The "violents" struggled on. In March, Smith's diary tells
that Wythe reported to Congress the "Preamble about Privateering," and Wythe and Lee proposed an amendment in
which the King was made "the Author of our Miseries instead of the Ministry . . ." As mentioned before, this was
opposed by Wilson and others on the grounds that it would
sever the King from the colonists forever and was debated
for four hours, when Maryland "interposed its Veto" and put
it off until the next day.

In his notes about the June debates on Lee's independence
resolution, Jefferson accords Wythe a prominent place. Regarding the motion itself he wrote: "It was urged by J.
Adams, (R. H.) Lee, Wythe and others . . ."

George Wythe left for Virginia, taking with him Jefferson's plan for the new government of Virginia. At the Convention, Wythe showed Jefferson's plan to those who had
"the chief hand" in the new plans already presented to the
Convention. Jefferson sent a draft of the Declaration of Independence to George Wythe. This is now in the New York
Public Library.

Wythe must have added his signature to the Declaration on parchment in September, as he did not return to Congress until the fourteenth of that month. In Rush's sketches of the Signers, Wythe is described as, "A profound lawyer and able politician. He seldom spoke in Congress, but when he did his speeches were sensible, correct, and pertinent. I have seldom known a man possess more modesty, or a more dove-like simplicity and gentleness of manner. He lived many years after he left Congress, the pride and ornament of his native State."

In November, 1776, Wythe was appointed by the Virginia Legislature to a committee to revise the state laws. The other members were Thomas Jefferson, Edmund Pendleton and two more, George Mason and Thomas Ludwell Lee, who did not serve. By June, 1779, one hundred twenty-six bills were prepared. Speaker of the house of delegates in 1777, Wythe was chosen the same year as one of the three judges of the Chancery Court of Virginia. On a reorganization, he became sole chancellor and held this post for more than twenty years.

Having lost almost everything he owned during the Revolution, Wythe supplemented his small income as chancellor by accepting the professorship of law at William and Mary College in 1779, teaching there for ten years. In 1783 he wrote to John Adams that he was helping "to form such characters as may be fit to succede those which have been ornamental and useful in the national councils of America. Adieu."

He resigned this post in 1789, as his judiciary work made it necessary for him to move to Richmond. In 1787 he served in the federal Constitutional Convention, but he did not sign the Constitution.

In the latter part of his life George Wythe freed his slaves, furnishing them with support until they could take care of themselves. In his eighty-first year, he was fatally poisoned, but no one was convicted of the crime. His great-nephew was tried for the murder but was acquitted.

Wythe left no descendants. Although he was married twice, his only child died in infancy. But he was well represented by his distinguished law students, including two presidents of the United States, Jefferson and Monroe, and Chief Justice Marshall.

Thomas Jefferson, one of these law pupils and a devoted adherent, made notes in 1821 for a biography of Wythe, which was never completed. In these notes Jefferson said: "No man ever left behind him a character more venerated than George Wythe. His virtue was of the purest tint; his integrity inflexible, and his justice exact; of warm patriotism, and devoted as he was to liberty, and the natural and equal rights of man, he might truly be called the Cato of his country . . . Such was George Wythe, the honour of his own, and model of future times."

Richard Henry Lee *1732–1794*

THE GREAT MOMENT of Richard Henry Lee's life, when he arose in Congress on June 7, 1776, to propose the independence resolutions, is scantily reported in the *Journal of Congress*. "It will naturally be inquired," John Adams wrote in his *Autobiography*, "why these resolutions, and the names of the gentlemen who moved and seconded them, were not inserted on the Journals. To this question, I can give no other answer than this, Mr. Hancock was President, Mr. Harrison, chairman of the committee of the whole house, Mr. Thomson the secretary, was cousin to Mr. Dickinson, and Mr. R. H. Lee and Mr. John Adams were no favorites of either."

For a free America, Lee was sacrificing his life, his fortune and the sacred honor of a family of extraordinary standing in the Colonies. Behind him were three generations of wealthy tobacco plantation owners, whose right to sit on the Council of Virginia was almost hereditary. Thomas Lee, President of Virginia (president of the Council) and afterward acting governor, was Richard Henry's father and the founder of the "Stratford" line, named for Stratford Hall, built by Thomas. John Adams described this branch of the Virginia Lees as "having more men of merit in it than any other family."

Thomas Lee's wife was Hannah Ludwell, whose grandfather, Colonel Philip Ludwell, had been twice expelled from the Council for opposing the royal governor. Her mother was a James River Harrison, of the family which was later to produce two Presidents of the United States.

At Stratford, built on the Potomac about 1725 and named for an English estate of the first Richard Lee, Thomas and Hannah brought up their six sons and two daughters. The building in which the sons received their early education is still standing—a little red brick cabin. A Scottish clergyman, Mr. Craig, was their schoolmaster and preceptor of behavior. Lessons began at seven for "one round" of the classroom before breakfast. With time out for dinner at two, instruction continued until five o'clock, accompanied by Bible readings. Four of the brothers, Philip Ludwell, Thomas Ludwell, Richard Henry and Arthur, supplemented their Stratford education with several years of study in England but Francis Lightfoot (later a Signer, with Richard Henry) and William had all their mental and part of their religious training at the plantation school.

From his twelfth to his nineteenth year, Richard Henry Lee attended an academy in Wakefield, England, established by Queen Elizabeth in 1592. He and his brothers Philip and Thomas were called back to Virginia in 1750 by the death of their father, the latter two becoming guardians of their younger brothers, to rear them "religiously and virtuously."

Richard Henry rented out the land he had inherited in Fauquier County and lived for ten years with his brother Philip in bachelor hall at Stratford, studying and enjoying a gay social round. Only one occupation appealed to him —public office. Preparing for service in the Virginia government was a tradition among the leading planter families and Richard Henry Lee was an outstanding example of the Virginia school of statesmanship. His notebook, in which he recorded comments of his favorite thinkers on government—Montesqieu and John Locke—is preserved in the Library of the University of Virginia.

His chance to enter public life came in 1757, at his election to the Virginia House of Burgesses, which met at Williamsburg. The other Westmoreland burgess was his cousin, "Squire" Richard of Lee Hall. His brother, Philip Ludwell Lee, had their father's seat on the Council, and two other brothers, Francis Lightfoot of Loudoun and Thomas Ludwell of Stafford, later served as well.

As Richard Henry Lee's abilities as an orator and legislator grew, he was dubbed a "Cicero." His gestures were so graceful that Edmund Pendleton is said to have accused the "harmonious Richard Henry Lee" of practicing before a mirror! In 1759 he made a speech in opposition to slavery, proposing "to lay so heavy a duty on the importation of slaves, as effectually to put an end to that iniquitous and disgraceful traffic within the colony of Virginia." This was a dangerous subject at that time and Lee's first sentence prophetically advised the House of Burgesses that, since the consequences of the debate "will greatly affect posterity, as well as ourselves, it surely merits our serious attention." And a century later, Robert E. Lee, born at Stratford and descended from Richard Henry's uncle, Henry Lee, *was* "greatly affected." Opposed to slavery himself, he was called upon to command the Confederate Army in the War between the States.

Later, Richard Henry Lee instigated an investigation to expose irregularities in the Virginia treasury. This promptly enhanced his standing with the popular party which had grown up in western Virginia and brought him in close association with Patrick Henry, but it also had important, far-reaching consequences that followed him on into the national scene.

Quick to see the danger to the Colonies in the Grenville tax program of 1763-64, Richard Henry Lee wrote to a friend in England in May, protesting that it was illegal under the British constitution to be taxed without representation. The acts of the royal government, designed to secure the dependence of the Colonies, he continued, might lead to independence instead.

Late in 1764, the House of Burgesses forwarded protests against the proposed Stamp Act to London. The petitions to the King and the House of Lords were written by Lee. Francis Fauquier, the royal governor, pronounced the protests "warm and indecent."

In the interim between the news of the passage of the Stamp Act and its enforcement on November 1, 1765, Richard Henry Lee became a fiery Son of Liberty. He said that Parliament "may take from me one shilling in the pound," to pay for the protection of the Colonies, "but what security have I for the other nineteen?" With Patrick Henry, he now became the leader of the Whigs.

At the end of February, 1766, an anti-Stamp Act Compact, called the Westmoreland Resolutions, was signed by more than a hundred well-known men, including its author, Richard Henry Lee. There was at least one signer from most of the great families on Virginia's Northern Neck. The Washingtons had four! The Act was repealed in March, 1766, but the landed aristocracy was ready to resent further attacks on colonial "liberties."

Of Richard Henry Lee, delegate to the First Continental Congress, Silas Deane of Connecticut wrote: "Col. Lee is said to be his (Patrick Henry's) equal in eloquence and in Virginia and to the southward they are styled the Demosthenes and Cicero of America. God grant they may not, like them, plead in vain for the liberties of their country."

Lee's years of oratory in the Virginia House made him a very polished speaker, and St. George Tucker felt sometimes that he was listening to "some being inspired with more than mortal powers of embellishment." But these years had also brought hardship to Lee. Established on a modest plantation, Chantilly, on the Potomac, about three miles from Stratford, he had not been very successful. His health was poor. His first wife, Ann Aylett Lee, had died in 1768, leaving four young children. At forty-two, his reddish hair unstreaked with gray, slim and six feet tall, he devoted himself tirelessly to the Patriot cause. His left hand, injured in an accident and swathed in a black handkerchief, quickly became a feature of Congress as it was used to gesticulate.

The Virginia delegates to the First Continental Congress were a distinguished group, Peyton Randolph (the President), Benjamin Harrison, Edmund Pendleton, George Washington, Richard Bland, and Patrick Henry, besides Richard Henry Lee.

In his initial speech before Congress in Carpenters' Hall, Patrick Henry said, "The distinctions between Virginians, Pennsylvanians, New Yorkers, and New Englanders, are no more. I am not a Virginian, but an American." Richard Henry Lee was one of the first members to address the body. His speech was on the advanced side, too.

The Adams-Lee association was very close and the two New Englanders and Lee worked zealously with other patriotic souls—including Roger Sherman, Patrick Henry of Virginia and Christopher Gadsden of South Carolina.

About the boycott of British goods, Lee felt "certain that the same ship which carried home the resolution will bring back the redress." With the two Adamses, he helped to draw up a Declaration of Rights. Then he was appointed chairman to prepare a petition to the King but his composition was too incendiary, so John Dickinson was added to the committee and he rewrote the paper. It was presented to the court by Franklin and Lee's brother Arthur, whose letters kept his brothers and other leaders informed on British sentiment.

"For my part," Richard Henry Lee wrote years later, "I must cease to live before I cease to love these proud Patriots with whom I early toiled in the vineyard of liberty." But thoughts of independence were abhorrent to the conservative majority, who were anxious for reconciliation.

Not at all discouraged, Richard Henry Lee felt that the grievances would be redressed. On leaving the First Continental Congress, his parting words to John Adams were: "We shall infallibly carry all our points. You will be completely relieved; all the offensive acts will be repealed—" But Britain did not give up her "foolish project," as he hoped.

At the Second Continental Congress, the Lee-Adams junto fought on. Patrick Henry's return to his home was a great loss to the Virginia faction but the delegation was joined by Thomas Jefferson, Francis Lightfoot Lee, and George Wythe, a reliable Patriot.

During the months preceding the Declaration, Richard Henry Lee was of vital importance to the independence party, but he was not popular with all Virginians, and Benjamin Harrison, who continued to feel that the country's best chance lay in reconciliation on honorable terms, seemed to be set up in determined opposition to him. "These feelings among the Virginia delegates were a great injury to us," John Adams recounts. "Mr. Samuel Adams and myself were very intimate with Mr. Lee, and he agreed perfectly with us in the great system of our policy, and by his means we kept a majority of the delegates of Virginia with us; but Harrison, Pendleton, and some others, showed their jealousy of this intimacy plainly enough at times. Harrison consequently courted Mr. Hancock . . ."

On May 9, the new government resolution was introduced "in concert between" Richard Henry Lee and John Adams, enabling the "forward men" to catch a fleeting glimpse of the "promised land." The Patriots complained that the "moderates" stalled in Congress, wasting time on trifles and matters of "frivolous importance."

Richard Henry Lee was appointed on the committee to prepare the preamble of the hotly contested measure on new governments, but he and the other member, Mr. Rutledge, named John Adams as penman, only stipulating that he "draw something short," as told before.

The day this preamble passed in Congress the Virginia House acted upon a suggestion Lee had made in a letter to Williamsburg. "You ask why we hesitate in Congress. I'll tell you . . . because we are heavily clogged with instructions from these shameful Proprietary people and this will continue till Virginia sets the example of taking up government and sending peremptory orders to their delegates to pursue the most effectual measures for the Security of America."

Virginia obliged with the independence resolutions which Lee moved in Congress. It was usual that the mover of a measure be appointed chairman and draftsman of the committee to carry it into execution but Lee was not even appointed a member of the body to prepare the Declaration.

The answer to this puzzling action is given by John Adams. Some say Lee had to withdraw from Congress due to the illness of his wife. Also, he stated in a letter that he had left Philadelphia because he wanted to be at Williamsburg to take part in the formation of the new Virginia government. But Adams maintained it was because of Lee's unpopularity with his Virginia colleagues that he was excluded.

Jefferson was chosen in preference to Harrison of the "cold" party and on July 8 he sent Lee a copy of the Declaration as he had originally written it and one as altered by Congress. Lee commiserated with the author on the changes made in the document by the delegates. Referring in particular to the disapproval of the denunciation of the slave trade, Lee's letter continued, "However the *Thing* in its nature is so good, that no Cookery can spoil the Dish for the palates of Freemen." He signed the letter "your affectionate friend," so dispelling any thought that he held a grudge against his close colleague for what must have been a crushing disappointment.

Richard Henry Lee served as a member of the Virginia House of Representatives in 1777 and again three years later. He supported the action of Virginia in ceding her title to the Northwest Territory to the federal government, maintaining that this area would provide land from which future states could be carved. He insisted that the Newfoundland fisheries and the navigation of the Mississippi from mouth to source be included in the Treaty of Peace. "These, sir, are the strong legs on which North America can alone walk securely in Independence," he wrote.

In 1784 Lee was again elected to Congress and went to serve at Trenton, New Jersey, although suffering from painful attacks of gout. In January the meeting place was changed to New York. Instead of choosing a president by state rotation, the members of Congress elected Richard Henry Lee President as the one most worthy of the position.

"President of Congress" was the top post in the United States and Lee entered into the dignity and prominence of his office with a revived vigor. The "old President," he commented, "has been converted into a young beau." His wardrobe became of great importance because of the entertaining expected of the head of the nation.

In 1787 the Northwest Ordinance and the Constitutional Convention at Philadelphia were giving Congress concern when Lee, racked with pain, returned to New York in July to attend the session of the governing body. He was largely responsible for the sound money principles and the veto on slavery north of the Ohio contained in the Northwest Ordinance.

Although strongly opposed to the adoption of the Federal Constitution without certain safeguards which he proposed, he accepted the nomination as senator from Virginia and so was one of the first pair of men to serve from that state.

The campaign for the ten amendments or Bill of Rights was Richard Henry Lee's last service to his country. When these were part of the Constitution he retired to his plantation, Chantilly. His home was an unpretentious wooden building, situated on a point, with one of the most beautiful views of the Potomac River. There he enjoyed the activities of his daughters. Mary married William Augustine Washington, General George Washington's nephew; Hannah, Corbin Washington, another nephew of the General; and Anne, her cousin Charles Lee, who became United States Attorney-General. Sarah Lee, a daughter of Lee's second wife—as was Anne—married her cousin, Edmund Jennings Lee. The Signer's son's wife was Flora Lee, sister of the "divine Matilda," whose husband was "Light Horse Harry" Lee. Richard Henry Lee died in 1794 and was buried near his loved home.

Chantilly is in ruins today, but the spirit and vision of its original owner have lived on, to be felt out over the Potomac, out across the Northwest Territory to the very shores of the Pacific, as part of the American dream—the same American dream of freedom to enjoy God-given rights which had brought the first Richard Lee to the Atlantic coast—once known as Virginia, from Nova Scotia to Florida.

Benjamin Harrison *1726–1791*

Bᴇɴᴊᴀᴍɪɴ ʜᴀʀʀɪsᴏɴ, "still counted among the cold party," as John Adams, his political opponent in early 1776, tells in his *Autobiography* under date of February 29, "was represented to be a kind of *nexus utriusque mundi,* a corner stone in which the two walls of party met in Virginia. He was descended from one of the most ancient, wealthy, and respectable families in the ancient dominion, and seemed to be set up in opposition to Mr. Richard Henry Lee." In American history, as a James River Harrison, Benjamin represents the transition from the aristocratic oligarchy of the colony to the republican Harrisons of the Republic, two of whom rose to the highest office in the land. His son, William Henry Harrison, became the ninth President, and his great-grandson, Benjamin Harrison, the twenty-third President of the United States.

Benjamin Harrison, of the third generation in the Colonies, settled at "Berkeley," in Charles City County, Virginia, on the James River, opposite Surry, where the original Harrison immigrant had lived. He increased the family estate and at his death was Speaker of the House of Burgesses. His son, Benjamin, married Anne, the daughter of Robert Carter of Corotoman, called "King Carter" because of his wealth and influence. They had a family of ten children of whom the eldest son was Benjamin, the Signer. One of their daughters married Peyton Randolph, President of the Continental Congress.

The Signer was born in the family mansion, Berkeley, in 1726. He went to the College of William and Mary but did not graduate, owing to his father's early death, when the management of the estate fell upon him. He was elected to the House of Burgesses, in which he served for many terms.

In November, 1764, he was a member of the committee which drew up the firm protests against the proposed Stamp Act. In 1774 he was a delegate to the First Continental Congress and he was present in Carpenters' Hall on the opening day when his brother-in-law, Peyton Randolph, was chosen president. John Adams had met Colonel Harrison and some of his colleagues the Friday before and records in his diary for that day: "These gentlemen from Virginia appear to be the most spirited and consistent of any. Harrison said he would have come on foot rather than not come. Bland said he would have gone . . . if it had been to Jericho."

At the second Virginia Convention in March, 1775, Harrison opposed Henry's resolutions to put the colony into a "posture of defence." But on their passage by a majority of five, he was appointed one of the committee of twelve to carry them into effect.

Early in May, Harrison went to Philadelphia for the Second Congress. He shared a house with two of his colleagues, George Washington and Peyton Randolph. When Randolph returned to Virginia and Hancock was elected president of Congress, it is told that the latter hesitated to take the presidential seat. Mr. Harrison, standing beside him, good-humoredly placed him in the chair.

Mr. Harrison served on many committees, including that chosen to put the militia in a proper state for the defense of America, and the one on the Continental Army. He was also chairman of the secret committee appointed "for the sole purpose of corresponding with our friends" abroad.

In his *Autobiography*, John Adams tells of the delaying tactics used by the then majority of those in Congress "who were either determined against all measures preparatory to independence, or yet too timorous and wavering to venture on any decisive steps." Adams recounts that around General Washington's headquarters there were some who were "weak and wavering" and that the General had chosen a fellow Virginian, Harrison of the "cold party," as his private confidential correspondent in Congress. "This (Harrison) was an indolent, luxurious, heavy gentleman, of no use in Congress or committee, but a great embarrassment to both."

Rush's sketch of Harrison fills in the background further —and a little more flatteringly: "He was well acquainted with the forms of public business. He had strong State prejudices, and was very hostile to the leading characters from the New England States. In private life he preferred pleasure and convivial company to business of all kinds . . . He was upon the whole a useful member of Congress and sincerely devoted to the welfare of his country."

A new Virginia delegate, Carter Braxton, elected in place of Peyton Randolph, who had died, took his seat in Congress on February 23. Of him Rush says: "He was not deficient in political information, but was suspected of being less detached than he should be from his British prejudices. He was a decent, agreeable and sensible speaker, and in private life an accomplished gentleman." He also had strong anti-New England prejudices, according to Rush. Regarding Braxton's selection as a delegate, Joseph Reed wrote to Washington on March 15: "It is said the Virginians are so alarmed with the Idea of Independence that they have sent Mr. Braxton on Purpose to turn the Vote of that Colony, if any Question on that Subject should come before Congress."

Carter Braxton was born in September, 1736, in King and

Queen County, Virginia, and inherited large estates from his father. His mother, who died when he was seven days old, was Mary Carter Braxton, daughter of Robert Carter, "King Carter," president of the King's Council in 1726. Young Braxton was educated at William and Mary. Left with two small daughters after the early death of his first wife, Braxton lived in England for over two years. On his return, he married Elizabeth Corbin, daughter of the King's receiver-general of taxes. As members of the Tidewater aristocracy, the family lived in great state on his plantations. By this marriage, Braxton had sixteen children, six of whom died in infancy.

Braxton first went to the House of Burgesses in 1761 and he served for many terms. When Patrick Henry marched on Williamsburg in reprisal for the Governor's taking the colony's powder on April 20, 1775, Braxton interceded and obtained from his father-in-law, the receiver-general, a bill on Philadelphia sufficient for reimbursement for the seized powder. He was one of eleven members of the Committee of Safety appointed by the General Convention of Virginia, and later he was elected to the Second Continental Congress.

After signing the Declaration, Braxton returned to Virginia. Although left out of the delegation to the Continental Congress due to his unpopular views on government, he was elected to Virginia's first House of Representatives under the state constitution. He was chairman of the committee on religion, and a member of others, including that on trade. In 1785 he supported Jefferson's Act for Religious Freedom in Virginia. He also served his state as a member of the Council for many years. His great fortune was swept away during the war when his vessels were captured by the enemy, and lost in unfortunate commercial enterprises. Debts due him were worthless in the depreciated currency and he became involved in endless litigation, into which his sons-in-law were drawn. Sunk under his misfortunes, he died in 1797.

In his *Autobiography*, John Adams told of his disappointment when Benjamin Harrison was first made chairman of the committee of the whole by President Hancock in March, 1776, in place of a staunch "violent," Governor Ward of Rhode Island. Ward became fatally ill with smallpox about this time, but Adams attributes his being superseded to the influence of Harrison and John Dickinson's "moderate" party, to whom Ward had become "obnoxious" because of his "zealous attachment" to Samuel Adams and Richard Henry Lee. Realizing that Harrison would often have the chairmanship of this important committee, Adams treated him with uniform politeness.

Although he was a "moderate," Harrison is listed in Richard Smith's diary as being one of the chief speakers for the amendment to the Privateering Preamble offered by Lee and Wythe, which named the British King as the author of the colonists' troubles instead of the Ministry. When the Privateering resolve was passed, Harrison became chairman of the committee to carry it into effect. John Adams wrote to Gates that day, ". . . for the future We are likely to wage three Quarters of a War," as quoted in the Prologue.

Regarding the choice of a chairman for the committee to prepare the Declaration of Independence, Adams explains in his *Autobiography* that the "violents" had decided on Jefferson, excluding Lee in order to "keep out" Harrison.

As chairman of the committee of the whole, Harrison reported the independence resolutions to Congress, and also the Declaration. And he and Braxton signed the Declaration on August 2.

The anecdote about the hanging scene described in the chapter on Elbridge Gerry must have been based on the disproved theory that a general signing took place on July 4.

Actually, Gerry was absent on August 2, and before he returned to Congress Harrison had gone home because he and Braxton had been "left out" as delegates to Congress at the state election in June. Among the explanations offered for their being dropped were the unpopularity of a political appointment attributed to Harrison and an address on government by Braxton. Another reason advanced was that it was an economy measure to reduce the delegation from seven to five. Still another suggests itself—the "forward" men were all re-elected.

Benjamin Harrison, omitted from the Virginia delegation to Philadelphia, was elected a councilor of the state in June, 1776, under the constitution. He wrote to Robert Morris that he did not even have a "Wish to return again into Public Business, except such as arise from Friendship."

On the resignation of Jefferson, Harrison was again elected to Congress. He was restored to his former positions, including the Board of War, of which he had been one of the five original members. Toward the end of 1777, Harrison retired from Congress and returned to Virginia.

He took his seat in the House of Delegates there and then was chosen Speaker, holding this office until late in 1781. He served three terms as Governor and at his death in 1791 was in the House of Representatives.

Colonel Harrison's wife was Elizabeth Bassett Harrison, related to Mrs. Washington's sister. They had a numerous family, of whom three sons and four daughters reached maturity. The Colonel also had two special pets, a small spaniel and a large cat! As was so often the case with the Signers, his fortune was greatly impaired and his estates were damaged during the war.

As a member of the Virginia Convention of 1788 which ratified the Federal Constitution, Harrison felt that the adoption of a bill of rights should precede, not follow, ratification. When overruled, he gave the Constitution his firm support and helped persuade other members who were pressing for immediate changes to use the Constitutional methods for obtaining amendments. Fifty-three years later, the Signer's third son, William Henry Harrison, the hero of Tippecanoe, took his oath of office as President, swearing to uphold the Constitution. To this had been added the Bill of Rights—which listed other "unalienable rights" given all men "by their Creator."

Thomas Jefferson *1743–1826*

THOMAS JEFFERSON, whose "masterly pen" wrote the original draft of the Declaration of Independence, had a distinguished and varied career—statesman, scientist, architect, inventor, author, educator, and builder of the Republic. Rush's Signer sketch tells us that Jefferson "possessed a genius of the first order. It was universal in its objects. He was not less distinguished for his political, than his mathematical and philosophical knowledge. . . . He seldom spoke in Congress, but was a member of all the important committees. He was the penman of the Declaration of Independence. He once showed me the original in his own handwriting. It contained a noble testimony against Negro slavery which was struck out in its passage through Congress. . . ."

Jefferson was born at "Shadwell," Albemarle County, Virginia, April 13, 1743, the son of Peter Jefferson, a surveyor to whom is accredited the first map of Virginia, and his wife, Jane Randolph Jefferson, daughter of Isham Randolph of the landed aristocracy. The Jeffersons were of the yeomanry, small independent farmers and landholders who had pushed on into Piedmont when slavery created the large plantations of the Tidewater. In Jefferson's *Autobiography,* written in 1821, he tells of a family tradition that the first Jefferson in this country came from Wales. The Randolphs, the writer continued, trace their ancestry far back in England and Scotland, "to which let everyone ascribe the faith and merit he chooses."

Self-taught himself, Peter Jefferson was anxious that his son have a good education. When Thomas was two years old, the family moved to Tuckahoe, elegant estate of the Randolphs on the James River. Peter had been chosen guardian of Thomas Mann Randolph, a minor, and supervisor of the estate. Baby Thomas Jefferson was carried on a pillow by a slave on horseback to Tuckahoe where he lived mostly for seven years. At five he went to an English school and at nine to a Latin school where his teacher was a Scotch clergyman named Douglas, who along with the rudiments of the Latin and Greek languages, taught the boy French.

About this time the Jefferson family moved their headquarters back to Shadwell again. There young Thomas had free range of his father's library. He pored over the Bible, Shakespeare and the works of Swift, Addison and Steele. Peter Jefferson also made sure that his son knew the ways of the forest and could hunt and fish. In these days the boy also met the many Indians who stopped at Shadwell and became their friend.

On the death of his father in 1757, young Jefferson studied for two years with the Reverend Maury, "a correct classical scholar" and Whig clergyman, who had come to Virginia to tutor the Monroe family. Thomas was a good student but he had a tendency to put off mastering his lessons. When the situation became serious, he would persuade other boys to apply for a holiday, and he would go into retirement until he was letter-perfect in the neglected work. Then he would triumphantly rejoin his class.

In March, 1760, Jefferson entered the College of William and Mary at Williamsburg and visitors today to the former Virginia capital can picture his life there. He studied at the college located at one end of town, was a favorite guest at the Governor's Palace at about the center and frequented the Capitol building at the other end of the main street. He wrote that it was his great good fortune and the circumstance that probably "fixed the destinies" of his life that Dr. William Small of Scotland, then professor of mathematics, became his friend and daily companion. Small gave him his first understanding of the range of science and the system of the universe. This learned scholar also introduced Jefferson to the leading Williamsburg lawyer, George Wythe, and to Governor Fauquier. The young Virginian from Albemarle County spent a great deal of time with these important men and absorbed much information from their conversation. A boy of his age was certainly an extraordinary youth to be accepted into such company!

Jefferson did not neglect his own contemporaries though and at one time shared a room with John Tyler, later a judge and the father of a future president. During his first year at college, Jefferson indulged too much in the pleasures and gaieties of the social and sporting life of the Virginia capital, as he admitted to his guardian when the bills mounted. In his second year he gave up his horse and fox-hunting, and even, it is said, his beloved fiddle, to study fifteen hours a day, so that he could graduate in April. Before returning to Europe in 1762, Dr. Small arranged to have his young friend study law with George Wythe.

Wythe was at the top of his profession when Jefferson began his five years of study under his guidance. An outline of instruction for a law student, prepared by Jefferson soon after he began to practice, gives an idea of the schedule he followed. From early rising until 8 A. M., reading was to be on agriculture, chemistry, anatomy, zoology, botany, ethics and natural religion, with Locke, Cicero and the Bible recommended. From eight until twelve, lawbooks were prescribed and the student was advised to copy into a commonplace book every case of value "condensed into the narrowest possible compass which will admit of presenting distinctly the principle of the case." This would accustom the student ". . . to an acquisition of the most valuable of all the talents, that of never using two words when one will do."

Jefferson's own Commonplace Book gives evidence that he followed this method, "after getting through Coke-Littleton, whose matters cannot be abridged . . ."

The study plan suggested that from twelve on to bedtime, there should be reading on politics, history, literature, criticism, rhetoric and oratory. Locke was again recommended, also Montesquieu, Greek and Roman historians and Gibbon's *Decline and Fall of the Roman Empire.*

In 1765, when Patrick Henry proposed the famous resolutions against the Stamp Act, his friend Jefferson, whom he had visited in Williamsburg, was still a law student. The latter attended the debate, as he reported it, "at the door of the lobby of the House of Burgesses, and heard the splendid display of Mr. Henry's talents as a popular orator. They were great indeed; such as I have never heard from any other man. He appeared to me to speak as Homer wrote."

Also the *Autobiography* tells more of Wythe and of Jefferson's law career. "Mr. Wythe continued to be my faithful and beloved mentor in youth, and my most affectionate friend through life. In 1767, he led me into the practice of the law at the bar of the General Court, at which I continued until the Revolution shut up the courts of justice." Jefferson was very successful as a lawyer, including among his clients Lord Fairfax, William Byrd, Benjamin Harrison and Richard Henry Lee. Two of his cases were especially significant to him. In the first, involving an issue of slavery, he argued that under the God-given law of nature all men are born free. The second, on the ecclesiastical jurisdiction of the General Court, aroused his interest in religious freedom.

Thomas Jefferson was elected in March, 1769, to represent

Albemarle County in the House of Burgesses. Over six feet tall with reddish hair and blue eyes, the young owner of a large plantation, and related to the best families in Virginia, he entered the Assembly at the age of twenty-six and plunged into the struggle for the colonists' rights.

He was chosen to draft the Assembly's reply to the Governor's Opening Address, and this, his first public paper, dated May 8, 1769, was humble and dutiful in tone, but the Governor pronounced it unsatisfactory. Never again would the rebuffed Jefferson's writings adopt a submissive tone!

In response to the resolutions of Parliament of 1768-69 on the Massachusetts resistance to the Townshend Acts, levying new duties, the Virginia House rushed through counter-resolutions denouncing taxation without representation and the proposal to send Americans to England for trial, and agreeing to the co-operation of the Colonies for redress. A petition to the King was also planned. The Governor immediately dissolved the Assembly but twenty-eight of the members, as told in Jefferson's *Autobiography,* met the next day in the Apollo Room of the Raleigh Tavern (where the writer had so often danced), formed a voluntary convention, and drew up articles of association against the use of any merchandise except paper imported from Great Britain. These articles were signed and recommended to the people, and strictly enforced until repeal of the Townshend Acts. Among the twenty-eight, besides Jefferson, were George Washington, Patrick Henry and Richard Henry Lee.

Jefferson was rebuffed a second time in his first term when he failed in trying to get from the House legal permission for slave-owners to free their slaves, if they wished to do so.

In February of the next year Jefferson's library and papers were burned at Shadwell. Of all his prized possessions, only his fiddle was saved. Since law student days he had been planning a home on a favorite mountain, about a mile and a half away. After the fire he moved into a finished pavilion of the future Monticello, consisting of just one room. And he sent to London for a catalogue to start rebuilding his library. A tiny outline in relief of Monticello, as completed, is to be seen on one side of the Jefferson nickel. Jefferson's beautiful home is now a museum.

On January 1, 1772, Jefferson married a young widow, Martha Wayles Skelton, who was attractive, well-educated and very musical. It is told that before they were married, two rivals calling on her at "The Forest," her father's fine estate, met in the hall leading to the drawing-room. On hearing Jefferson playing the violin and Martha singing inside, they looked at each other in consternation and, accepting their fate, departed, leaving Jefferson in undisputed possession of the field.

The Jeffersons' daughter, Martha, was born in September, 1772. Of the Jeffersons' six children, only she and her sister Maria lived to grow up.

In the spring of 1773, Jefferson felt that the colonists had fallen into a state of false security, in spite of the duty on tea and the act asserting the right of Parliament to bind the Colonies by law which were still suspended over them. The Virginia Assembly was then considering a Rhode Island court of inquiry which was empowered to send Americans to England to be tried for offences committed in the Colonies as a matter which demanded Virginia's attention.

"Not thinking our old and leading members up to the point of forwardness and zeal which the times required," Jefferson recounted, "Mr. Henry, Richard Henry Lee, Francis L. Lee, Mr. Carr and myself agreed to meet in the evening, in a private room of the Raleigh, to consult on the state of things." With perhaps one or two other members, these outstanding Patriots drew up the resolutions which, when passed by the Assembly, originated the inter-colonial Committees of Correspondence. The new Governor, Lord Dunmore, dissolved the Assembly, but in the words of the

Autobiography, "The committee met the next day, prepared a circular letter to the speakers of the other colonies, inclosing to each a copy of the resolutions."

It was the news of the Boston Port Bill, in retaliation for the famous Tea Party, however, that brought the Colonies together, face to face. The Virginia Legislature was in session when the news arrived and the "forward" members agreed that they "must boldly take an unequivocal stand in the line with Massachusetts . . ." They met in the council chamber to consult on proper measures. They "cooked up" a resolution, designating June 1, 1774, the day on which the port was to be closed, as "a day of fasting, humiliation and prayer, to implore Heaven to avert from us the evils of civil war . . ." This was passed by the House, which was then dissolved by the Governor, "as usual." The "forward" members, says Jefferson, retired to the Apollo Room as before, agreed to an association and instructed the Committee of Correspondence to propose to the committees of all the other Colonies the appointment of deputies to meet in a Congress annually. It was further recommended that the several counties elect deputies to meet at Williamsburg on the first of August, to choose delegates to a general Congress.

The people of Albemarle met in July. Jefferson wrote the "forward" resolution and he was chosen to represent the county. He prepared a draft of instructions for the delegates to be elected to Congress and sent this to the convention. He was unable to be present himself because of illness. Intended as a petition to the King, the paper listed the complaints "excited by many unwarrantable encroachments and usurpations . . . upon the rights which God, and the laws, have given equally and independently to all." It exhorted George III not to "be a blot on the page of history," and in concluding declared: "The God who gave us life, gave us liberty at the same time: the hand of force may destroy, but cannot disjoin them." Considered too bold at that time, the instruc-

tions were published in pamphlet form at Philadelphia under the title, *A Summary View of the Rights of British
America,* but they were not entered on the record of the convention.

This pamphlet had great influence in the Colonies and in
England. Delegates in the First Continental Congress read
and discussed the work, which established its author as a
Patriot leader. In Parliament it won for Jefferson a place on
a proposed list of those whose lives and property were forfeit.
He had been declared headed for the Tower of London!

In March, 1775, at the Virginia Convention in St. John's
Church, Richmond, Jefferson argued "closely, profoundly
and warmly" in support of Henry's position after the "Lib-
erty or Death" speech, according to the Edmund Randolph
Manuscript. The "forward" men won—but by a majority of
only five votes! Peyton Randolph, slated to be president of
the Second Continental Congress, was also speaker of the
Virginia House. Since Randolph might be called home,
Jefferson was added to the colony's delegation to the next
Congress.

Randolph left Philadelphia in May to attend the Virginia
Assembly, which was summoned by Governor Dunmore to
consider Lord North's "conciliatory propositions." Jefferson,
"pressed" by Randolph, prepared Virginia's answer, which
was carried through the House, with "long and doubtful
scruples" on the part of two of the members, "and a dash of
cold water on it here and there, enfeebling it somewhat, but
finally with unanimity, or a vote approaching it." Jefferson
immediately went on to Congress, taking his seat on June 21,
1775.

On June 26 Jefferson and Dickinson were added to the
committee to prepare a declaration of the causes of taking
up arms, since the first draft had been disapproved. Jefferson's draft "was too strong for Mr. Dickinson . . . (who) was
greatly indulged even by those who could not feel his

scruples." Dickinson then drew up "an entire new statement," retaining only the last paragraphs of Jefferson's.

The *Autobiography* tells that on July 22 Franklin, Adams, R. H. Lee and Jefferson were appointed to report on Lord North's conciliatory resolution. When Congress approved Jefferson's answer for Virginia, he was requested to prepare this report "which will account for the similarity of feature in the two instruments."

Jefferson, who had been in Virginia since December, returned to Congress on May 14, 1776, just in time for the May 15 new government resolution. Three days later he wrote to Page that he had been so long out of the political world that he was "almost a new man in it."

Not knowing that at that very moment Thomas Nelson, Jr., was riding to Philadelphia with the May 15 Virginia Resolutions for "independency" and the formation of a new government for the colony, Jefferson wrote to Nelson on May 17. He suggested that the Convention recall their delegates for a short time if a new form of government were proposed, as "it is a work of the most interesting nature and such as every individual would wish to have his voice in." He told of his anxiety about his wife's health and his hope that Nelson would bring up the question of independence in the Assembly.

Ten days later Nelson laid the Virginia instructions to her delegates before Congress, as well as the resolution regarding a new government for the colony. Jefferson quickly drew up an outline of a constitution for Virginia, with a preamble. He sent this off to his colony with Wythe, in case "it might suggest something worth incorporation into that before the Convention."

Jefferson's *Autobiography* gives invaluable notes on the debates on the "Independency" resolutions which were presented by Richard Henry Lee, as authorized by the new instructions. John Adams, Lee, Wythe and others were the principal speakers for an immediate Declaration but as certain colonies were not yet ready for a separation, final consideration was postponed until July 1—"but, that this might occasion as little delay as possible, a committee was appointed to prepare a Declaration of Independence. The committee were John Adams, Dr. Franklin, Roger Sherman, Robert R. Livingston, and myself," is Jefferson's brief account of what followed. He continues, "The committee for drawing the Declaration of Independence, desired me to do it—"

Thomas Jefferson was only thirty-three when this honor fell to him. John Adams says in his *Autobiography* that during their time in Congress he never heard Jefferson "utter three sentences together," and that it would naturally be asked how he happened to be appointed to this important committee. There were several reasons, Adams explains. Besides the Frankfort advice given the Massachusetts delegates to let Virginia take the lead in important measures, the young Virginian had the "reputation of a masterly pen. . . Another reason was that Mr. Richard Henry Lee was not beloved by the most of his colleagues from Virginia, and Mr. Jefferson was set up to rival and supplant him." This could only be done by the pen, Adams observes, as Jefferson could not compete in "elocution and public debate." As Adams pithily sums the selection up, "Jefferson was chairman because he had most votes and he had most votes because We united in him, to the exclusion of R. H. Lee in (or)der to keep out Harrison." These early Patriots were only human and disagreed among themselves, some to the point of quarrels and bitter personal feuds—even as today—but they were inevitably drawn together by the inspiration of their common cause.

The great Virginian was then living in a second-floor apartment of the "Graaf" house, at the corner of Market and Seventh Streets in Philadelphia. He usually worked in the parlor. The portable writing desk he used when composing the priceless document was his own invention. This desk is now on display at the National Museum in Washington, D. C., but the house was torn down in 1883—attracting the notice of only one souvenir hunter, a Mr. Hall, who was given a joist or small wooden beam.

Writing to James Madison in 1823, Jefferson tells that the Declaration committee "pressed on myself alone to undertake the draught. I consented; I drew it . . ." He then submitted the draft separately to Dr. Franklin and Mr. Adams "because they were the two members of whose judgments and amendments I wished most to have the benefit." The pair made a few changes and the committee then passed it unaltered. Jefferson laid the draft before Congress on June 28.

In the same letter Jefferson wrote to Madison regarding the observations of Pickering and Adams on the composition. He said that he was not to be the judge that his draft "contained no new ideas . . . it's sentiments hacknied in Congress for two years before, and it's essence contained in Otis' pamphlet." He had never seen Otis' pamphlet, Jefferson stated, and did not know whether he had "gathered his ideas From reading or reflection . . ." He knew only that he turned to "neither book nor pamphlet while writing it." He did not consider it as part of his charge to invent new ideas or to offer any new sentiments. Writing to Joseph Delaplaine in 1817, Jefferson disclaimed undue credit for the composition, "for that alone was mine; the sentiments were of all America."

After voting independence on July 2, Congress again became a committee of the whole to consider the Declaration of Independence. The debate continued through the third and on into the fourth. Jefferson's notes on the amendments made by Congress tell that passages censuring the people of England were struck out, as "the pusillanimous idea that we had friends in England worth keeping terms with, still haunted the minds of many." The anti-slavery clause was struck out also, because of Southern opposition.

Seeing that Jefferson "was not insensible to these" and other changes in his draft, Dr. Franklin, who was sitting next to him, told him a favorite anecdote about John Thompson, the hatter, which is related in the Prologue.

Jefferson says that Adams "supported the declaration with zeal & ability, fighting fearlessly for every word." As for its author, he was "writhing a little under the acrimonious criticism on some of it's parts," although somewhat soothed by Franklin's humor!

The Declaration was adopted on the evening of July fourth, since celebrated as Independence Day. On the eighth, Jefferson sent to Richard Henry Lee, as has been told, copies of the Declaration. "You will judge whether it is the better or worse for the critics," was his restrained comment. Later he quoted Lee as charging that the Declaration was copied from Locke. Lee, however, while regretting that the manuscript had been so "mangled," declared it to be so good that it could not be spoiled.

John Page congratulated the author in a letter of July 20, "God preserve the united States—We know the Race is not to the swift nor the Battle to the strong—Do you not think an Angel rides in the Whirlwind & directs this Storm?"

To Jefferson, proclaiming independence was only the first step. A blueprint for the Republic had to be drawn and implemented. The plan he had made for the new government in Virginia, and sent to Williamsburg by Wythe, had reached the Assembly too late to be considered but his preamble was added to the state constitution.

Worried about his wife's health, Jefferson returned to Virginia as soon as he could after the Signing and took up his work there to fight for reforms in the state government. In October his bill to abolish entail or settlement of land on a person and his descendants forever, without any recourse, was introduced in the Virginia Assembly. In 1779 he was elected governor of the state. His Bill for Religious Freedom was introduced and he, with his fellow revisers, reported the new code of laws for the state. This seems a worthy record to offer in answer to Washington's query, "Where is Jefferson?" unthinkingly uttered at a time when he was distressed by the procrastinations in Congress.

In 1781 Jefferson ordered out the militia to repel the British invasion. Warned of Tarleton's plan to capture him at Monticello, he escaped just in time, on horseback by a back road. In June he resigned as governor and also declined an appointment as Peace Commissioner. His wife died the following year and his daughter Martha became his close companion and hostess, both at Monticello and abroad.

Jefferson lavished time, skill and money on Monticello. At an early period he began to keep open house and his extensive hospitality later led him to the verge of bankruptcy. Today many visitors still find their way to Monticello to see the beauty he created. Some of Jefferson's many inventions are on display there also—the dumbwaiter he designed and installed in the dining-room mantel, the revolving buffet and the clock with cannon balls for weights.

In 1784 Jefferson's *Notes on Virginia* were ready for publication, and in 1787 he endorsed the new Constitution for the United States but urged inclusion of a Bill of Rights.

Thomas Jefferson's further career can only be highlighted in this brief sketch—he ably and loyally served his country as Minister to France, Secretary of State in George Washington's Administration, Vice-President of the United States, and President, 1801-1809.

Implementing his ideas on education, Jefferson planned the University of Virginia, at Charlottesville, Virginia, and was the architect of its original buildings. The seal he designed gives an idea of his political philosophy. Circling the bold initials T J is inscribed the motto, "Rebellion To Tyrants Is Obedience To God."

In 1824, writing from Monticello, Jefferson thanked another President, John Quincy Adams, for two facsimile copies of the Declaration, sent to him under a resolution of Congress— "I contemplate with pleasure the evidence afforded of reverance for that instrument, and view in it a pledge of adhesion to it's principles, and of a sacred determination to maintain and perpetuate them."

Thomas Jefferson and John Adams, who had made up their political feud years before, both died on July 4, 1826— the fiftieth Anniversary of the Declaration of Independence. Jefferson requested that the inscription on his tombstone should read—

" 'Author of the Declaration of American Independence
of the Statute of Virginia for religious freedom
& Father of the University of Virginia'

because by these, as testimonials that I have lived, I wish
most to be remembered."

Abraham Lincoln said on the eve of the War between the States, "The principles of Jefferson are the definitions and axioms of a free society."

Joseph Hewes *1730–1779*
John Penn *1740–1788*

Writing to thomas jefferson in 1819 on the recent discovery of the Mecklenburg County, North Carolina, "Declaration of Independence," a document supposed by some to antedate Jefferson's Declaration, John Adams said, "and you know that the unanimity of the States finally depended upon the vote of Joseph Hewes, and was finally determined by him." But history has reserved a special moment for Joseph Hewes.

Signer Hewes's parents, Aaron and Providence Worth Hewes, were members of the Society of Friends. Aaron was the third generation of his family to live in New Jersey. The Hewes's first child was a daughter, Sarah. Joseph was born at Kingston, New Jersey, in January, 1730, the second in a family of six.

After finishing school, Joseph was apprenticed to a Philadelphia merchant and later went into business successfully for himself. Sometime before 1763, he moved to Edenton, North Carolina, taking his nephew, Nathaniel Allen, Jr., the son of his sister Sarah Hewes Allen, to live with him there.

In 1766 he began service as a borough member of the Assembly, and in 1774 he was chosen to represent North Carolina in the First Continental Congress, with Richard Caswell and William Hooper. Rush described Hewes as "A plain, worthy merchant, and well acquainted with business. He seldom spoke in Congress, but was very useful upon committees."

The same delegation appeared for North Carolina at the opening of the Second Continental Congress. In September, 1775, however, John Penn was appointed to succeed Richard Caswell. In the Second Congress, Hewes was active on the committee for fitting out armed vessels. He also served on the secret committee and that on claims.

In February, 1776, Joseph Hewes wrote to Samuel Johnston, president of the North Carolina Provincial Assembly, that William Hooper, while returning from a visit to Cambridge, Massachusetts, to see his mother, had sent him a letter from New York which painted "things in the strongest colours to me . . . I have furnished myself with a good musket & Bayonet . . ." Hewes also sent Johnston a "Curiosity," the pamphlet *Common Sense*—but just one copy, as he did not know how Johnston might "relish independency."

Finding that his colleague John Penn had a "fondness" for *Common Sense*, Hewes agreed to send copies to North Carolina and let the Council decide about distributing them.

From Halifax, North Carolina, where the Assembly was to meet, Johnston wrote his brother-in-law that he had received powder, drums and colors for the troops. He told of hearing from Hewes about his despair of a reconciliation, and that no peace commissioners were appointed in December by Parliament, whose meetings were then postponed until late January. *"All our people here,"* Johnston continued, *"are up for independence . . ."*

North Carolina was the first colony to authorize her delegates "to concur with the Delegates of the other Colonies in declaring Independency . . ." as resolved by the Provincial

Congress on April 12. Johnston explained that the House had passed this motion and also signified approval of foreign alliances after receiving some very important intelligence.

Joseph Hewes had not attended the Provincial Congress. He had remained in Philadelphia because, as he stated in a letter earlier, close attention to business every day in Congress and work on committees almost every evening and frequently in the morning were too much for his constitution. "However," he added, "my country is entitled to my services, and I shall not shrink from her cause, even though it should cost me my life."

Hewes reported to Johnston on May 16 that he had received his letters and the independence resolutions, which he laid before Congress at the earliest opportunity. But the *Journal of Congress* shows that the new instructions from North Carolina were not laid before Congress until May 27, at the same time as the Virginia resolutions of May 15.

North Carolina, however, was not united on the measure, and a pamphlet citing the horror of independence and the "happier nature" of a reunion was circulated by the reconciliation party in June among some of the leading men of North Carolina.

It was during the debate on Lee's independence motion, that Hewes's great moment to serve his country came. "But America is a great unwieldy body," John Adams had written of the Second Congress. "Its progress must be slow . . . like a coach and six, the swiftest horses must be slackened, and the slowest quickened, that all may keep an even pace." During the Lee debate, the Colonies stood at six to six—North Carolina would determine whether America was to be independent or slip back into dependency.

North Carolina's delegation of one—Joseph Hewes—was opposed, notwithstanding the April instructions. Hooper had not yet returned from North Carolina to Philadelphia; neither had Penn, who was for the motion. On Hewes's vote, the fate of the colony and the fate of the country rested—and Hewes was negative!

In a letter written in March, 1813, to William Plumer, John Adams replies to the question whether "every member of Congress did, on the 4th of July, 1776, in fact, cordially approve of the declaration of independence" as follows:

"The measure had been upon the market for months, and obstinately opposed from day to day. Majorities were constantly against it. For many days the majority depended on Mr. Hewes, of North Carolina. As described in the Prologue, while a member (Samuel Adams), one day, was speaking, and reading documents from all the colonies, to prove that the public opinion, the general sense of all, was in favor of it, Mr. Hewes, who had hitherto constantly voted against it, started suddenly upright, and lifting up both hands to Heaven, as if he had been in a trance, cried out, 'It is done! and I will abide by it.' I would give more for a perfect painting of the terror and horror upon the faces of the old majority, at that critical moment, than for the best piece of Raphael. The question, however, was eluded by an immediate motion for adjournment. . . ."

John Penn, back in Congress, wrote to Johnston: "I arrived here several days ago in good health & found Mr. Hewes well . . . The first day of July will be made remarcable then the question relative to Independance will be agitated and there is no doubt but a total seperation from Britain will take place . . ." That same day Hewes predicted: "On Monday the great question of independency . . . will come on. It will be carried, I expect, by a great majority, and then, I suppose we shall take upon us a new name."

Hewes and Penn voted for independence and all three North Carolina delegates signed on August 2.

The Declaration was proclaimed in Halifax on August 1. According to a contemporary account, at noon, Cornelius Harnett mounted a rostrum set up in front of the Court

House, and as he opened the scroll upon which were written the "immortal words" of the Declaration, the enthusiasm of the immense crowd broke in "one swell of rejoicing and prayer."

Hewes was appointed on the committee to prepare a plan for confederation. He was active on the naval committee and in the affairs of North Carolina, then menaced by the enemy and distracted by civil war. At his own expense, he sent gunpowder and other war supplies to the republican troops, being reimbursed afterward by Congress. Following an absence from Congress, he was again elected, taking his seat in July, 1779. His health failed and he died that same year while in Congress, and was buried in Christ Church cemetery in Philadelphia. Three Signers, Robert Morris, Benjamin Franklin and Francis Hopkinson, rented pews in this church.

Joseph Hewes never married. He was engaged to Isabella Johnston, sister of Governor Samuel Johnston, but she died a few days before their wedding. Hewes, it is said, never recovered from this blow.

He took his nephew, Nathaniel Allen, Jr., into partnership in Hewes, Smith and Allen. Hewes's considerable fortune was partly left to this nephew, including water lots, wharf, warehouses and personal belongings.

John Penn, the only child of Moses and Catherine Taylor Penn, was born in Caroline County, Virginia, on May 6, 1740. When his father died, John Penn, at eighteen, had had only a few years of country school education. Inheriting a comfortable fortune, he was anxious to continue his studies and was given free range of the library of his relative, Edmund Pendleton. He decided to take up law, and at the age of twenty-one obtained a license to practice. He married Susannah Lyme and in 1774 the couple moved to Granville

County, North Carolina, where some of John's relatives had gone to live.

Rush estimated Penn as "A good humored man, very talkative in company, but seldom spoke in Congress except it was to whisper to the member who sat next to him. He was honest, and warmly attached to the liberties of his country."

"Brother Penn" wrote from Philadelphia to Thomas Person in February, 1776, that making foreign alliances would perhaps mean a total separation from Britain but that some sort of alliance might be necessary to provide for their defense— "My first wish is that America may be free; the second that we may be restored to peace . . . upon Just and proper terms. . . ."

Penn and Hooper, members of the North Carolina Congress as well as the Continental Congress, appeared in Halifax, North Carolina, and took their seats on April 15. Penn wrote to John Adams about his tedious journey, due to bad roads and wet weather. He reported that the feeling for independence was even stronger in North Carolina than in Virginia, because of the "trouble and danger" the people in his colony had undergone for some time.

John Penn served in Congress until 1777 and was again elected the following year. When Lord Cornwallis invaded North Carolina in 1780, Penn was on the state board of war. Great responsibility fell to him and he discharged his trust with credit. He was appointed receiver of taxes for North Carolina by Robert Morris in 1784 but resigned after a few weeks. Of his children, only his daughter Lucy, who married her cousin, Colonel John Taylor of Hazelwood, Caroline County, left descendants.

Rush called William Hooper "A sensible, sprightly lawyer, and a rapid, but correct speaker." Originally from Boston, where his father was rector of Trinity Church, William had graduated from Harvard in 1760 and studied law with James

Otis. In 1764 he moved to Wilmington, North Carolina, to practice law, rapidly rising to prominence. He was active in opposing the "Regulators" in 1771 and represented Wilmington in the General Assembly of 1773.

In March, 1776, Hooper, one of the "orators" of Congress, wrote Johnston that he most earnestly wished "peace and reconciliation" upon honorable terms. "Heaven forbid" that he should submit to any other!

Hooper served on many committees in Congress until he resigned in 1777 and returned to his home on Masonborough Sound, about eight miles from Wilmington, but he was driven from there soon afterward by the enemy. He later moved to Hillsborough, where he died in 1790.

A startling postscript to the colonial history of North Carolina came to light in 1819—the Mecklenburg Declaration of Independence. The two Carolinas, originally founded by eight nobles in 1663, were formally separated, with different governors, in 1711, and North Carolina became a royal province in 1729. Passed by the Provincial Assembly, the April 12, 1776, resolutions authorized the North Carolina delegates to concur with the other Colonies in voting for independence, which those present did on July 2. The so-called Mecklenburg Declaration purported to be resolutions for independence approved by a meeting in that county on May 20, 1775, more than a year before.

Of the Mecklenburg Declaration, as printed in the *Essex Register* of June 5, 1819, John Adams wrote to Jefferson: "May I inclose you one of the greatest curiositys and one of the deepest mysterys that ever occurred to me . . . How is it possible that this paper should have been concealed from me to this day—had it been communicated to me in the time of it . . . it would have been printed in every Whig Newspaper upon this Continent . . . I would have made the Hall of Congress Echo . . . and re-echo, with it fifteen months before your Declaration . . . Richard Caswell, William Hooper, and Joseph Hughs, the then Representatives of North Carolina in Congress you know as well as I do . . ." And Adams tells how the unanimity of the States depended upon Hewes. In another letter, to William Bentley, he says: "Its total concealment from me is a mystery, which can be unriddled only by the timidity of the delegates in Congress from North Carolina, by the influence of Quakers and proprietary gentlemen in Pennsylvania, the remaining art and power of toryism throughout the continent at that time."

Jefferson answered: "I believe it is spurious. I deem it to be a very unjustifiable quiz . . . when mr Henry's resolutions, far short of independance, flew like lightning thro every paper and kindled both sides of the Atlantic, this flaming declaration of the same date . . . altho' sent to Congress too, is never heard of. . . . would not every advocate of independance have rung the glories of Mecklenburg county . . . in the ears of the doubting Dickinson and others, who hung so heavily on us? . . . the paper speaks too of the continued exertion of their delegation, 'in the cause of liberty and independance.' now you remember as well as I do, that we had not a greater tory in Congress than Hooper. that Hughes was very wavering, sometimes firm, sometimes feeble, according as the day was clear or cloudy; that Caswell indeed was a good whig, and kept these gentlemen to the notch, while he was present; but that he left us soon, and their line of conduct became then uncertain till Penn came, who fixed Hughes and the vote of the state. I must not be understood as suggesting any doubtfulness in the state of N. Carolina. no state was more fixed or forward . . ."

Adams wrote to Bentley again, saying: "The plot thickens . . . I was on social, friendly terms with Caswell, Hooper, and Hewes, every moment of their existence in Congress; with Hooper, a Bostonian, and a son of Harvard, intimate and familiar. Yet, from neither of the three did the slightest hint of these Mecklenburg resolutions ever escape . . . The Declaration of Independence made by Congress . . . is a document . . . that ought not to be disgraced or trifled with."

The Mecklenburg resolutions were investigated further in 1831, under the direction of the General Assembly of North Carolina and a report was published. It seems that all that could be definitely established was that resolutions of an advanced nature were passed sometime in May by citizens of Mecklenburg County, according to John H. Hazelton in *The Declaration Of Independence—Its History.*

Joseph Hewes, who certainly was in a position to hear of the Mecklenburg paper, wrote to a friend six months later, in December, 1775, that "no plan of Seperation has been offered, the Colonies will never Agree to Any 'till drove to it by dire Necessity. I wish the time may not come too soon, I fear it will be the case if the British Ministry pursue their present diabolical Schemes . . ."

Arthur Middleton *1742–1787*
Edward Rutledge *1749–1800*

Rush describes arthur middleton as a "man of a cynical temper, but of upright intentions towards his country. He had been educated in England and was a critical Latin and Greek scholar. He read Horace and other classicks during his recess from Congress. He spoke frequently, and always with asperity or personalities. He disliked business, and when put upon the Committee of Accounts he refused to serve and gave as a reason for it that he hated accounts, that he did not even keep his own accounts, and that he knew nothing about them."

The Middletons of South Carolina are remembered not only for having on the distinguished family tree a Signer who did not have to worry about "accounts," but also because of the beautiful gardens of Middleton Place, which are to be seen today near Charleston.

The first of the line in America was Edward Middleton, who inherited large properties in England, but went to Barbados and then to Carolina in 1678, with his brother Arthur. Edward obtained a large grant of land in Berkeley County and became a member of the grand council. In 1719, his son Arthur, as president of the popular convention, helped to overthrow the government of the proprietors, and South Carolina was made a royal colony. Arthur's second son, Henry, inherited his father's determined spirit and ample fortune. While he was a member of the Council of Safety and of the Provincial Congress, by his position, wealth and powerful family connection, he did much to turn the balance in South Carolina in favor of the American party.

At a convention held in July, 1774, Henry Middleton, Christopher Gadsden, Thomas Lynch, John and Edward Rutledge, "Esquires," were elected to represent their colony in the First Continental Congress at Philadelphia. In October, 1774, Henry Middleton was elected president of Congress and the following May he was again offered the presidency but declined. He served as president of the South Carolina Provincial Congress, 1775-1776.

The Signer, Arthur Middleton, was the eldest of the children of Henry Middleton and his wife, Mary Williams Middleton, the only child of a wealthy South Carolina planter. Arthur was born on June 26, 1742, at Middleton Place on the Ashley River, the seat of his father, who owned about fifty thousand acres. He had one brother and several sisters. Among the latter was Henrietta Middleton, who married Edward Rutledge, Arthur's fellow Signer.

As was customary among wealthy planters in those days, Arthur was sent "home" to England to be educated. He studied at an academy in Hackney and was admitted to the Middle Temple to read law. After a two-year tour of Europe, he returned to South Carolina in 1763, and the following year he married Mary Izard, daughter of Walter Izard. That same year Arthur Middleton was elected to the Assembly, in which he became a member of the committee to correspond with the colonial agent in London. He took his wife to London in 1768 and they also spent some time in Rome.

On their return to South Carolina, they settled down at Middleton Place, which he had inherited through his mother. Becoming very active in the Patriot cause, he was appointed by the Provincial Congress in April, 1775, to a secret committee of five men authorized to place the colony in a "posture of defence" in the face of the royal government. Under this committee's direction, the royal magazine of arms and ammunition was appropriated for the defense of the colony.

In June, Middleton was one of thirteen chosen for the Council of Safety. When it was discovered by the Patriots that the new royal governor, Sir William Campbell, though seemingly friendly, was expecting troops from England and wanted the "friends of the royal government," including those in border counties and Indians, to delay any action until their arrival, Middleton made a motion that "the governor should be immediately taken into custody." This bold move, made despite the fact that the Governor's wife, Sarah Izard Campbell, and Mrs. Arthur Middleton were first cousins, was defeated—a majority were still loyal to religious and commercial ties and wanted protection from the French and Indians. The Governor, however, retired on board a British sloop of war soon afterward.

Edward Rutledge, Middleton's brother-in-law, was born on November 23, 1749, in or near Charleston. He was the youngest son of Dr. John Rutledge, who had come to South Carolina from Ireland about 1735. Dr. Rutledge practiced medicine in Charleston and married Sarah Hext, known for her piety and wisdom, and possessor of a small fortune. She was left a widow at twenty-seven, with seven children to raise.

After a classical education under David Smith of New Jersey, Edward read law with his eldest brother John, who represented South Carolina in the Stamp Act Congress in 1765. Following the example of John and another brother Hugh, a well-known jurist, Edward was sent to England in

1767 to complete his legal studies at the Middle Temple. While in London he went often to Parliament, where he heard the orators of the day.

Admitted to the bar, he returned home in 1773 and began to practice. On March 1, 1774, he married Henrietta Middleton, and was chosen, at twenty-four, a delegate to the First Congress, with his brother, John, and his father-in-law, Henry Middleton.

Adams, in Philadelphia for Congress, tells in his diary that on his first day there "Mr. Lynch, Mr. Gadsden, Mr. Middleton, and young Mr. Rutledge came to visit us . . . Mr. Middleton was silent and reserved; young Rutledge was high enough. A promise of the King was mentioned. He started! 'I should have no regard for his word; his promises are not worth anything,' &c. This is a young, smart, spirited body."

To Yankee eyes, John Rutledge had "nothing of the profound, sagacious, brilliant, or sparkling" in his first appearance, and two days later Adams commented on his "air of reserve, design and cunning . . ."

Thomas Lynch, "a hearty friend to America," whom Adams had met in Boston, is described as a "solid, firm, judicious man." Christopher Gadsden, a delegate to the Stamp Act Congress nine years before, received a visit at his lodgings from John Adams, who recorded, "Gadsden is violent against allowing to Parliament any power of regulating trade, or allowing that they have anything to do with us." In the debates on nonimportation, Gadsden is quoted as saying, "I am for being ready, but I am not for the sword. The only way to prevent the sword from being used, is to have it ready." This advice has proved a prophetic forerunner of America's offensive strength policy of today.

South Carolina's rice and indigo crops proved stumbling blocks to agreement in the association for nonexportation. When the members were signing, all the South Carolina delegates, except Gadsden, withdrew and the colony was on the point of being excluded when, by a compromise, rice was removed from the list forbidden for export. The indigo cultivators raised a violent struggle in the Provincial Congress over this discrimination.

Edward Rutledge wrote to Judge Bee about his attitude in this Congress, saying that he was not attached to the most violent party. "I long to tell you what we have done, but am prevented, from silence having been imposed upon us all by consent, the first week in congress . . . the province will not be able to account for our conduct until we explain it, though it is justifiable upon the strictest principles of honour and policy. Don't be alarmed; we have done no mischief, though I am sure, if Mr. —— had had his way, we should. But you may thank your stars you sent prudent men, and I trust the youngest is not the least so. The gentleman to whom you alluded is, if possible, worse than ever; more violent . . ." According to the Sanderson-Waln *Biography,* the gentleman alluded to was Mr. Gadsden.

On October 24, after a day of the usual "nibbling and quibbling" in Congress, John Adams wrote, "Young Ned Rutledge is a perfect Bob-o-Lincoln—a swallow, a sparrow, a peacock . . ."

South Carolina sent the same delegates to the Second Continental Congress, which met in Philadelphia on May 10, 1775. News of the Battle of Lexington had not reached Charleston by then, but it had its full effect on the Congress and South Carolina's representatives there.

At the early sessions, John Rutledge "in more than one public speech" approved John Adams' bold plans to retaliate for Lexington—plans which led toward independence. Mr. Lynch, Mr. Gadsden and Mr. Edward Rutledge appeared "to be of the same mind." This caused alarm in the "moderate" party, and Mr. Dickinson himself told Adams later that when "we first came together the balance lay with

South Carolina." All the "moderates'" efforts were employed to "convert the delegates" from that colony.

When George Washington was elected Commander-in-Chief of the newly-created Continental Army, Thomas Lynch was one of a committee, with John Adams and Patrick Henry, to inform him of this appointment.

John Adams, in describing the debating in Congress, says that Edward Rutledge was "tedious upon frivolous points. . . . Much precious time is indiscreetly expended; points of little consequence are started and debated with warmth. Rutledge is a very uncouth and ungraceful speaker; he shrugs his shoulders, distorts his body, nods and wiggles with his head, and looks about with his eyes from side to side, and speaks through his nose, as the Yankees sing. His brother John dodges his head too . . . and both of them spout out their language in a rough and rapid torrent, but without much force or effect." There was unflattering comment among Congressmen in those days, too!

But Rush's sketch of Edward Rutledge is complimentary: "A sensible young lawyer, of great volubility in speaking, and very useful in the business of Congress."

Richard Smith's diary entry of February 21, 1776, shows that Edward Rutledge was one who opposed the motion to publish the oration on General Montgomery, who had fallen at Quebec, because in the oration Congress was portrayed as wishing to continue dependent on Great Britain.

Christopher Gadsden, who was always on John Adams' side during the struggle toward independence in Congress, was called home to take command of his regiment, and left Philadelphia on January 18, 1776. Arriving in South Carolina with the first copy of *Common Sense,* Gadsden took part in the debate in the Provincial Congress on the proposed new government. According to Drayton's *Memoirs of the American Revolution,* he "boldly declared himself, not only in favour of the form of government; but, for the absolute Independence of America. This last sentiment came like an explosion of thunder upon the members of Congress . . ." for the majority of members had no thoughts of "aspiring at independence" at that time. One distinguished member declared he "abhorred the idea . . ." He was willing, he said, to ride to Philadelphia to assist in reunion, and another member made unflattering comments about the author of *Common Sense*. The few who wished for independence thought Colonel Gadsden imprudent in suddenly declaring for it at a time when the house was unprepared.

Within a week, a new election was held by the Provincial Congress, of which Henry Middleton was president. Thomas Lynch, John and Edward Rutledge were re-elected to the Continental Congress; John, despite his previous request to be withdrawn. He remained at home, becoming president of the newly-formed temporary government. Arthur Middleton, who served on the committee to prepare the new government, was chosen when his father asked that he be excused from holding office because "of infirmities of age." Thomas Heyward, Jr., was also elected—and Christopher Gadsden was "left out"!

Edward Rutledge wrote from Philadelphia of the illness of Thomas Lynch, who was stricken by apoplexy, and on receipt of his letter the Provincial Congress passed new instructions, empowering the majority or any one of the delegates "to concert, agree to, and execute, every measure which they or he, together with a majority of the Continental Congress, shall judge necessary, for the defence, security, interest, or welfare of this Colony in particular, and of America in general." Thomas Lynch, Jr., was elected a sixth delegate and went to Philadelphia to take care of his father.

That the new instructions did not mean to work for independence was shown by the fact that the new South Carolina government, established a few days later, was to exist only until the "unhappy differences between Great Britain and America" were resolved. But in a letter of April 12, a South Carolinian is quoted as saying that the people there had "no expectation of ever being reconciled with Britain again but only as a foreign State."

On April 23, the Chief Justice, John Drayton, at the opening of the courts in Charleston, went further, charging the grand jury, "The law of the land authorizes me to declare, and it is my duty to declare the law, that George the Third . . . has abdicated the government, that he has no authority over us, and we owe no obedience to him . . . True reconcilement never can exist between Great Britain and America, the latter being in subjection to the former. The Almighty created America to be independent of Britain; to refuse our labors in this divine work, is to refuse to be a great, a free, a pious, and a happy people!"

The *Autobiography* of John Adams tells more of the political situation of the South Carolina delegates during this Congress, telescoping the proceedings somewhat! The "proprietary gentlemen, Israel Pemberton and other principal Quakers now united with Mr. Dickinson" to influence all the members of Congress they could, even some of the Massachusetts delegates, but most of all the delegates from South Carolina. "Mr. Lynch had been an old acquaintance of the Penn family, particularly of the Governor. Mr. Edward Rutledge brought his lady with him, a daughter of our former President Middleton. Mr. Arthur Middleton, her brother, was now a delegate in place of his father. The lady and the gentlemen were invited to all parties, and were visited perpetually by the party, and we soon began to find that Mr. Lynch, Mr. Arthur Middleton, and even the two Rutledges, began to waver and to clamor about independence." Adams continues that he became the "terror" of the "moderate" party while "Arthur Middleton became the hero of Quaker and proprietary politics in Congress. He had little information, and less argument; in rudeness and sarcasm his forte lay, and he played off his artillery without reserve. I made it a rule to return him a Roland for every Oliver, so that he never got, and I never lost, any thing from these rencounters. We soon parted, never to see each other more—I believe, without a spark of malice on either side; for he was an honest and generous fellow, with all his zeal in this cause."

Edward Rutledge was chosen, with John Adams and Richard Henry Lee, on the committee to prepare the preamble to the new government resolution and he approved Adams' report, which was passed on May 15, after further heated debate.

During the first day's debate on Lee's independence motion, as Rutledge wrote that same evening, the "sensible" part of the House opposed the motion. The "moderates" did not object to proposing a treaty to France or to a confederation of the Colonies but they saw no "Wisdom" in declaring independence. When the debate was resumed the following Monday, Rutledge planned to move for a postponement of three weeks or months. He did not know whether he would succeed in this, but felt he had to do what was right in his "own Eyes." On the "moderate" side, he and three others had sustained the "whole Argument."

Edward Rutledge's motion to postpone consideration of Lee's motion did pass, as has been told, and Thomas Jefferson's notes reveal that, as New York, New Jersey, Pennsylvania, Delaware, Maryland "& South Carolina were not yet matured for falling from the parent stem, but that they were fast advancing to that state," it was decided to wait a while and postpone final action to July 1. Jefferson apparently added "& South Carolina" later, since these words are in darker ink than the rest. Doubtless this was because it occurred to him that South Carolina's delegates were also opposed at the time. However, the notes as originally written presumably were correct, as Congress evidently did not expect to hear from South Carolina during the three weeks' postponement.

On June 29, not knowing that a naval force under General Sir Henry Clinton, accompanied by the former royal governor, had been repulsed in an attack on Charleston, Edward Rutledge wrote requesting a certain New York "moderate" to hurry to attend Congress, as the independence resolution and the two others would be brought up on Monday, July 1. "Whether we shall be able effectually to oppose the first . . . will depend in a great measure upon the exertions of the . . . sensible part of the Members," he explained.

In "the greatest Debate of all," on July 1, Edward Rutledge asked John Adams to sum up the arguments for the New Jersey delegates just arrived, as related in the Prologue. The Lee motion was then carried in the committee of the whole by nine colonies—South Carolina and Pennsylvania voted against it. Jefferson's notes tell that "m̄r Edward Rutledge of S. Carolina then requested the determination might be put off to the next day, as he believed his collegues, tho' they disapproved of the resolution, would then join in it for the sake of unanimity." And on the following morning — "S. Carolina concurred in voting for—" independence.

Signing for South Carolina on August 2 were Arthur Middleton, Edward Rutledge, Thomas Lynch, Jr., and Thomas Heyward, Jr. They sent a copy of the Declaration, with a covering letter, to their colony. Sounding almost timid about its reception, they wrote, ". . . and a very important Declaration, which the King . . . has at last reduced us to the necessity of making. . . . P.S. The express is to be paid for every day that he is detained in Carolina."

But the time was propitious. The repulse of the British attack on Charleston had brought war to the colony—on the very day the Declaration had been laid before Congress. A celebration was held at the long-famed Liberty Tree in Mazyckborough, "just beyond Gadsden's and Lynch's pasture," on August 5. The gathering was opened by prayers and the Declaration was proclaimed to a cheering audience.

A contemporary member of Congress said of Thomas Heyward, Jr., one of the new delegates, "On him we could always depend for sound measures, though he seldom spoke in public." The son of a wealthy planter of English descent, Heyward was born on July 28, 1746, at "Old House," his father's seat in Granville County. After receiving a classical education, he took up law, completing his studies at the Middle Temple in London. Following a tour of Europe, he returned to South Carolina to practice law. He was elected to the first provincial assembly and was a member of the Committee of Safety. Retiring from Congress in 1778, he was appointed a judge and later presided at a treason trial at which the defendants were convicted and executed, according to the Sanderson-Waln *Biography*. Wounded by a musket ball in the Beaufort skirmish in 1779, he was captain of a battalion of volunteers at the siege of Charleston the following year. Taken prisoner on May 12, at the surrender of the city, he was sent to St. Augustine, Florida, where, to pass the time, he composed patriotic words to *God Save The King* and other British songs. While he was held there, a party of British plundered his plantation, "White Hall," and carried off his slaves. After his release, he was elected to the Jacksonborough Assembly of 1782 and resumed his judicial duties. In Rush's sketch Heyward is described as a "firm Republican of good education and most amiable manners. He possessed an elegant poetical genius, which he sometimes exercised with success upon the various events of the war."

Rush's account of Thomas Lynch, Jr., is not as flattering: "A man of moderate talents and timid in difficult circumstances of his country." Educated at Eton and Cambridge, Lynch studied law at the Temple in London but returned home in 1772 before finishing the course. He devoted himself to cultivating a plantation on the North Santee River, given to him by his father. His grandfather had been the first to cultivate rice in the South Carolina lowlands. Lynch, commissioned a captain in the first regiment of South Carolina provincials, in 1775, contracted swamp fever during his service. Although in poor health himself, he succeeded his father in Congress but was forced to leave in the fall of 1776. As a last hope for a cure, he embarked with his wife in late 1779 for St. Eustatius, in the West Indies, to take passage in a neutral ship for the south of France, but the vessel in which they sailed was lost at sea.

After capturing Long Island, on August 27, 1776, Lord Howe invited Congress to send representatives to confer with him, as private gentlemen, upon peace with Great Britain. Edward Rutledge, Thomas Lynch, Thomas Stone and several others spoke in favor of accepting; John Adams, Benjamin Rush, Dr. Witherspoon and George Ross argued against the proposal—"with uncommon eloquence." The motion to send a committee was carried with modifications. Edward Rutledge, Dr. Franklin and John Adams were selected to find out what Howe's proposals were and what constituted his authority to make them to members of Congress. John Adams was reluctant to go, but "All sides agreed in sending me," he wrote to James Warren. "Enemies to the measure . . . pushed for me, that as little evil might come of it as possible. . . ."

On September 9, Rutledge and Franklin in "chairs"—one-horse chaises—and Adams on horseback proceeded to Staten Island, to see "that rare curiosity, Lord Howe." At New Brunswick the inn was so crowded that Franklin and Adams were obliged to sleep in one bed in a tiny room with one window. When Adams closed the window, Franklin objected, " 'don't shut the window, we shall be suffocated.' I

answered," wrote Adams, "I was afraid of the evening air."
Franklin opened the window and expounded his theories of
colds to the amused Adams, who soon fell asleep.

The conference took place in the Billopp mansion on
Staten Island, a large room of which had been prepared by
his lordship "by spreading a carpet of moss and green sprigs
. . . till he had made it not only wholesome, but romantically
elegant . . ." But nothing came of the talks, as Howe was not
empowered to treat with representatives of the independent
United States. Adams assured his lordship that "America
would never treat in any other character than as independent
States. . . . Mr. Rutledge concurred in the same opinion."

When Howe said that, if America should fall, he would
lament the loss like that of a brother, Franklin, with "a bow,
a smile, and all that naiveté which sometimes appeared in his
conversation, and is often observed in his writings, replied,
'My Lord, we will do our utmost endeavors to save your lordship that mortification.' "

The committee reported to Congress on the failure of the
mission. To one member Lord Howe's peace conference was
"a bubble, an ambuscade, a mere insidious manoeuvre, calculated only to decoy and deceive . . ." The enemy, having
built up their military position, then attacked and took New
York on September 15, 1776.

Edward Rutledge, appointed in June, 1776, to the first
board of war, served in Congress until November. As a captain in the Charleston artillery, he assisted in dislodging
British regulars from the island of Port Royal in 1779. During the British siege of Charleston in May, 1780, he was sent
by General Lincoln to speed up the reinforcements but was
captured by the enemy. He was imprisoned at St. Augustine,
with other prominent rebels, for nearly a year and on his
exchange he went to live in Philadelphia, as South Carolina
was mostly in the hands of the British and beset by civil

war. A member of the legislature which convened in Jacksonborough in 1782, he served in the state assembly as a representative for fourteen years. When Charleston was evacuated in December, 1782, he resumed his practice of law there. On his return he found that his mother had been held by the British as dangerous to their cause.

A member of the state conventions of 1788 and 1790, he drafted the law abolishing primogeniture, property inheritance by the oldest son exclusively, in the state. In 1798 he became governor of South Carolina but did not live to finish his term.

Edward Rutledge had three children by his first wife, and remarried after her death. In appearance he was taller than average and inclined to be stout. A Latin inscription, planned by the Bar of Charleston, describes the "Piety, Virtue, Temper, and Benevolence" of his character.

Arthur Middleton attended Congress until the end of 1777 and the following year was offered the governorship of South Carolina under a new constitution, but he declined. Active in the defense of Charleston in 1780, he was captured and taken as a prisoner of war to St. Augustine and later confined in a prison ship. "Middleton Place" was on the line of march of the British and occupied by them. Although the buildings were spared, Middleton's valuable collection of paintings was mutilated.

On his exchange in July, 1781, Middleton again became a delegate to Congress. After witnessing the devastation caused by the British campaigns in his state, he submitted a resolution to Congress that Lord Cornwallis should be regarded as a "barbarian, who had violated all the rules of modern warfare, and had been guilty of innumerable cases of wanton cruelty and oppression," and that he should not be exchanged. Middleton's family and estate were then at the mercy of a British commissioner. The resolution was not passed.

Later Middleton served in the state senate. He was a skilled stenographer and recorded many of the debates in which he took part. He also wrote several political essays signed "Andrew Marvell." He died at Goose Creek in 1787, two years after the birth of his younger son, John Izard Middleton, who became an author. Middleton's elder son, Henry, was a governor of South Carolina, a representative in the United States Congress and minister to Russia.

Lyman Hall *1724–1790*
Button Gwinnett *1735–1777*

ON MAY 20, 1776, John Adams noted in his *Autobiography* that "Lyman Hall and Button Gwinnet appear as delegates from Georgia, both intelligent and spirited men, who made a powerful addition to our phalanx." This was a critical time in the affairs of the Continental Congress. The next day dispatches were forwarded by General Washington, including intelligence from England and copies of treaties by "His Britannic Majesty" for foreign mercenaries. General Washington was summoned to Congress from New York, and Lyman Hall was on the committee appointed to confer with Washington, Major-General Gates and Brigadier-General Mifflin, to map out a plan of military operations for the ensuing campaign.

Lyman Hall had worked long and untiringly to have Georgia represented in the Continental Congress. Born in Connecticut in 1724, the son of John and Mary Street Hall of Wallingford, he was descended from a John Hall who came to Boston in 1633. He received a classical education and graduated from Yale in 1747. Lyman studied theology under his uncle, Reverend Samuel Hall, and became a minister. This choice of career did not work out for him and he took up the practice of medicine instead.

In 1752 Hall married Abigail Burr, daughter of Thaddeus and Abigail Burr of Fairfield, Connecticut, at whose brother Thaddeus' house John Hancock and Dorothy Quincy were married during the Revolution. Abigail Hall died the following year and Hall remarried.

With his second wife, Hall then moved to Dorchester, South Carolina, a community to which a number of people had emigrated from the vicinity of Boston in 1697. About the time Hall joined the colony, these former New Englanders migrated to the Midway District of Georgia and later founded the town of Sunbury, on the coast. Hall settled at Sunbury, where he acquired a large medical practice. He also had a plantation in Midway. After Georgia became a royal colony in 1752, upon the surrender of the Trustees' Charter, and later was divided into eight parishes, the Midway district became St. John's Parish.

Hall did not hesitate to risk everything in adopting the colonists' cause, although the Parish of St. John, a narrow coastal settlement, was doubly exposed—to the hostile Creek Indians inland, and to invasion by sea. Georgia—first established by General James Oglethorpe on February 12, 1733 (Georgia Day)—consisted of just a thin line of settlements, extending about two hundred miles up the Savannah River and one hundred miles along the coast.

After the news of the Intolerable Acts reached Georgia, a meeting in opposition to the royal governor was called, to consider the critical situation of the Colonies, due to these arbitrary acts punishing Boston and, also, to the current acts for raising a "perpetual revenue, without the consent of the people or their representatives . . ." It was felt that these measures were "particularly calculated to deprive the American subjects of their constitutional rights and liberties, as a part of the British empire." Everyone in the province was requested to "attend at the *Liberty Pole* at Tondee's tavern in Savannah," in July, 1774, to act on such constitutional measures, "as may then appear to be most eligible." The notice was signed by Noble W. Jones, Archibald Bulloch, John Houstoun and George Walton (later a Signer).

This meeting appointed a committee to start correspondence with the different parishes, inviting their co-operation in acting with the other Colonies. To counteract this, Governor Wright sent messengers to the parishes to obtain signatures on a pledge of loyalty to the royal cause.

As the representative of St. John's Parish, Dr. Hall attended this meeting and he was present at the Savannah provincial convention in January, 1775, which failed to adopt the Continental Association as passed by the First Congress at Philadelphia. Hall's report after the January meeting created such dissatisfaction among his constituents that they applied (in a letter signed by Hall) to the Committee of Correspondence in Charleston, South Carolina, requesting permission to join with them and to concur in the nonimportation act. The South Carolina Committee, while praising the patriotism of the Georgia parish and urging the residents to continue their "laudable exertions," decided that it would be a violation of the Continental Association to act with a part of a province, as the articles of association specified an undivided colony or province.

Their request denied by South Carolina, Dr. Hall and his fellow inhabitants were forced to trade with the other parishes of Georgia, but St. John's passed resolutions binding themselves not to purchase any slave imported into Savannah nor to trade with that city or elsewhere except for absolute necessities.

The next move of the parish was the appointment of a delegate to represent St. John's in Congress at Philadelphia, and on March 21 Lyman Hall was elected unanimously.

Governor Wright wrote to the Earl of Dartmouth about the situation in St. John's Parish. He said that a few descendants of New Englanders there were sending Lyman Hall of "New England extract" to Philadelphia and that he expected Hall would receive the same treatment from Congress which was given the representatives of these "poor, insignificant fanatics" at Charleston.

On May 13, Dr. Hall produced his credentials at the Second Continental Congress and, contrary to the Governor's prediction, was admitted as a delegate from the Parish of St. John, subject to the determination of Congress as to his voting. After some debate, Dr. Hall stated that, since he represented only a portion of a colony, he did not insist on voting for the whole colony. He was satisfied to take part in the debates and to vote only on those occasions when the vote was not taken by colonies. He concluded by expressing the earnest hope that the example of St. John's Parish would soon be followed by the rest of the colony of Georgia.

This transplanted New Englander did not have long to wait for his wish to come true. In July, Georgia's Provincial Congress voted to join the sister Colonies in the great and important cause of liberty, and elected five delegates, including Hall, to the Continental Congress.

Re-elected in February, 1776, Dr. Hall, a member of the "violent" phalanx, was present in Congress to vote for and sign the Declaration of Independence. He was again appointed to serve that fall.

When the British occupied Georgia after the capture of Savannah, Hall was forced to move his family to the North. He had to sacrifice his medical practice and also suffered confiscation of his property, including his rice plantation, by the enemy.

In 1782 he returned to Georgia, before the evacuation of Savannah, and he was elected governor of Georgia the following year. Withdrawing later from public life, he settled in Burke County, where he died in 1790. His only son died a short while later.

Dr. Hall and the Parish of St. John, in joining with the Continental Congress, set an example soon followed by the other parishes. When Georgia, as a whole, sent representatives to Congress, the United Colonies became unanimous in their opposition to British oppression. On the adoption in 1777 of the first constitution of the state of Georgia, the Parish of St. John was incorporated into a county suitably called Liberty County. Other parishes were renamed as counties in honor of members of the British Parliament who had advocated the rights of British colonists in America— Chatham, Effingham, Burke, Richmond, Wilkes, Glynn and Camden. In recognition of Dr. Hall's contribution to freedom, a Georgia county established later was named for him.

Elected delegates from Georgia to the Second Congress, with Lyman Hall, were Archibald Bulloch, John Houstoun, the Reverend Doctor Zubly and Noble W. Jones. On September 13, 1775, Bulloch, Houstoun and Zubly attended Congress and two days later Richard Smith of New Jersey remarked in his diary that two of the "Georgia Delegates are possessed of Homespun Suits of Cloaths, an Adornment few other Members can boast of, besides my Bro^r. Crane and myself." Bulloch was one of the pair clothed "in American manufacture," according to John Adams' diary.

One Sunday evening late in September, John Houstoun and Samuel Adams "disputed the whole time in good humor. They are both dabs at disputation." Houstoun was for acting offensively, if Dickinson's petition to the King was rejected, and he and Bulloch gave "a melancholy account of the State of Georgia and South Carolina." Bulloch, "a solid, clever man," later president of Georgia, was an ancestor of President Theodore Roosevelt.

At first thought to be a "zealous spirit," Zubly disclosed the secrets of Congress to the royal governor of Georgia. When this was discovered toward the end of October, he fled from Congress. According to the Sanderson-Waln *Biography,* Houstoun was dispatched to Georgia after Zubly, to counteract any damage he might do.

In February, the Georgia Congress, meeting at Savannah, elected Archibald Bulloch, Lyman Hall, John Houstoun and two new members, George Walton and Button Gwinnett. On behalf of the Provincial Congress, Bulloch sent a circular letter to the Georgia delegates in April, reminding them of the dangers confronting the colony. Because of the "remote Situation," no particular instructions were given and Bulloch concluded that the Congress relied on the delegates' "Patriotism, Abilities, Firmness and Integrity, to propose, join and concur in all such measures as you shall think calculated for the common good, and to oppose such as shall appear destructive."

As has been told, Hall and Gwinnett took an active part in the moves for independence in the Continental Congress at Philadelphia. Gwinnett was appointed to the committee to prepare and report a plan for the confederation of the Colonies.

George Walton reached Congress by the end of June. He brought a letter to John Adams from Bulloch, which Adams answered on July 1—the day Lee's motion was again considered— "Your colleagues, Hall and Gwinnet, are here in good health and spirits, and as firm as you yourself could wish them. . . ."

This reply to Bulloch, evidently written before Congress met, declares that "This Morning is assigned for the greatest Debate of all."

On the second and fourth of July, Hall, Gwinnett and Walton cast the vote of Georgia for independence and the Declaration. Walton, with Hall, signed the document on August 2, and Gwinnett about the same time. The Journal for that day says that Mr. Walton was "appointed a member of the marine committee in the room of Mr Gwinnet, who is absent," but Button may have signed in the morning, before leaving.

Because of the distance from Philadelphia, a copy of the Declaration, sent by John Hancock, was not received in Georgia until August 8. It was first read by President Bulloch to the Council in the council-chamber in Savannah, then in the square before the Assembly House. After that the Declaration was proclaimed at the Liberty Pole and at the Battery in the Trustees' Gardens, with suitable salutes from field pieces and cannon. In the evening, before the courthouse, a mock burial of George III's political existence was conducted, ". . . corruption to corruption, tyranny to the grave, and oppression to eternal infamy . . . let us remember America is free and independent, that she is, and will be, with the blessing of the Almighty, GREAT among the nations of the earth. . . . May God give us his blessing . . ." Nowhere in the state was the Declaration proclaimed with greater approval than in St. John's Parish, the home of Lyman Hall and Button Gwinnett—and the first parish of Georgia to be represented in the Continental Congress.

In 1848 a statue of the state's three Signers was placed in Augusta, Georgia.

George Walton was born in Prince Edward County, Virginia, in 1741. Left an orphan at an early age, he was apprenticed to a carpenter, who released him so that he could attend a local school. Walton later moved to Savannah, Georgia, where he studied law and was admitted to the bar in 1774. He was an active Patriot, taking a leading part in the meetings of July and August that year. Elected to the Continental Congress in 1776, he arrived in Philadelphia in time to vote and sign for independence.

In December, 1778, Walton, a colonel of militia, commanded his troops when the enemy captured Savannah. Badly wounded, he was taken prisoner and held at Sunbury. Since he was prominent on account of his seat in Congress and his signature on the Declaration, the British demanded a brigadier-general in exchange for him. He was finally exchanged for a navy captain, in September, 1779.

After the unsuccessful siege of Savannah by the American and French forces under General Lincoln and Comte D'Estaing, in October, George Walton was elected governor of Georgia by one faction. In 1783 he became chief justice of the state. Six years later he served as governor again and he was United States Senator in 1795.

Button Gwinnett was, if possible, a "Whig to excess," according to his friend, Lyman Hall. He was born in England about 1735, the son of Reverend Samuel Gwinnett, of Down Hatherley, and his wife, Ann Emes Gwinnett, who was related to people of importance in Herefordshire. Button received an excellent education and engaged in mercantile pursuits for a while in Bristol and Wolverhampton. Later he emigrated to Savannah, Georgia, and was established there as a merchant by 1765. In October of that year, Gwinnett bought St. Catherine's Island, a tract of thirty-six square miles off Sunbury, in St. John's Parish, and became a planter. He was never able to clear up the debt incurred by this purchase.

Said to have been influenced by Dr. Hall, Gwinnett adopted the colonists' cause in 1776 at certain risk to himself and his family, as his possessions on the island could not have been defended from the mainland.

Gwinnett was first elected by the Provincial Congress to represent Georgia in February, 1776. He voted and signed for independence in July and August of the same year. As a member of the committee to prepare the plan for Confederation, he was present in the early debates. Contemporary notes tell that he was in favor of giving to Congress "the power of regulating the trade and managing all affairs of the Indians."

Although re-elected to Congress in October, there is no record of his attendance there for that term. He was a member of the Georgia Council of Safety and was elected speaker of the state constitutional convention which met that fall. In January, 1777, Gwinnett was chairman of the committee to reconsider and revise the constitution draft. The committee report, as amended by the Assembly, was adopted in February. He also helped to defeat the plan for a union of Georgia and South Carolina.

After the death of Archibald Bulloch, Gwinnett was commissioned president of Georgia and commander-in-chief of its army. Two months later he was defeated for re-election as governor by one of his own party.

The failure of the recent military expedition to Florida was investigated by the Assembly. Gwinnett and General Lachlan McIntosh, his personal enemy, testified. The Assembly sustained Gwinnett, who was publicly insulted by McIntosh, and he challenged the general to a duel. Both duellists were wounded. McIntosh recovered, but Mr. Gwinnett died on May 19, 1777, as a result of this deplorable custom of "honor," leaving his wife, Ann Bourne Gwinnett, and a daughter.

Because of his early death, Button Gwinnett is in some ways one of the least known of the Signers. But this same fact brought him nationwide fame in the present century. His autograph, about the rarest among the Signers, was sold at auction for twenty-eight thousand, five hundred dollars.

General James Oglethorpe alone among the founders of the Colonies was living to see the colony he had established join the American Republic. He was then in England, where he had returned ten years after establishing Georgia as a haven for debtors and a place where prisoners might obtain a new start. It was laid out on religious lines.

Oglethorpe's colony had taken a vital part in the June debates on Lee's motion for independence in 1776. As Edward Rutledge revealed in a contemporary letter, the "whole Argument" for independence at that time was sustained "by the Power of all N. England, Virginia & Georgia . . ."

Lyman Hall and Button Gwinnett were the Georgia delegates then in Congress. They both had the wisdom to know from their own experience just what the guiding star of America was—

Equal opportunity under God—

XXIX

The Declaration of Independence

THE CHILD INDEPENDENCE, said John Adams, was born when James Otis made his electrifying protest against the writs of assistance, based on the colonists' God-given rights.

Fifteen years later, the fifty-six Signers witnessed the birth certificate of the independent United States of America. They established a way of life based solely on "certain unalienable rights" endowed by their Creator. Knowing that hardship and possible death awaited them, these Patriots signed the Declaration of Independence, which follows, with a "firm reliance on the protection of divine Providence—"

May we never surrender these God-given rights.

DECLARATION OF INDEPENDENCE

IN CONGRESS, JULY 4, 1776.

The Unanimous Declaration of the Thirteen United States of America,

WHEN, in the course of human events, it becomes necessary for one people to dissolve the political bands which have connected them with another, and to assume, among the powers of the earth, the separate and equal station to which the laws of nature and of nature's God entitle them, a decent respect to the opinions of mankind requires that they should declare the causes which impel them to the separation.

We hold these truths to be self-evident:—That all men are created equal; that they are endowed by their Creator with certain unalienable rights; that among these are life, liberty, and the pursuit of happiness. That, to secure these rights, governments are instituted among men, deriving their just powers from the consent of the governed; that, whenever any form of government becomes destructive of these ends, it is the right of the people to alter or to abolish it, and to institute a new government, laying its foundation on such principles, and organizing its powers in such form, as to them shall seem most likely to effect their safety and happiness. Prudence, indeed, will dictate, that governments long established should not be changed for light and transient causes; and accordingly all experience hath shown that mankind are more disposed to suffer while evils are sufferable, than to right themselves by abolishing the forms to which they are accustomed. But when a long train of abuses and usurpations, pursuing invariably the same object, evinces a design to reduce them under absolute despotism, it is their right, it is their duty, to throw off such government, and to provide new guards for their future security. Such has been the patient sufferance of these colonies; and such is now the necessity which constrains them to alter their former systems of government. The history of the present King of Great Britain is a history of repeated injuries and usurpations, all having in direct object the establishment of an absolute tyranny over these states. To prove this, let facts be submitted to a candid world.

He has refused his assent to laws the most wholesome and necessary for the public good.

He has forbidden his governors to pass laws of immediate and pressing importance, unless suspended in their operation till his assent should be obtained; and when so suspended, he has utterly neglected to attend to them.

He has refused to pass other laws for the accommodation of large districts of people, unless those people would relinquish the right of representation in the legislature—a right inestimable to them, and formidable to tyrants only.

He has called together legislative bodies at places unusual, uncomfortable, and distant from the depository of their public records, for the sole purpose of fatiguing them into compliance with his measure.

He has dissolved representative houses repeatedly, for opposing, with manly firmness, his invasions on the rights of the people.

He has refused, for a long time after such dissolutions, to cause others to be elected, whereby the legislative powers, incapable of annihilation, have returned to the people at large for their exercise; the State remaining, in the mean time, exposed to all the dangers of invasions from without, and convulsions within.

He has endeavored to prevent the population of these States; for that purpose obstructing the laws for the naturalization of foreigners; refusing to pass others to encourage their migration hither, and raising the conditions of new appropriations of lands.

He has obstructed the administration of justice, by refusing his assent to laws for establishing judiciary powers.

He has made judges dependent on his will alone for the tenure of their offices, and the amount and payment of their salaries.

He has erected a multitude of new offices, and sent hither swarms of officers to harass our people and eat out their substance.

He has kept among us in times of peace, standing armies, without the consent of our legislatures.

He has affected to render the military independent of, and superior to, the civil power.

He has combined with others to subject us to a jurisdiction foreign to our constitutions, and unacknowledged by our laws; giving his assent to their acts of pretended legislation:

For quartering large bodies of armed troops among us;

For protecting them, by a mock trial, from punishment for any murders which they should commit on the inhabitants of these States;

For cutting off our trade with all parts of the world;

For imposing taxes on us without our consent;

For depriving us, in many cases, of the benefits of trial by jury;

For transporting us beyond seas, to be tried for pretended offences;

For abolishing the free system of English laws in a neighboring province, establishing therein an arbitrary government, and enlarging its boundaries, so as to render it at once an example and fit instrument for introducing the same absolute rule into these colonies;

For taking away our charters, abolishing our most valuable laws, and altering, fundamentally, the forms of our governments;

For suspending our own legislatures, and declaring themselves invested with power to legislate for us in all cases whatsoever.

He has abdicated government here, by declaring us out of his protection, and waging war against us.

He has plundered our seas, ravaged our coasts, burned our towns, and destroyed the lives of our people.

He is at this time transporting large armies of foreign mercenaries to complete the works of death, desolation and tyranny, already begun with circumstances of cruelty and perfidy scarcely paralleled in the most barbarous ages, and totally unworthy the head of a civilized nation.

He has constrained our fellow-citizens, taken captive on the high seas, to bear arms against their country, to become the executioners of their friends and brethren, or to fall themselves by their hands.

He has excited domestic insurrection among us, and has endeavored to bring on the inhabitants of our frontiers the merciless Indian savages, whose known rule of warfare is an undistinguished destruction of all ages, sexes, and conditions.

In every stage of these oppressions we have petitioned for redress in the most humble terms; our repeated petitions have been answered only by repeated injury. A prince whose character is thus marked by every act which may define a tyrant, is unfit to be the ruler of a free people.

Nor have we been wanting in our attentions to our British brethren. We have warned them, from time to time, of attempts by their legislature to extend an unwarrantable jurisdiction over us. We have reminded them of the circumstances of our emigration and settlement here. We have appealed to their native justice and magnanimity; and we have conjured them, by the ties of our common kindred, to disavow these usurpations, which would inevitably interrupt our connections and correspondence. They, too, have been deaf to the voice of justice and consanguinity. We must, therefore, acquiesce in the necessity which denounces our separation, and hold them, as we hold the rest of mankind, enemies in war, in peace friends.

We, therefore, the Representatives of the United States of America, in General Congress assembled, appealing to the Supreme Judge of the world for the rectitude of our intentions, do, in the name and by the authority of the good people of these colonies, solemnly publish and declare, That these united Colonies are, and of right ought to be, free and independent states; that they are absolved from all allegiance to the British crown, and that all political connection between them and the state of Great Britain is, and ought to be, totally dissolved; and that, as free and independent states, they have full power to levy war, conclude peace, contract alliances, establish commerce, and do all other acts and things which independent states may of right do. And, for the support of this declaration, with a firm reliance on the protection of Divine Providence, we mutually pledge to each other our lives, our fortunes, and our sacred honor.

The foregoing Declaration was, by order of Congress, engrossed, and signed by the following members:

JOHN HANCOCK

NEW HAMPSHIRE
JOSIAH BARTLETT
WILLIAM WHIPPLE
MATTHEW THORNTON

MASSACHUSETTS
SAMUEL ADAMS
JOHN ADAMS
ROBERT TREAT PAINE
ELBRIDGE GERRY

RHODE ISLAND
STEPHEN HOPKINS
WILLIAM ELLERY

CONNECTICUT
ROGER SHERMAN
SAMUEL HUNTINGTON
WILLIAM WILLIAMS
OLIVER WOLCOTT

NEW YORK

WILLIAM FLOYD
PHILIP LIVINGSTON
FRANCIS LEWIS
LEWIS MORRIS

NEW JERSEY

RICHARD STOCKTON
JOHN WITHERSPOON
FRANCIS HOPKINSON
JOHN HART
ABRAHAM CLARK

PENNSYLVANIA

ROBERT MORRIS
BENJAMIN RUSH
BENJAMIN FRANKLIN
JOHN MORTON
GEORGE CLYMER
JAMES SMITH
GEORGE TAYLOR
JAMES WILSON
GEORGE ROSS

DELAWARE

CÆSAR RODNEY
GEORGE READ
THOMAS M'KEAN

MARYLAND

SAMUEL CHASE
WILLIAM PACA
THOMAS STONE
CHARLES CARROLL, of
   Carrollton

VIRGINIA

GEORGE WYTHE
RICHARD HENRY LEE
THOMAS JEFFERSON
BENJAMIN HARRISON
THOMAS NELSON, JR.
FRANCIS LIGHTFOOT LEE
CARTER BRAXTON

NORTH CAROLINA

WILLIAM HOOPER
JOSEPH HEWES
JOHN PENN

SOUTH CAROLINA

EDWARD RUTLEDGE
THOMAS HEYWARD, JR.
THOMAS LYNCH, JR.
ARTHUR MIDDLETON

GEORGIA

BUTTON GWINNETT
LYMAN HALL
GEORGE WALTON

Resolved, That copies of the Declaration be sent to the several assemblies, conventions, and committees, or councils of safety, and to the several commanding officers of the continental troops; that it be proclaimed in each of the United States, at the head of the army.

Index

[306]

DOROTHY HORTON McGEE

*was born at West Point, New York, where her father, a
graduate of the United States Military Academy, was an
instructor in law at the Military Academy. She has lived
mostly on the north shore of Long Island and attended
the Green Vale School, Glen Head; the Brearley School,
New York City; and the Fermata School, Aiken, South
Carolina.*

*Dorothy McGee's favorite hobby is sailing. She be-
gan sailing at the age of eight, at Quisset on Cape Cod,
where her family had a cottage for the summer. She has
enjoyed many seasons of racing and sailing at the Seawanhaka-Corinthian Yacht Club at Oyster Bay, of which
she is a member. She has sailed on many kinds of
boats, from a dinghy to a cup-defender, and in many
waters, from Long Island Sound to the New England
Atlantic Coast and Nantucket, as well as at Nassau, Ber-
muda and the inland lakes of Minnesota and the Adi-
rondacks. A racing skipper in her own right, she has
raced sailboats of several classes, including Star, Herreshoff Fish, Atlantic, Herreshoff "S" and Six Metre,
the latter with a crew of four, and has won the "S" class
at Larchmont Race Week and the Season Champion-
ship in the "S" class at the Seawanhaka-Corinthian
Yacht Club.*

*Dorothy McGee is also greatly interested in Ameri-
can history. A member of several historical and genealogical societies, she is assistant historian of the Long
Island village in which she lives.*